MATHEMATICAL ECONOMICS TEXTS
5

COLLECTIVE CHOICE AND SOCIAL WELFARE

MATHEMATICAL ECONOMICS TEXTS

Editors

K. ARROW, Professor of Economics, Harvard University, U.S.A.
F. HAHN, Professor of Economics, London School of Economics, U.K.
J. JOHNSTON, Professor of Econometrics, University of Manchester, U.K.
R. M. SOLOW, Professor of Economics, Massachusetts Institute of Technology, U.S.A.

Students of mathematical economics and econometrics have two unnecessary difficulties. One is that much of what they have to read is spread over the journals, often written in different notations. The second is that the theoretical and the empirical writings often make little reference to each other, and the student is left to relate them.

The main object of this series is to overcome these difficulties. Most of the books are concerned with specific topics in economic theory, but they relate the theory to relevant empirical work. Others deal with the necessary mathematical apparatus of economic theory and econometrics. They are designed for third-year undergraduates and postgraduate students.

The editors are drawn from both sides of the Atlantic and are people who are known both for their contribution to economics and for the emphasis they place on clear exposition.

Titles in the series

Other titles are in preparation

COLLECTIVE CHOICE
AND
SOCIAL WELFARE

AMARTYA K. SEN

Delhi School of Economics
University of Delhi

WITHDRAWN

HOLDEN-DAY, INC.
SAN FRANCISCO

Library of Congress Catalog Card No. 70-114684

First published 1970
© Copyright 1970 by Holden-Day, Inc.,
500 Sansome Street, San Francisco, California.

Printed in the United States of America

ISBN 0-8162-7765-6

34567890 MP 79876543

To
Nabaneeta

PREFACE

The theory of collective choice belongs to several disciplines. Economics is one of them but not the only one. While this book is part of a series in "mathematical economics texts," no attempt has been made to confine the treatment to economic problems exclusively. Indeed the approach of this book is based on the belief that the problem cannot be satisfactorily discussed within the confines of economics. While collective choice is a crucial aspect of economics (notably of welfare economics, planning theory and public economics), the subject relates closely to political science, in particular to the theory of the state and the theory of decision procedures. It also has important philosophical aspects, related to ethics and especially to the theory of justice.

The book is divided into starred chapters which contain formal analyses, and unstarred ones which are quite informal. They alternate. A nontechnical reader can get an intuitive idea of the main arguments from the unstarred chapters. However, for precise statement of results as well as proofs, the starred chapters have to be read.

The partitioning of the book into formal and informal chapters is a stylistic experiment. Many problems of collective choice require a rigorous and formal treatment for definiteness, and informal arguments can indeed be treacherous, but once the results are obtained, their meaning, significance and relevance can be discussed informally. In fact, a purely formal discussion of significance would be unnecessarily narrow. The book attempts to cater to two distinct groups of readers, viz., those who are primarily interested in the relevance of the results rather than in their formal statement and technical derivation, and those who are also concerned with the latter. Thus, the partitioning of the book into starred and unstarred chapters does have some rationale, aside from reflecting the author's incurable schizophrenia.

The mathematics used in the book mainly involves the logic of relations. The main results of mathematical logic employed in proving theorems on collective choice are stated, discussed and proved in Chapter 1*. The book is in this sense self-contained.

The field of collective choice is vast. It has not been possible to cover all the branches, and still less to discuss all of them equally thoroughly. While it is hoped that the book covers the major branches of the literature adequately, it must be recognized that the judgment of the relative importance of different branches represents the author's own bias.

For facilities of typing and duplication of two versions of this manuscript I am grateful to the Delhi School of Economics and to the Harvard Institute of Economic Research. The actual typing of the two versions was done very efficiently by Mr. C. G. Devarajan and Mrs. Helen Bigelow, respectively.

I must express my indebtedness to people who have influenced this book. My interest in the problem was first aroused by some stimulating discussions with Maurice Dobb when I was an undergraduate at Trinity College, Cambridge, about a decade and a half ago, and I have had discussions with him intermittently ever since. My debt to Kenneth Arrow is immense, not merely because his pioneering work has opened up several avenues of research in the field of collective choice, but, more personally, because he has gone through the entire manuscript and has suggested many important improvements. John Rawls read entirely the first version of the manuscript, which was prepared during 1966–1967, and has put me right on several questions, especially on the philosophical side of the problem. During 1967–1968, Tapas Majumdar, James Mirrlees and Prasanta Pattanaik read the first draft of the manuscript and suggested numerous improvements both of substance and style, and the final version of the book reflects the impact of their comments. I have also benefited from the joint seminar on this subject that Arrow, Rawls and I conducted at Harvard University during 1968–1969, in particular from the participation of Franklin Fisher, A. Gibbard, Stephen Marglin, Howard Raiffa, Jerome Rothenberg, Ross Starr, David Starrett and Richard Zechhauser. I have also had useful discussions with, or helpful comments from, Dipak Banerji, Robert Cassen, Partha Dasgupta, Peter Diamond, Jan Graaff, Frank Hahn, Bengt Hansson, John Harsanyi, Hans Herzberger, Ken-Ichi Inada, Tjalling Koopmans, Abba Lerner, Paul Samuelson, Thomas Schelling, and Subramanian Swamy. But I am, alas, reconciled to the fact that none of these gentlemen can be held responsible for the errors and shortcomings of this work.

A. K. S.

Delhi School of Economics
1st August, 1969

CONTENTS

Chapter 1

INTRODUCTION

1.1. Preliminary Remarks

There is something in common between singing romantic songs about an abstract motherland and doing optimization exercises with an arbitrary objective function for a society. While both the activities are worthy, and certainly both are frequently performed, this book, I fear, will not be concerned with either. The subject of our study is the relation between the objectives of social policy and the preferences and aspirations of members of a society.

It is, of course, possible to take the view that a society is an entity that is independent of the individuals in it, and that social preference need not be based on the preference of the members of the society. Or that there might be a dependence, but one could abstract from it, and simply "assume" that society has a personality and a preference of its own.[1] Anyone who finds his fulfillment in this assumption is entirely welcome to it, and this book must bore him. This study is concerned precisely with investigating the dependence of judgments on social choice and of public policy on the preferences of the members of the society.

Judgments on collective choice, while related to the needs and desires of the members of the community, can, however, take widely differenct form. The calm economic technician who states that imposing a tax on commodity α will be inoptimal provides a judgement on collective choice of one type. The angry crowd which, on July 14, 1789, responded to De Launay, the governor of Bastille, by shouting, "Down with the second drawbridge!"[2]

---

[1] While this position is taken in some of the socialist literature, it was sharply rejected by Marx: "What is to be avoided above all is the re-establishing of 'Society' as an abstraction vis-a-vis the individual." (Marx (1844), p. 104.)

[2] G. Lefebvre, *The Coming of the French Revolution*, trans. by R. R. Palmer, Vintage Books, New York, 1957, p. 101.

1

was involved in a collective choice of a somewhat different kind. The subject is wide enough to cover both, but the approach to these problems must, of course, differ substantially. This diversity is an essential aspect of the subject of collective choice, and indeed a great deal of the richness of the field is related to this.

A study of different relations between individual preferences and social choice is one of our chief concerns. Varieties here are enormous. For example, someone might take the view, implicitly or explicitly, that only his aspirations should count in social choice. Or only the homogeneous interests of a particular class, or a group. Or one might argue that everyone's preference "should count equally," but that statement itself can be interpreted, as we shall presently see, in many different ways. And corresponding to each interpretation we get a different system of making collective choice. This book is much concerned with these systems—their nature, their operations, and their implications.

1.2.   Ingredients of Collective Choice

To assert that social choices should depend on individual preferences leaves the question open as to what should be the form in which individual preferences would be relevant. In his classic study, Arrow (1951) takes orderings of the individuals over the set of alternative social states to be the basic constituent of collective choice. He is concerned with rules of collective choice which make the preference ordering of the society a function of individual preference orderings, so that if the latter set is specified, the former must be fully determined.

An ordering is a ranking of all alternatives vis-a-vis each other. The formal properties of an ordering are discussed in Chapter 1*,[3] but we might briefly state here that the ranking relation must satisfy three characteristics to count as an ordering. Consider the relation "at least as good as." First, it must be "transitive," i.e., if x is at least as good as y, and y is at least as good as z, then x should be at least as good as z. This condition of rationality is analyzed in some detail in Chapter 1*. Second, the relation must be "reflexive," i.e., every alternative x must be thought to be at least as good as itself. This requirement is so mild that it is best

---

[3] The reader can also consult Tarski (1965); Arrow (1951), Chapter 2; or Debreu (1959), Chapter 1.

looked at as a condition, I imagine, of sanity rather than of rationality. Third, the relation must be "complete,"[4] i.e., for any pair of alternatives x and y, either x is at least as good as y, or y is at least as good as x (or possibly both). A man with a preference relation that is complete knows his mind in choices over every pair.

It is important to distinguish between indifference and lack of completeness. Our daily language is often loose enough to fail to distinguish between the two. If I "don't know" which one to choose, this could possibly mean that I am indifferent, though a more natural meaning is that I cannot make up my mind. The logical difference between the two is simple enough. Consider the two statements:

(1) x is at least as good as y
(2) y is at least as good as x

In the case of "indifference" both are being asserted, and in the case of lack of "completeness," neither.

Each individual is assumed to have an ordering over the alternative social states, and society is supposed to have an ordering based on the set of individual orderings, as the problem is posed by Arrow. We shall have to depart from this classic framework in some respects. First, for consistent choice it is not needed that the society should have an ordering. For example, if x is preferred to y, y is preferred to z, and z is indifferent to x, then there is a best alternative in every choice situation, but transitivity is violated. If the choice is over the pair (x, y), x can be chosen; if over (y, z), y is to be preferred; if over (z, x) either can be chosen; and if it is a choice from the set of all three alternatives (x, y, z), then x is to be selected, for it is the only alternative which is at least as good as the two others. Is this a satisfactory basis of choice? It is difficult to decide, for while it is a sufficient basis, it does violate some rationality property. The precise property it violates (property β) is spelt out in Chapter 1*. We shall discuss this question in detail in terms of its implication in Chapter 4, but at this stage simply note that the problem can be considered without requiring that social preference be fully transitive. We shall indeed take the problem in this general form, introducing

---

[4] Logicians seem to prefer the expression "connected" to "complete," but there is then the danger of a confusion with the topological property of "connectedness."

transitivity as a special assumption later on, e.g., in Chapter 3.

Second, for some choice problems we do not even need completeness. Suppose that x is preferred to y and also to z, but y and z cannot be compared, then the preference ordering will be incomplete, but still we can choose a best alternative, viz., x, given the choice between x, y, and z. However, should the choice be between y and z, then we are in trouble. Whether we can dispense with completeness depends on the nature of the choice. Obviously completeness is a desirable characteristic of social preference, but we shall not make a fetish of it. A preference relation that is reflexive and transitive but not necessarily complete is called a quasi-ordering, and its formal properties are studied in Chapter 1*. Exercises with incomplete social preferences will figure in Chapters 2, 8, and 9, and in the corresponding starred chapters.

Third, it is arguable that social choice should depend not merely on individual orderings, but on their intensities of preference. Cardinal welfare functions for individuals may be considered. As an example it may be said that if person 1 wants very strongly that society should choose x rather than y, while person 2 wants very marginally that y be chosen and not x, then in this two-person world there is a good case for choosing x. This argument is somewhat misleading, for in this exercise we are not merely specifying preference intensities of the individuals, we are making interpersonal comparisons between these. There may or may not be any harm in this, but the fact remains that the persuasive nature of the argument is based on the additional feature of interpersonal comparisons and not on the purely personal measures of preference intensity. The use of cardinality with interpersonal comparisons will be discussed in Chapter 7 and that without it in Chapter 8, and in the corresponding starred chapters.

Fourth, the question of interpersonal comparisons is itself an interesting one. It can be used even without cardinality (Chapters 7, 7*, 9, and 9*), and it can be applied in various doses (Chapters 7 and 7*). If collective choice depends not merely on individual orderings but also on interpersonal comparisons of levels of welfare or of marginal gains and losses of welfare of individuals, a new set of possibilities open up.

The use of interpersonal comparisons is widely thought to be arbitrary, and many people view these comparisons as "meaningless" in not being related to acts of choice. One way of giving meaning to such comparisons is to consider choices between being person A in social state x or being person B in social state y. For example, we could ask: "Would you prefer to be Mr. A, an unemployed laborer, in state x, or Mr. B, a well-paid employed engineer, in state y?" While the answer to the question does involve interpersonal comparisons, I should hazard the view that it is not entirely beyond our intellectual depth to be able to think systematically about this choice. It is possible to introduce preferences involving such alternatives into the mechanism of collective choice. This approach will be taken up in Chapters 9 and 9*.

We would, therefore, consider alternative frameworks for collective choice with alternative views on the necessary *ingredients* of such choice, varying from purely individual orderings, as in the system of Arrow, to individual welfare functions with or without cardinality and with or without interpersonal comparability of various types.

1.3. The Nature of Individual Preferences

It is possible to argue that a theory of collective choice should be concerned merely with the derivation of social preference from a set of individual preferences, and need not go into the formation of individual preferences themselves. This view has attractions, not the least of which is its convenience in limiting the exercise. However, it is a somewhat narrow position to take, and the genesis of individual preferences may indeed be relevant for postulating rules for collective choice. We shall find that the effectiveness of different rules of collective choice depends much on the precise configuration of individual preference orderings, and these configurations will, in general, reflect the forces that determine individual preferences in a society. Just as social choice may be based on individual preferences, the latter in their turn will depend on the nature of the society. Thus, the appropriateness of alternative rules of collective choice will depend partly on the precise structure of the society.

The content of individual preferences is also an important issue. In some studies of social choice a distinction is made between individual preferences as they actually are and what they would be if people tried to place themselves in the position of others.

This is an important distinction and one that will be examined in some detail (see Chapters 9 and 9*), but it will be a mistake to assume that preferences as they actually are do not involve any concern for others.   The society in which a person lives, the class to which he belongs, the relation that he has with the social and economic structure of the community, are relevant to a person's choice not merely because they affect the nature of his personal interests but also because they influence his value system including his notion of "due" concern for other members of society.[5]   The insular economic man pursuing his self-interest to the exclusion of all other considerations may represent an assumption that pervades much of traditional economics,[6] but it is not a particularly useful model for understanding problems of social choice.   No attempt will be made in this study to rule out interpersonal inter-dependences.

A useful preliminary exercise is a study of the logical properties of preference relations, and this is what is presented, with an eye to subsequent use, in Chapter 1*.   Many of these results are well-known, though quite a few are not, mainly because the development of the study of preference relations in the standard literature has been largely motivated by consumption theory and demand analysis, which is not always helpful for problems of collective choice.

---

[5] This is, of course, an important issue for historical studies; see, for example, Hobsbawm (1955).

[6] Formally, this takes the form of ruling out externalities.   See also Arrow's contrast between "tastes" and "values" (Arrow (1951), p. 18).

Chapter 1*

PREFERENCE RELATIONS

1*1. Binary Relations

Let $x\,R\,y$ represent a binary relation between x and y, e.g., "x is at least as good as y," or "x is greater than y." If this relation does not hold, e.g., if "x is not at least as good as y," or if "x is not greater than y," we write $\sim(x\,R\,y)$.

One way of specifying such a binary relation over a set S is to specify a subset R of the square of S, denoted $S \times S$, defined as the set of all ordered pairs (x, y) such that x and y both belong to S. Instead of saying $x\,R\,y$ holds, we can then say that (x, y) belongs to R. The study of binary relations on S does not, therefore, differ essentially from the study of subsets of $S \times S$. While we shall not study preference relations in this manner, the reader is free to do the translation should it appear more convenient.

The notation given below will be used in what follows. For a discussion of the underlying concepts, the reader is referred to any standard introduction to mathematical logic, e.g., Carnap (1958), Church (1956), Hilbert and Ackermann (1960), Quine (1951), Suppes (1958), or Tarski (1965).

∃	the existential quantifier ("for some")
∀	the universal quantifier ("for all")
→	conditional ("if, then")
↔	equivalence ("if and only if")
∼	negation ("not")
∨	alternation (the inclusive "or")
&	conjunction ("and")
=	identity ("the same as")
∈	element of ("belongs to")
⊂	subset of ("is contained in")
∩	intersection of ("elements belonging to both sets")
∪	union of ("elements belonging to either set")

One can think of a variety of properties that a binary relation may or may not satisfy.   The following have been found important in different contexts:

(1)   *Reflexivity:* $\forall x \in S: x R x$.
(2)   *Completeness:* $\forall x, y \in S: (x \neq y) \rightarrow (x R y \vee y R x)$.
(3)   *Transitivity:* $\forall x, y, z \in S: (x R y \ \& \ y R z) \rightarrow x R z$.
(4)   *Anti-symmetry:* $\forall x, y \in S: (x R y \ \& \ y R x) \rightarrow x = y$.
(5)   *Asymmetry:* $\forall x, y \in S: x R y \rightarrow \sim(y R x)$.
(6)   *Symmetry:* $\forall x, y \in S: x R y \rightarrow y R x$.

Consider, as an illustration, the relation "at least as tall as" applied to the set of all mountain peaks with measured heights. The relation is reflexive, since a peak is as tall as itself.   It is complete, for if peak A is not at least as tall as peak B, then peak B will be at least as tall as (in fact, taller than) peak A.   It is transitive, since peak A, being at least as tall as peak B which is itself at least as tall as peak C, must imply that peak A is at least as tall as peak C.[1]   It is not anti-symmetric since peaks A and B could be of the same height without being the same peaks.   Nor is it asymmetric, since A being at least as tall as B does not preclude the possibility that B will be as tall as A.[2]   Nor is it symmetric, since A being at least as tall as B does not at all impose any compulsion that B must be at least as tall as A.

It may be easily checked that the relation "taller than" would satisfy transitivity, anti-symmetry, and asymmetry, but not reflexivity, completeness, and symmetry.

Binary relations of certain standard types (i.e., with given properties) have been assigned specific names for convenience. Unfortunately the terminology varies from author to author, and there are some important inconsistencies which one must be aware of.   For example, for Arrow (1951) an "ordering" is reflexive, transitive, and complete (irrespective of anti-symmetry), while for Debreu (1959) an "ordering" is reflexive, transitive, and anti-symmetric (irrespective of completeness).

---

[1] The relation "being brother of" applied to men, while occationally thought to be transitive, is not really so.   Person A may be brother of B and B brother of A, so that by transitivity A should be brother of himself—a luxury that, alas, must be denied to A.

[2] Note that asymmetry implies anti-symmetry, but not vice versa. If $x R y \rightarrow \sim(y R x)$, then the antecedence $(x R y \ \& \ y R x)$ is always false, and hence the implication is logically correct in the case of anti-symmetry.

We specify below the terminology to be used in this book and also note a few alternative names used in the literature.[3]

Properties satisfied	Name to be used in this work	Other names used in the literature
1. reflexivity and transitivity	quasi-ordering	pre-ordering
2. reflexivity, transitivity and completeness	ordering	complete pre-ordering; complete quasi-ordering; weak ordering
3. reflexivity, transitivity and anti-symmetry	partial ordering	ordering
4. reflexivity, transitivity, completeness and anti-symmetry	chain	linear ordering; complete ordering; simply ordering
5. transitivity and asymmetry	strict partial ordering	
6. transitivity, asymmetry and completeness	strong ordering	ordering; strict ordering; strict complete ordering

1*2   Maximal Elements and Choice Sets

Corresponding to the binary relation of "weak preference" R ("at least as good as"), we can define relations of "strict preference" P and of "indifference" I.

DEFINITION 1*1. $x P y \leftrightarrow [x R y \ \& \ \sim(y R x)]$

DEFINITION 1*2. $x I y \leftrightarrow [x R y \ \& \ y R x]$

The elements of a set which are not dominated by any others in the set may be called the maximal elements of the set with respect to the binary relation in question.

DEFINITION 1*3.   *An element x in S is a maximal element of S with respect to a binary relation R if and only if*

$$\sim[\exists y: (y \in S \ \& \ y P x)]$$

The set of maximal elements in S is called its maximal set, and is denoted $M(S, R)$.

---

[3] See for example, Birkhoff (1940), Bourbaki (1939), Tarski (1965), and Church (1956), and in the economic literature, Arrow (1951) and Debreu (1959).

An element x can be called a "best" ("greatest," in the context of size relations) element of S if it is least as good (great) as every other element in S with respect to the relevant preference relation R.

DEFINITION 1*4.   *An element x in S is a best element of S with respect to a binary relation R if and only if*

$$\forall y: (y \in S \rightarrow x\,R\,y)$$

The set of best elements in S is called its choice set, and is denoted $C(S, R)$.

Two comments might be worth making for the purpose of clarification.   First, a best element is also a maximal element but not vice versa.   If $x\,R\,y$ for all y in S, then clearly there is no y in S such that $y\,P\,x$.   On the other hand, if neither $x\,R\,y$ nor $y\,R\,x$, then x and y are both maximal elements of the set (x, y), but neither is a best element.   Thus, $C(S, R) \subset M(S, R)$.

Second, $C(S, R)$ or $M(S, R)$ may well be empty.   For example, if $x\,P\,y$, $y\,P\,z$ and $z\,P\,x$, there is neither a best element, nor any element not bettered by any other.   If transitivity holds, $M(S, R)$ could be empty if the set is infinite, e.g., $x_2\,P\,x_1$, $x_3\,P\,x_2$, ..., $x_n\,P\,x_{n-1}$, ...   On the other hand, even with transitivity and finiteness, $C(S, R)$ may be empty, e.g., $\sim(x\,R\,y)$ & $\sim(y\,R\,x)$, which makes both x and y members of the maximal set of (x, y) but neither a member of the choice set of (x, y).

1*3.   A Set of Results for Quasi-Orderings

We shall now derive certain elementary results for quasi-orderings.   These will apply, naturally, to orderings, chains, and partial orderings as well, since these are special cases of quasi-orderings.

LEMMA 1*a.   *If R is a quasi-ordering, then for all $x, y, z \in S$*

  (1) $x\,I\,y$ & $y\,I\,z \rightarrow x\,I\,z$
  (2) $x\,P\,y$ & $y\,I\,z \rightarrow x\,P\,z$
  (3) $x\,I\,y$ & $y\,P\,z \rightarrow x\,P\,z$
  (4) $x\,P\,y$ & $y\,P\,z \rightarrow x\,P\,z$

Proof.

  (1) $x\,I\,y$ & $y\,I\,z \rightarrow (x\,R\,y$ & $y\,R\,z)$ & $(y\,R\,x$ & $z\,R\,y)$
                $\rightarrow x\,R\,z$ & $z\,R\,x$
                $\rightarrow x\,I\,z$

(2) $\qquad x P y \ \& \ y I z \to x R y \ \& \ y R z$

$\qquad\qquad\qquad \to x R z$

So (2) can be false only if $z R x$, i.e., only if $x I z$. Suppose this is the case; then $x I y$, since $x I z \ \& \ y I z \to x I y$, by (1). But $x I y$ is false.

(3) The proof is exactly similar to that of (2).

(4) It can be seen that $x P y \ \& \ y P z \to x R y \ \& \ y R z \to x R z$. So (4) can be false only if $z R x$, i.e., only if $x I z$. However, if $x I z$, then $z P y$, given (3) and $x P y$. But $z P y$ is false.

We shall refer to the four properties (1)–(4) as *II*, *PI*, *IP*, and *PP*, respectively.

The following two results are elementary:

LEMMA 1*b. *Any finite quasi-ordered set has at least one maximal element.*[4]

Proof. Let the elements be $x_1, x_2, \ldots, x_n$. Let us put $a_1 = x_1$. We now follow the recursive rule that $a_{j+1} = x_{j+1}$, if $x_{j+1} P a_j$, and $a_{j+1} = a_j$, otherwise. By construction, a_n must be maximal.

LEMMA 1*c. *If R is reflexive, then $x P y \leftrightarrow [x] = C([x, y], R)$.*[5]

Proof.

$$x P y \to x R y \ \& \ \sim(y R x)$$

$$\to [x] = C([x, y], R)$$

since $x R x$ by reflexivity.

$$[x] = C([x, y], R) \to x R y \ \& \ \sim(y R x)$$

since $y R y$ by reflexivity,

$$\to x P y$$

Thus x is the only element of the choice set of $[x, y]$ if and only if x is preferred to y.

The relation between maximal sets and choice sets is important for some exercises. We have noted already that $C(S, R) \subset M(S, R)$. We may note further the following result:

LEMMA 1*d. *If for a quasi-ordering R, $C(S, R)$ is nonempty, then $C(S, R) = M(S, R)$.*

---

[4] See Theorem 1.4 in Birkhoff (1940), p. 8. Birkhoff speaks of "partially ordered systems," but the proof does not use the property of anti-symmetry.

[5] See Lemma 2 in Arrow (1951), p. 16.

Proof. Suppose $x \in C(S, R)$. Then

$$z \in M(S, R) \to \sim(x P z)$$
$$\to x I z$$

since $x R z$,

$$\to \forall y: [y \in S \to z R y]$$

by Lemma 1*a and the fact of $x \in C(S, R)$,

$$\to z \in C(S, R)$$

Hence, $M(S, R) \subset C(S, R)$. It follows now from the fact that $C(S, R) \subset M(S, R)$, that $C(S, R) = M(S, R)$.

The following result is also convenient:

LEMMA 1*e. *For any quasi-ordering R over a finite set S,*

$$\forall x, y: [x, y \in M(S, R) \to x I y] \leftrightarrow [C(S, R) = M(S, R)]$$

Proof. Suppose to the contrary, $C(S, R) \neq M(S, R)$, but $\forall x, y: [x, y \in M(S, R) \to x I y]$. Then by Lemma 1*d, $C(S, R)$ is empty. Let $x_0 \in M(S, R)$. Now, clearly, $\sim[x_0 \in C(S, R)] \to \exists x_1 \in S: \sim(x_0 R x_1)$. Since x_1 cannot belong to $M(S, R)$, as that would have implied $x_0 I x_1$, clearly x belongs to its complement $C_M(S, R)$. But this implies that: $\exists x_2 \in S: x_2 P x_1$. Yet x_2 cannot belong to $M(S, R)$, since that would have impled $x_0 I x_2$ and thus $x_0 P x_1$. So x_2 belongs to $C_M(S, R)$. By similar reasoning, $\exists x_3 \in S: [x_3 P x_2 \& x_3 \in C_M(S, R)]$.

Proceeding this way when there are n alternatives in $C_M(S, R)$, we obtain the last alternative x_n such that $x_n \in C_M(S, R)$ and $x_n P y$ for all y in $C_M(S, R)$. Furthermore, $\sim(x_0 P x_n)$ since $x_0 P x_n$ would lead, by transitivity of P, to $x_0 P x_1$, which is false. Since all elements of S except x_0 belong, by our demonstration, to $C_M(S, R)$, it now follows that x_n *is* after all a maximal element. But x_n is supposed to belong to the complement set $C_M(S, R)$. This contradiction establishes one part of the lemma. (Note that the finiteness of S is not necessary for the proof, and only the finiteness of $C_M(S, R)$ is used. Lemma 1*e can, thus, be appropriately generalized.)

The converse is immediate. Let $C(S, R) = M(S, R)$. Hence $x, y \in M(S, R) \to x, y \in C(S, R)$, so that $x R y \& y R x$, which implies $x I y$.

1*4. Subrelations and Compatibility

Consider two quasi-orderings Q_1 and Q_2. We now introduce the notion of being a "subrelation."

DEFINITION 1*5. *Let Q_1 be a subrelation of Q_2 if and only if for all $x, y \in X$,*
(1) $x\, Q_1\, y \rightarrow x\, Q_2\, y$
(2) $[x\, Q_1\, y\ \&\ \sim(y\, Q_1\, x)] \rightarrow \sim(y\, Q_2\, x)$
That is, whenever x is "at least as good as" (or alternatively, "better than") y according to Q_1, it is so according to Q_2 as well, but not necessarily vice versa.

It is important also to note the concept of compatibility of a quasi-ordering with an ordering.

DEFINITION 1*6. *If Q, a quasi-ordering, is a subrelation of an ordering R, then R is said to be compatible with Q.*

Next, we shall note two standard results without proving them here.

LEMMA 1*f. *For every quasi-ordering Q, there is an ordering R compatible with Q.*[6]

LEMMA 1*g. *If Q is a quasi-ordering such that $\forall x, y \in S \subset X$: $x\, Q\, y \leftrightarrow x = y$, and T is an ordering of elements of S, then there is an ordering R of all elements of X such that R is compatible with both Q and T.*[7]

For any particular application the two lemmas are trivial, but they are not so in their full generality. Lemma 1*g, it may be noted, subsumes Lemma 1*f, and asserts that any quasi-ordering can be completed consistently with an ordering of a subset over which the quasi-ordering in question is incomplete for every pair.

We can define the compatibility of two quasi-ordering as follows:

DEFINITION 1*7. *Two quasi-orderings Q_1 and Q_2 are compatible if and only if there is an ordering compatible with each.*

The following results are immediate:

LEMMA 1*h. *If a quasi-ordering Q_1 is a subrelation of a quasi-ordering Q_2, then Q_1 and Q_2 are compatible.*

---

[6] See Szpilrajn (1930), pp. 386–389. Szpilrajn is concerned with partial orderings, but the proof for quasi-orderings is similar.

[7] Arrow (1951), pp. 64–68.

LEMMA 1*i.   *If Q is a quasi-ordering such that $\forall x, y \in S \subset X$: $x Q y \leftrightarrow x = y$, and T is a quasi-ordering of elements of S, then there is an ordering R of all elements of X such that R is compatible with both Q and T.*

Lemma 1*i is a slight extension of 1*g. By Lemma 1*f, an ordering T^* can be defined over S such that T^* is compatible with T, and by Lemma 1*g there is an ordering R defined over X such that R is compatible with Q and T^*. It is trivial to prove that if R is compatible with T^* over X, and T is a subrelation of T^*, then R is compatible with T. What it does mean, however, is that if we take two quasi-orderings such that each violates completeness for every pair of alternatives for which the other is complete, then they are compatible. In social choice this may be important in permitting the use of a number of independent principles of preference.

1*5.   Choice Functions and Quasi-Transitivity

In Section 1*2 we defined a choice set. We can now define a choice function.

DEFINITION 1*8.   *A choice function $C(S, R)$ defined over X is a functional relation such that the choice set $C(S, R)$ is nonempty for every nonempty subset S of X.*

To say that there exists a choice function $C(S, R)$ defined over X is thus equivalent to saying that there is a best element in every nonempty subset of X. The existence of a choice function is obviously important for rational choice.

If a preference relation violates completeness, clearly a choice function will not exist. There will be some pair x, y in X, for which neither $x R y$, nor $y R x$, so that the choice set of this pair (x, y) will be empty. Similarly a violation of reflexivity will make a choice function impossible, since there will then be some alternative x, such that it would not be regarded as good as itself.

If on top of reflexivity and completeness, we also assume transitivity, then we get an ordering. Before we consider the possibility of getting a choice function in spite of violating transitivity, an elementary result on orderings is noted.

LEMMA 1*j.   *If R is an ordering defined over a finite set X, then a choice function $C(S, R)$ is defined over X.*

The proof is similar to that for Lemma 1*b and is omitted here. When the set X is not finite, the existence of an ordering over X does not, of course, guarantee a choice function; for example, we might have $x_j \, P \, x_{j-1}$ for $j = 2, 3, \ldots, \infty$.

While given reflexivity and completeness, transitivity is a sufficient condition for the existence of a choice function over a finite set, it is not a necessary condition.   A weaker sufficiency condition is noted below.

DEFINITION 1*9.   *If for all* $x, y, z \in X$, $x \, P \, y$ & $y \, P \, z \rightarrow x \, P \, z$, *then* R *is quasi-transitive.*

This condition was earlier referred to as PP, in the context of Lemma 1*a.

LEMMA 1*k.   *If R is reflexive, complete and quasi-transitive over a finite set X, then a choice function $C(S, R)$ is defined over X.*[8]

Proof.   Let there be n alternatives in $S \subset X$, viz., $x_1, \ldots, x_n$. Consider first the pair (x_1, x_2).   By reflexivity and completeness of R, there is a best element in this pair.   The proof is now completed by induction through showing that if $(x_1, \ldots, x_j)$ has a best element, then so does $(x_1, \ldots, x_j, x_{j+1})$.   Let a_j be a best element of the former set, so that $a_j \, R \, x_k$, for $k = 1, \ldots, j$.   Either $x_{j+1} \, P \, a_j$, or $a_j \, R \, x_{j+1}$.   If the latter, then a_j is a best element of $(x_1, \ldots, x_{j+1})$ as well.   If the former, then x_{j+1} can fail to be a best element of $(x_1, \ldots, x_{j+1})$ only if $x_k \, P \, x_{j+1}$ for some $k = 1, \ldots, j$.   Then by quasi-transitivity of R, we must have $x_k \, P \, a_j$, which contradicts $a_j \, R \, x_k$.   This completes the proof.

It is to be noted that while quasi-transitivity is sufficient, it is not necessary for a choice function to exists for a finite set.   Indeed it can be shown that no condition defined over only triples can be necessary for the existence of choice functions.   The property of *acyclicity* may now be introduced.

DEFINITION 1*10.   *R is acyclical over X if and only if the following holds:*

$$\forall x_1, \ldots, x_j \in X: \ [\{x_1 \, P \, x_2 \ \& \ x_2 \, P \, x_3 \ \& \ \cdots \ \& \ x_{j-1} \, P \, x_j\} \rightarrow x_1 \, R \, x_j]$$

---

[8] See Sen (1969), Theorem II; also Pattanaik (1968).   For infinite sets it is necessary that P be "founded," i.e., no infinitely long descending chains are permitted.   This is one aspect of the concept of well-ordering of Whitehead and Russell (1913).   On this and other questions concerning choice functions, see Herzberger (1968).

LEMMA 1*l. *If R is reflexive and complete, then a necessary and sufficient condition for C(S, R) to be defined over a finite X is that R be acyclical over X.*

Proof. First the proof of necessity. Suppose R is not acyclical. Then there is some subset of j alternatives in X such that $x_1 P x_2, \ldots,$ $x_{j-1} P x_j$, $x_j P x_1$. Clearly there is no best element in this subset, so that a choice function does not exist over X. The proof of sufficiency can begin with noting that if all the alternatives are indifferent to each other then they are all best, so that we need be concerned only with cases where there is at least one strictly ordered pair, say, $x_2 P x_1$. Now, x_2 can fail to be the best element of S only if there is some element, say x_3, in X such that $x_3 P x_2$. If $x_1 P x_3$, then by acyclicity $x_1 R x_2$, which is a contradiction. Thus, x_3 is a best element of (x_1, x_2, x_3). Proceeding this way we can exhaust all the elements of S without the choice set becoming empty. So acyclicity is necessary and sufficient.

It may be noted that acyclicity over triples only, i.e., $\forall x, y, z \in X$: $[x P y \ \& \ y P z \to x R z]$, is not a sufficient condition for the existence of a choice function, for acyclicity over triples does not imply acyclicity over the whole set. Consider, for example, the set of four alternatives x_1, x_2, x_3, x_4, such that $x_1 P x_2$, $x_2 P x_3$, $x_3 P x_4$, $x_4 P x_1$, $x_1 I x_3$ and $x_2 I x_4$. No triple violates acyclicity, but the whole set violates it, and there is no best element in the whole set.

Finally, it follows from Lemma 1*k and 1*l that quasi-transitivity, which is a condition on triples, does imply acyclicity. The converse, however, does not follow.

1*6. Preference and Rational Choice

The existence of a choice function is in some ways a condition of rational choice. A choice function has been defined here on the basis of a binary preference relation, so that the existence of a nonempty choice set is equivalent to the existence of some alternative which is regarded as at least as good as every other one in the set. This is itself a rationality property, noted in the context of majority rule by Condorcet as early as 1785.

We can, however, also define certain rationality conditions in terms of the properties of the choice function (see Arrow (1959)). For this purpose we take $C(S)$ as any choice function defined over some X, not necessarily derived with respect to some binary preference relation. It is, of course, easy to consider choice functions that cannot possibly be derived from any binary relation, e.g., $C([x, y, z]) = [x]$, and $C([x, y]) = [y]$. To guarantee that not only can we choose, but we can choose rationally, certain properties of the choice function may have to be specified. We consider (see Sen (1969)):

Property α: $x \in S_1 \subset S_2 \rightarrow [x \in C(S_2) \rightarrow x \in C(S_1)]$, for all x
Property β: $[x, y \in C(S_1)$ & $S_1 \subset S_2] \rightarrow [x \in C(S_2) \leftrightarrow y \in C(S_2)]$, for all x, y

Property α states that if some element of subset S_1 of S_2 is best in S_2, then it is best in S_1. This is a very basic requirement of rational choice, and in a different context has been called the condition of "the independence of irrelevant alternatives."[9] Property β is also appealing, though it is perhaps somewhat less intuitive than property α. It requires that if x and y are both best in S_1, a subset of S_2, the one of them cannot be best in S_2 without the other being also best in S_2. To give an example, property α states that if the world champion in some game is a Pakistani, then he must also be the champion in Pakistan, while property β states that if some Pakistani is a world champion, then *all* champions of Pakistan must be champions of the world.

The remainder of this chapter leans heavily on Sen (1969).

LEMMA 1*m. *Every choice function $C(S, R)$ generated by a binary relation R satisfies property α but not necessarily property β.*

Proof. If x belongs to $C(S, R)$, clearly $x R y$ for all y in S and therefore $x R y$ for all y in any subset of S. Hence property α is satisfied.

Now consider a triple, x, y, z such that $x I y$, $x P z$, and $z P y$. It is clear that $[x, y] = C([x, y], R)$, and $[x] = C([x, y, z], R)$. This violates property β.

There seems to be a close relationship between a choice function fulfilling property β and the underlying preference relation satis-

---

[9] See Nash (1950), Chernoff (1954), Radner and Marschak (1954), and Luce and Raiffa (1957). This condition should not, however, be confused with Arrow's (1951) condition of the same name, which is a condition on the functional relationship between social preference and individual preferences; see Chapter 3*.

fying condition *PI*, which was mentioned in the context of Lemma 1*a.

DEFINITION 1*11.   *Relation R is PI-transitive over X if and only if for all x, y, z in X, $x\,P\,y$ & $y\,I\,z \rightarrow x\,P\,z$.*

LEMMA 1*n.   *A choice function C(S, R) generated by a binary relation R satisfies property β if and only if R is PI-transitive.*[10]

Proof. It has been noted earlier that a binary relation must be complete and reflexive to generate a choice function. Now suppose that *PI* is violated. Then there is a triple x, y, z such that $x\,P\,y$, $y\,I\,z$ and $z\,R\,x$. Obviously $[y, z] = C([y, z], R)$. Further, $z \in C([x, y, z], R)$, but $\sim[y \in C([x, y, z], R)]$. Thus property β is violated.

Conversely, suppose that property β is violated. Then we have a pair x, y such that $x, y \in C(S_1, R)$, $x \in C(S_2, R)$, and $\sim[y \in C(S_2, R)]$ when $S_1 \subset S_2$. Clearly, there exists some z in S_2 such that $z\,P\,y$ & $x\,R\,z$. We know that $x\,I\,y$, since $x, y \in C(S_1, R)$. Now, $z\,P\,y$ & $y\,I\,x \rightarrow z\,P\,x$, by *PI*-transitivity. But we know that $x\,R\,z$. Hence R cannot possibly satisfy *PI*. This completes the proof of the lemma.

What is the precise interrelationship between *PP* (quasi-transitivity), *PI*, and transitivity?

LEMMA 1*o.   (*a*)   *In general, PP and PI are completely independent of each other.*
    (*b*)   *Together, PP and PI imply transitivity, given completeness of R.*

Proof. Statement (*a*) is proved by considering two examples. Consider $x\,P\,y$, $y\,P\,z$ and $z\,P\,x$. This violates *PP*, but not *PI*. Next consider $x\,P\,y$, $y\,I\,z$ and $x\,I\,z$. This violates *PI*, but not *PP*.

Statement (*b*) is proved by making the contrary supposition that *PI* and *PP* hold, but transitivity does not. Then for some triple x, y, z we must have $x\,R\,y$, $y\,R\,z$ and $\sim(x\,R\,z)$, i.e., $z\,P\,x$, by the completeness of R. Now, $x\,R\,y$ implies $x\,P\,y \lor x\,I\,y$. Suppose $x\,P\,y$. Then from $z\,P\,x$ and by virtue of *PP* we must have $z\,P\,y$. But this is false. Therefore $x\,I\,y$. Then from $z\,P\,x$ and by virtue

---

[10] Sen (1969), Theorem III.

of *PI* we must have $z P y$, which is the same false statement. This contradiction establishes the result, and this completes the proof of the lemma.

However, if *R* must generate a choice function, then there is a close relationship between *PI* and *PP*, viz., *PI* implies *PP* (though the converse does not hold). Thus, *PI* is then equivalent to full transitivity.

LEMMA 1*p. *If a binary relation R generates a choice function, then PI-transitivity implies that R is an ordering.*[11]

Proof. Reflexivity and completeness of *R* are trivial. By Lemma 1*o we need only show that *PI* implies *PP*.

Suppose *PP* is violated. Then there is a triple *x, y, z*, such that $x P y$, $y P z$ and $z R x$. If $z P x$, then $C([x, y, z], R)$ will be empty. Hence $z I x$ holds. But $[y P z \ \& \ z I x] \rightarrow y P x$, by *PI*. We know, however, that $x P y$. Thus *PI* must also be violated. Thus *PI* implies *PP*, so that *PI* also implies that *R* is an ordering (in view of Lemma 1*o), which completes the proof.

From Lemmas 1*n and 1*p we immediately obtain the following result as a corollary:

LEMMA 1*q. *A choice function C(S, R) derived from a binary relation R satisfies property β if and only if R is an ordering.*[12]

To extend the picture on the different aspects of transitivity, we also note some further entailment relations which hold whether or not a choice function exists.

LEMMA 1*r. *If R is complete, then* (a) $PI \leftrightarrow IP$; (b) $PI \rightarrow II$; *and* (c) $PP \ \& \ II \rightarrow PI$.

The proofs are omitted here, but for (a) can be found in Sonnenschein (1965) and Lorimer (1967), and for (b) and (c) are given in Sen (1969). They are all straightforward.[13]

Finally, we show in the form of two diagrams the main relations between *PP*, *PI*, *II*, *IP*, and transitivity *T* of *R*, the existence of $C(S, R)$ over a finite *S*, and the fulfillment of the rationality conditions α and β. The direction of the arrow represents the direction

---

[11] Sen (1969), Theorem IV.

[12] Sen (1969). See also Arrow (1959).

[13] Some important results on preference and choice, which we do not go into here, will be found in Herzberger (1968) and Hansson (1969).

of implication.   In Diagram 1*2, the implications within the box
hold if the choice function $C(S, R)$ exists.

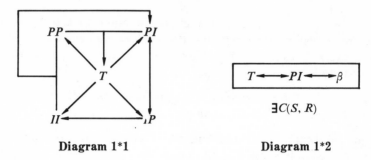

Diagram 1*1   **Diagram 1*2**

Chapter 2

UNANIMITY

2.1. The Pareto Criterion

A very simple criterion of comparison of social welfare is associated with the name of Pareto (Pareto (1897)). In this approach the two following rules are used: (a) if everyone in the society is indifferent between two alternative social situations x and y, then the society should be indifferent too; and (b) if at least one individual strictly prefers x to y, and every individual regards x to be at least as good as y, then the society should prefer x to y. This criterion has an obvious appeal. When (a) is satisfied, it does not matter for anyone which of the two alternatives is chosen by the society; hence it is safe to choose either. When (b) is satisfied, it is in no one's interest to be at y rather than at x, and it is in someone's interest to be at x rather than at y; hence it seems reasonable to say that the society, as an aggregate of the individuals, does prefer x to y.

To get our terminology unambiguous, when (a) is fulfilled we shall say that the society is Pareto-wise indifferent between x and y, and when (b) is fulfilled that x is Pareto-wise better than y. We can now consider the concept of *Pareto-optimality*. In a given choice situation, consider the set of alternatives X from which choice would have to be made. An alternative x belonging to that set will be described as Pareto-optimal if there is no other alternative in the set which is Pareto-wise better than x. That is, x is Pareto-optimal if we cannot choose an alternative that everyone will regard to be at least as good as x and which at least one person will regard to be strictly better than x.

A great deal of modern welfare economics has been based on this approach. The "optimality" of a system or of a policy is often judged in terms of whether it achieves Pareto-optimality or not.[1] This may seem alright as far as it goes, but how far does it go? If one individual prefers x to y, and another prefers y to x, then we cannot compare them socially using the Pareto rule no matter how the rest of them evaluate x vis-a-vis y and no matter how many of them there are. It is clear that the social preference relation derived from the Pareto criterion, while reflexive and transitive (given that each individual has a quasi-ordering), may not have the property of completeness, even when all the individuals constituting the society have complete preference orderings. Precisely how incomplete the Pareto criterion will be depends on how unanimous the individuals are. On the one extreme lies the case in which everyone has the same preference ordering,[2] when the social ordering will in fact be, for this special case, complete. At the other end lies the case in which two individuals have strictly opposite preferences,[3] when no alternatives whatever could be compared with each other by using the Pareto rule. Neither extreme may be common, and in an intermediate case some comparisons can be made by using the Pareto rule, but not all. How many comparisons can be made will depend on the precise circumstances.

In the difficult field of welfare economics even small mercies count, so that there is much to commend in the Pareto criterion, in spite of its incompleteness. But there is a danger in being exclusively concerned with Pareto-optimality. An economy can be optimal in this sense even when some people are rolling in luxury and others are near starvation as long as the starvers cannot be made better off without cutting into the pleasures of the rich. If preventing the burning of Rome would have made Emperor Nero feel worse off, then letting him burn Rome would have been Pareto-optimal. In short, a society or an economy can be Pareto-optimal and still be perfectly disgusting.

2.2. Pareto-Inclusive Choice Rules

We shall call methods of going from individual orderings to social

---

[1] See the literature on the optimality of competitive equilibrium, e.g., Arrow (1951a), Debreu (1959).

[2] It does not have to be strictly the same, as long as whenever x is preferred to y by some individual, all others regard x to be at least as good as y.

[3] More explicitly, of the two individuals each has a strong ordering over the entire range of alternatives, and whenever one prefers one alternative to another, the other individual prefers the latter to the former.

preference "collective choice rules" (CCR). For example, the "method of majority decision" (MMD) is one such CCR whereby x is declared as socially at least as good as y if and only if at least as many people prefer x to y as prefer y to x. The MMD often yields intransitive social preference, but it is always "decisive" over every pair in the sense that it yields complete preference orderings, i.e., either x is socially at least as good as y, or y is socially at least as good as x. The Pareto criterion, taken on its own, also generates a CCR, but it is not pair-wise decisive, because of the possible incompleteness of the Pareto relation. The Pareto-optimal elements are not ranked vis-a-vis each other.

A CCR that subsumes the Pareto relation, but possibly goes beyond it will be called a Pareto-inclusive CCR. The MMD is a Pareto-inclusive CCR. If x is Pareto-superior to y, then x must strictly win over y in a majority vote, but x and y may be Pareto-wise incomparable and still one of the two will win over the other (or the two will tie, indicating social indifference) in a majority vote. If the Pareto criterion is found to be compelling, then our interest should focus on Pareto-inclusive CCRs.

One way of getting a "best" alternative specified from a Pareto-optimal set with more than one element is to order the Pareto-optimal alternatives. We may wish, for example, to take note of considerations of income distribution,[4] since the Pareto criterion is efficiency-oriented and neutral between income distributions. There are difficulties in this, some of which we shall discuss later on.

A particularly simple way of extending the Pareto relation is to declare all Pareto-optimal points as indifferent. This will amount to a deliberate exclusion of distributional considerations. I cannot believe that this will appeal to many people, but I do not doubt that it might appeal to some, if the almost exclusive concern with the Pareto relation in modern welfare economics is any indication. We shall have the occasion to examine it more closely in Chapters 5 and 5*.

It is also possible to have CCRs that are not "decisive," but which generate preference relations that are more extensive than the Pareto relation and subsume it. This can be seen in certain criteria of aggregate welfare (Chapters 7 and 7*), of bargaining solutions (Chapters 8 and 8*), and of justice (Chapters 9 and 9*). It is fair

---

[4] See Fisher (1956) and Kenen and Fisher (1957).

to say that most CCRs that are usually considered are Pareto-inclusive, at least in a weaker form.

In the weaker form of the Pareto principle, x may be declared as socially better than y, if *everyone* strictly prefers x to y. This criterion says less than the usual Pareto criterion since nothing is stated about a case where someone prefers x to y and everyone regards x to be at least as good as y.

If x is Pareto-superior to y in this more demanding sense, it will be difficult to argue that x should not be socially preferred to y. If everyone in the society wants x rather than y, in which sense can society prefer y to x, or even be indifferent or undecided?[5] This is a fairly compelling argument, but I would doubt that it is altogether unexceptionable.   If the choice between a pair of alternatives must be based exclusively on individual preferences over that pair only, then the problem looks simple enough.   But if one thinks of a CCR such that the social choice over x and y depends also on individual preferences over other pairs (e.g., x and z, and y and z), then the picture is not that clear.   It is perhaps too complicated an argument to go into without some further study of collective choice rules, and we postpone a discussion on this until Chapter 6.   For the moment we shall take the Pareto criterion as compelling.   The fact remains, however, that it is severely incomplete and something more is needed.

2.3.   Consensus as a Basis of Collective Action

In spite of this incompleteness of the Pareto quasi-ordering, arguments have been put forward in recent years in favor of exclusive reliance on general consensus or unanimity as a basis of social action.   Buchanan and Tullock (1962), in particular, have produced a very painstaking analysis of the consequences of such an approach, which they have contrasted favorably with other approaches.   Departures from the unanimity rule are tolerated by them only when it is too expensive to reach decisions unanimously.

> The individualistic theory of the constitution we have been able to develop assigns a central role to a single decision-making rule—that of general consensus or unanimity.   The other pos-

---

[5] Cf. Cassen (1967).

> sible rules for choice-making are introduced as variants from the unanimity rule. These variants will be rationally chosen, not because they will produce 'better' collective decisions (they will not), but rather because on balance, the sheer weight of the costs involved in reaching decisions unanimously dictates some departure from the 'ideal' rule. (Buchanan and Tullock (1962), p. 96)

When there is a unanimity of views on some issue, clearly this provides a very satisfactory basis for choice.   Difficulties in social choice arise precisely because unanimity does not exist on many questions.   What do we do then?   One answer is to insist on unanimity for a *change*, and if there is no such unanimity for any proposed change, then to stick to the *status quo*.   The rule for social choice then can be summed up thus: Given that some prefer an alternative x to the status quo y and no one regards x to be worse than y, x is socially preferred to y; and when this condition is not satisfied, the status quo y is preferred to the other alternative x.

This method is one of supreme conservatism.   Even a single person opposing a change can block it altogether no matter what everybody else wants.[6]   Marie Antoinette's opposition to the First Republic would have saved the monarchy in France, and the world would have seen very little change.   Clearly there is something grotesquely unsatisfactory about a social decision rule like this.

It has been argued by Buchanan and Tullock that "modern political theorists have perhaps shrugged off the unanimity requirement too early in their thinking" (Buchanan and Tullock (1962), p. 250) and that "the existence of conflicts of interest does not preclude the attainment of unanimity" (Buchanan and Tullock (1962),

---

[6] Buchanan and Tullock (1962) refers to the "paradoxical result *that the rule of unanimity is the same as the minority rule of one*" (p. 259). But they point out the important logical distinction between the power of "taking action" and that of "blocking action," and it is for the latter that unanimity gives such power to each. What is, however, doubtful is Buchanan and Tullock's statement that this distinction "represents the difference between the power *to impose external costs on others* and the power *to prevent external costs from* being imposed" (p. 259). It depends much on what kind of action is involved. Buchanan and Tullock discuss cases of compulsory contribution, e.g., for road repair. However, if an antipollution move is lost for lack of unanimous support, one individual (e.g., the owner of a smokey factory) will be exercising power to impose an *external* cost on others.

p. 255).   It is certainly true that even when unanimity of views
does not exist to start with, discussions and bargaining may even-
tually bring it about.   It is also true that this process of compromises
and "trades" among themselves is essentially "equivalent to the
logrolling process."[7]   I can eschew my mild opposition to your
proposal in return for your support for mine about which I feel
more strongly.   Indeed, unanimity can emerge when none existed
to start with.

This is a valuable point, and a theory of collective choice must
take into account such compromises.   Two explanatory observations are, however, worth making in this context.   First, a collective
choice rule, as we have envisaged it, is based on individual orderings over complete descriptions of social states x, y, etc., which
represent all possible combinations of decisions on separate issues,
and this includes logrolling compromises.   What the Buchanan-
Tullock argument points out is that over some choices involving
such compromises unanimity might exist even though there are
conflicts of interests in separate issues.   This does not, of course,
mean that the individual orderings must be, in general, largely
unanimous.[8]

Second, it could not be overemphasized that what compromises
people are ready to accept depends much on their own assessment
of their relative bargaining power.   The fact that all members of
a community come to accept a certain social situation does not
necessarily mean that it is unanimously preferred to other social
alternatives.   A laborer in a monopsonistic labor market may accept certain terms of agreement feeling that he cannot hope to get
anything better, but this does not mean that it is unanimously
preferred to an alternative set of terms.   This is a simple enough
point but it does indicate that the general acceptance of a compromise solution should not be interpreted as universal endorsement.   In Chapters 8 and 8* bargaining solutions will be examined
in the light of the requirements of an ethical model.

---

[7] Buchanan and Tullock (1962), p. 255.   See Chapter 10 of their book for an
illuminating discussion of this process.   See also Wilson (1968), (1968a), (1968b).

[8] In the context of the "impossibility theorem" of Arrow, to be discussed in
the next chapter, Buchanan and Tullock have asserted that when "votes are
traded," "the particular type of irrationality described by Arrow is impossible"
(Buchanan and Tullock (1962), p. 332; also footnote 14, p. 359).   This seems to
be based on a misinterpretation of the nature of the alternatives over which the
individual preferences are defined.   On this question, see Arrow (1963), p. 109.

It is, however, interesting to enquire into implications of taking Pareto-incompleteness as equivalent to social indifference.   We shall do this in Chapter 5, and we shall present in Chapter 5* a set of axioms that are necessary and sufficient for this rather arbitrary rule.

Chapter 2*

COLLECTIVE CHOICE RULES AND PARETO COMPARISONS

2*1. Choice and Pareto Relation

Let X be the set of social states.   The preference relation of the ith individual is R_i, and let there be n such persons, $i = 1, \ldots, n$. Let R refer to the social preference relation.   We assume that each individual has an ordering, i.e., for each i, R_i is reflexive, transitive, and complete.   For the relation of social preference R, no such assumption is easy to make, and indeed it is part of our exercise to see whether R will have these characteristics or not.   We do not, therefore, demand at this stage[1] that R must be an ordering.

DEFINITION 2*1. *A collective choice rule is a functional relation f such that for any set of n individual orderings $R_1, \ldots, R_n$ (one ordering for each individual), one and only one social preference relation R is determined, $R = f(R_1, \ldots, R_n)$.*

DEFINITION 2*2. *A collective choice rule is decisive if and only if its range is restricted to complete preference relations R.*

We now define Pareto preference ($\bar{P}$), indifference ($\bar{I}$), and preference or indifference ($\bar{R}$).

DEFINITION 2*3. *For all x, y in X*

(1) $x \bar{R} y \leftrightarrow [\forall i: x R_i y]$
(2) $x \bar{P} y \leftrightarrow [x \bar{R} y \ \& \ \sim(y \bar{R} x)]$
(3) $x \bar{I} y \leftrightarrow [x \bar{R} y \ \& \ y \bar{R} x]$

We can derive a collective choice rule from the Pareto relation by requiring that $x \bar{R} y \leftrightarrow x R y$.   We can, alternatively, merely require that $x \bar{R} y \rightarrow x R y$, or that $x \bar{P} y \rightarrow x P y$, or that $x \bar{I} y \rightarrow x I y$,

---

[1] In Chapter 3* we shall examine the particular case when R is required to be an ordering, which corresponds to Arrow's "social welfare function."

without the converse implication. This will be a *condition* on a collective choice rule, rather than a rule itself.

It is easy to check that $\bar{R}$ must be a quasi-ordering.

LEMMA 2*a. *Relation $\bar{R}$ is a quasi-ordering for every logically possible combination of individual preferences.*

Proof. Since $\forall x \in X:\ x\,R_i\,x$, $\bar{R}$ is reflexive. Further,

$$\forall x, y, z \in X:\ [x\,\bar{R}\,y\ \&\ y\,\bar{R}\,z] \to \forall i:\ [x\,R_i\,y\ \&\ y\,R_i\,z]$$
$$\to \forall i:\ x\,R_i\,z$$
$$\to x\,\bar{R}\,z$$

Relation $\bar{R}$ is not necessarily an ordering, for it may violate completeness. When will $\bar{R}$ be an ordering?

LEMMA 2*b. *A necessary and sufficient condition for $\bar{R}$ to be an ordering and for $R = \bar{R}$ to be a decisive collective choice rule is that*

$$\forall x, y \in X:\ [(\exists i:\ x\,P_i\,y) \to (\forall j:\ x\,R_j\,y)]$$

Proof. For any pair x, y, if $x\,I_i\,y$ for all i, then the condition is trivially fulfilled, and also $x\,\bar{I}\,y$. If, on the other hand, $\exists i:\ x\,P_i\,y$, then $\forall j:\ x\,R_j\,y$, and hence $x\,\bar{R}\,y$. On the other hand, if the condition is violated, then $\exists i:\ x\,P_i\,y\ \&\ \exists j:\ y\,P_j\,x$, and $\sim(x\,\bar{R}\,y)\ \&\ \sim(y\,\bar{R}\,x)$, and completeness is violated. Thus the condition is sufficient *and* necessary.

We can define a weaker version of the strict Pareto relation.

DEFINITION 2*4. *For all x, y in X*

$$x\,\bar{\bar{P}}\,y \leftrightarrow \forall i:\ x\,P_i\,y$$

We note, without proofs, two results. The proofs are obvious.

LEMMA 2*c. *Both $\bar{P}$ and $\bar{\bar{P}}$ are strict partial orderings (transitive and asymmetric) for every logically possible combination of individual preferences.*

LEMMA 2*d. $\qquad \forall x, y \in X:\ x\,\bar{\bar{P}}\,y \to x\,\bar{P}\,y$

To assume that $x\,P\,y \leftrightarrow x\,\bar{\bar{P}}\,y$ for all x, y, does not define a collective choice rule. This is because $\sim(x\,\bar{\bar{P}}\,y)$ leaves it undecided as to whether $y\,R\,x$. We know that $x\,P\,y \leftrightarrow [x\,R\,y\ \&\ \sim(y\,R\,x)]$, so that $\sim(x\,P\,y)$ can coexist with incompleteness, i.e., $\sim(x\,R\,y)\ \&$

$\sim(y\,R\,x)$, or with indifference, $x\,I\,y$. We can assume that $x\,R\,y \leftrightarrow x\,\bar{\bar{P}}\,y$, or $x\,R\,y \leftrightarrow \sim(y\,\bar{\bar{P}}\,x)$, or something in between. These are collective choice rules, and note that in the first case R may be incomplete, while in the second case, it must be complete.

We can make similar observations about $\bar{P}$, and similarly consider $x\,R\,y \leftrightarrow x\,\bar{P}\,y$, or $x\,R\,y \leftrightarrow \sim(y\,\bar{P}\,x)$, or something else. Once again R under the first may violate completeness, while R under the second cannot.

Traditional welfare economics has been essentially "Paretian" in the sense of taking $x\,R\,y$ whenever $x\,\bar{R}\,y$ and $x\,P\,y$ whenever $x\,\bar{P}\,y$. We can call the class of collective choice rules satisfying these conditions Pareto-inclusive choice rules.

DEFINITION 2*5.   *A collective choice rule is Pareto-inclusive if and only if its range is restricted to social preference relations R such that the Pareto relations $\bar{R}$ is a subrelation of R, i.e.,*

$$\forall x, y \in X:\ [(x\,\bar{R}\,y \to x\,R\,y)\ \&\ (x\,\bar{P}\,y \to x\,P\,y)]$$

Social states are Pareto-optimal if they are not Pareto-inferior to any other alternative in S.

DEFINITION 2*6.   *For any n-tuple of individual preferences $(R_1, \ldots, R_n)$, a state $x \in S$ is Pareto-optimal in S if and only if $\sim[\exists y \in S: y\,\bar{P}\,x]$. A Pareto-optimal state is also called economically efficient.*

LEMMA 2*e.   *For every set of individual preferences $(R_1, \ldots, R_n)$ over any finite set of social states S, there is at least one Pareto-optimal state.*

Proof.   By Lemma 2*a, the Pareto preference relation $\bar{R}$ is a quasi-ordering. And the Pareto-optimal subset is merely the maximal set of S with respect to $\bar{R}$, i.e., $M(S, \bar{R})$, as defined in Chapter 1*. By Lemma 1*b, $M(S, R)$ must be nonempty when S is finite and R is a quasi-ordering.

2*2.   Compensation Tests

We turn now to a set of attempts at extending the Pareto rule in the form of "compensation tests." Let $S(x)$ be all the social states that can be reached through redistribution starting from x. Of course, $x \in S(x)$. The compensation test as developed by Kaldor (1939) declares x to be superior to y if and only if we can reach a state z through redistribution from x such that $z\,P\,y$ according to the Pareto criterion, i.e., if there is a move from y to x the gainers can compensate the losers and still retain some gain.

DEFINITION 2*7. *According to the Kaldor compensation test for any* $x, y \in X$:

$$[x\,P\,y] \leftrightarrow \exists z: [z \in S(x) \;\&\; \forall i: z\,R_i\,y \;\&\; \exists i: z\,P_i\,y]$$

This subsumes the strict preference relation generated by the Pareto criterion in the sense that if $x\,\bar{P}\,y$, then x is better than y in terms of the Kaldor criterion. This is obvious since $x \in S(x)$. We may note, now, a sad result, first demonstrated by Scitovsky (1941).

LEMMA 2*f. *The Kaldor test is inconsistent with every possible CCR under some configuration of preferences.*

Proof. This follows from the fact that we may have $x\,P\,y$ and $y\,P\,x$ according to the Kaldor test. Take $x, y \in X$ such that $\exists z \in S(x): z\,\bar{P}\,y$, according to the Pareto criterion, and $\exists w \in S(y): w\,\bar{P}\,x$, according to the Pareto criterion.[2] The inconsistency is immediate.

This inconsistency is eliminated by the Scitovsky compensation test.

DEFINITION 2*8. *According to the Scitovsky compensation test, for any* $x, y \in X$: $x\,P\,y$ *if and only if* $x\,P\,y$ *&* $\sim(y\,P\,x)$ *according to the Kaldor compensation test.*

However, the preference relation generated by the Scitovsky compensation test may not be transitive, not even quasi-transitive (see Gorman (1955)).

LEMMA 2*g. *The Scitovsky compensation test may yield an intransitive* P.

Proof. It is readily checked that there is no contradiction in assuming that for some $x, y, z \in X$:

(1) $[\exists x' \in S(x): x'\,\bar{P}\,y] \;\&\; \sim[\exists y' \in S(y): y'\,\bar{P}\,x]$
(2) $[\exists y' \in S(y): y'\,\bar{P}\,z] \;\&\; \sim[\exists z' \in S(z): z'\,P\,y]$
(3) $\sim[\exists x' \in S(x): x'\,\bar{P}\,z]$

Clearly, $x\,P\,y$, $y\,P\,z$, but not $x\,P\,z$, according to the Scitovsky test.

---

[2] For the factual plausibility of this inconsistency, see Scitovsky (1941), and Little (1950).

A sufficient condition for the transitivity of P under the Scitovsky test is given below.[3]

LEMMA 2*h. *If for all x, y in X*

$$[\exists x' \in S(x): x' \, \bar{P} \, y] \to \forall y' \in S(y): [\exists x'' \in S(x): x'' \, \bar{R} \, y']$$

then P, under the Scitovsky test, is a strict partial ordering.

Proof. For any triple $x, y, z \in X$,

$$x \, P \, y \ \& \ y \, P \, z \to \exists x' \in S(x): x' \, \bar{P} \, y \ \& \ \exists y' \in S(y): y' \, \bar{P} \, z$$
$$\to \exists x'' \in S(x): x'' \, \bar{R} \, y' \ \& \ y' \, \bar{P} \, z$$

by assumption,

$$\to \exists x'' \in S(x): x'' \, \bar{P} \, z$$

Hence $x \, P \, z$, unless $\exists z' \in S(z): z' \, \bar{P} \, x$. But this assumption, if true, will imply that $\exists z'' \in S(z): z'' \, \bar{R} \, x' \ \& \ x' \, \bar{P} \, y$. But we know that $\sim[\exists z'' \in S(z): z'' \, \bar{P} \, y]$, since $y \, P \, z$, according to the Scitovsky test. This contradiction establishes $x \, P \, z$, and hence the lemma.

In fact, with the quoted assumption, the Kaldor preference relation and the Scitovsky preference relation are identical, since $x \, P \, y \to \sim (y \, P \, x)$ in the Kaldor test. The Kaldor test is perfectly consistent in this particular case.

---

[3] Cf. Samuelson (1950). Samuelson is not concerned with transitivity as such, but his condition of a complete outward movement of the "utility possibility frontier" is, in fact, sufficient for transitivity of strict preference.

Chapter 3

COLLECTIVE RATIONALITY

3.1. The Bergson-Samuelson Welfare Function

A rational and systematic way of thinking about social welfare is to try to define an ordering for the society over all possible alternative states. This fundamental idea, among others, was expressed in a seminal paper by Bergson (1938), though he put it somewhat differently. Social welfare can be thought to be a real-valued welfare function, W, "the value of which is understood to depend on all the variables that might be considered as affecting welfare" (Bergson (1948), p. 417). Such a social welfare function W may subsume the Pareto relation, if Pareto catches our fancy, though there is no real compulsion to assume even this. It can be defined in many alternative ways using many alternative criteria. The approach is very general (see Samuelson (1947), Chap. 8).

As an example of the use of this approach, we can refer to the literature on "social indifference curves." Using the Pareto indifference rule, one way of defining social indifference is that everyone in the society be indifferent. Scitovsky was concerned with this problem in a classic paper (1942) and required two alternative bundles of commodities to belong to the same social indifference curve if and only if everyone were indifferent between the two bundles for some distribution of each over the individuals. This concept can be extended by using the Bergson social welfare function. While person 1 may be better off in x than in y, and person 2 may be better off in y than in x, society might still be indifferent if the overall social judgment is that the gain of one exactly compensates the loss of another. Samuelson (1956), Graaff (1957), and others have analyzed the difference between keeping social walfare constant in the sense of Scitovsky and doing so in the sense of Bergson. If the Bergson social welfare function is Pareto-inclusive, as it is generally assumed to be, then social indifference in the sense

33

of Scitovsky implies *that* in the sense of Bergson, but not vice versa. This corresponds to the statement that the Pareto quasi-ordering is subsumed by a Pareto-inclusive social ordering (see Chapter 2*).

The concept of a Bergson welfare function is simple, perhaps deceptively so, and some observations in clarification may be called for. First, the *form* of the welfare function is not yet specified, and only a framework of rational thought is suggested. If nothing more were to be said than the conception of a Bergson welfare function, we would not have gone much further.[1] "Specific decisions on ends" (Bergson (1948), p. 417) have to be systematically introduced, thereby specifying the characteristics of the relation, and this is where difficulties are likely to be experienced.[2]

Second, nothing whatever is said in this analysis as to *who* provides the ends represented by the social welfare function. It may represent the views of an ethical observer, or the decisions of a consistent majority, or the dictates of an oligarchy, or the whims of a dictator, or the values of a class, or even be given simply by tradition. Nothing is specified about the genesis of the social ordering.

Finally, on a rather technical point, the particular method of representation chosen is unnecessarily restrictive. For the purpose of being able to choose between alternative social states, it is not really necessary that a real-valued W function must exist. What is needed is a complete social ordering R over all possible alternatives,[3] and this can exist without there being any real-valued walfare function corresponding to it.[4] For example, a complete "lexicographic ordering" over a two-dimensional real space cannot be represented by any real welfare function.

---

[1] See Samuelson (1947), p. 222.

> The subject could end with these banalities were it not for the fact that numerous individuals find it of interest to specify the form of W, the nature of the variables, z, and the nature of the constraints.

[2] See, for example, Graaff (1957) on the relevance of the convexity of "Bergson frontiers" in the context of the theory of index numbers.

[3] What is really needed for choice is not even an ordering, but a preference relation that specifies a "best" alternative in every choice situation. We discussed this in Chapter 1 and we shall go into it more deeply in Chapter 4.

[4] If risk is present, the ordering referred to should be over all possible "lotteries," and not merely over the certain alternatives.

A simple example of a lexicographic ordering is the following: Let the welfare levels of two persons be represented respectively by W_1 and W_2, and let it be decided that the social objective is: (a) maximize W_1, and (b) given the same value of W_1, maximize W_2. Suppose W_1 and W_2 can each take any value in the range 0 to 1, and the object is to represent social welfare W as a real-valued function of W_1 and W_2 representing the lexicographic ordering specified. No such representation is possible.[5] There is a perfectly fine social ordering R, but there is no social welfare function in this case as defined by Bergson. I do not believe, however, that we would do any injustice to Bergson's and Samuelson's ideas if we simply take R as a social welfare function rather than taking its real-valued representation W.[6]

3.2. Arrowian Social Welfare Function

The concept of a social welfare function W as proposed by Bergson (1938) and developed by Samuelson (1947) cleared up several barriers to rational thought on social choice. It was an important step in the history of welfare economics ending a rather confused debate begun by Robbins' (1932) celebrated attack on utilitarianism. In extending this idea, Arrow (1951) asked the question: What should determine the particular Bergson social welfare function to be used? In particular, how would the function W (or more generally the social ordering R) depend on individual preference orderings? Or, in other words, what should be the collective choice rule (as we defined it in the last chapter)?

Before we proceed further, two warning notes are due. First, Arrow's use of the expression social welfare function is different from that of Bergson and Samuelson.[7] A collective choice rule that specifies *orderings* for the society is called a social welfare function (hereafter, SWF) by Arrow. Any ordering for the society (more accurately, its real-valued representation) is a Bergson-Samuelson social welfare function (hereafter, swf). An Arrow

---

[5] See Debreu (1959). See also Little (1949), Chipman (1960), Banerji (1964), and Richter (1966).

[6] Bergson and Samuelson were writing at a time when it was common to assume that all orderings were representable by a utility function. Compare Hicks' (1939) concern with "ordinal utility" rather than with orderings. Samuelson himself was a pioneer in bringing about the change of approach.

[7] On this see Arrow (1951), pp. 23-24, and Samuelson (1967).

SWF determines a Bergson swf (or the ordering R underlying it) on the basis of individual orderings. The relation between the two is simple enough, but the two are not the same, and the terminology has been responsible for some confusion. Since our chief concern is with exercises of the kind that Arrow considered, we shall use the unqualified term social welfare function in his sense, but it is merely a matter of convenience and we resist the temptation to go into the semantic suitability of one use vis-a-vis the other.

Second, Arrow's SWF is a particular type of collective choice rule such that each social preference that is determined is an ordering, i.e., reflexive, transitive and complete. While Arrow is exclusively concerned with SWFs, some of the problems with which Arrow is involved apply more generally to all CCRs. There are, however, others (including the famous "impossibility theorem") which are specific to SWFs only.

While from the point of view of logic a SWF or a CCR can be defined in any consistent way we like, consistency is not the sole virtue that a collective choice mechanism has to satisfy. For example, it is logically perfectly alright to postulate the following SWF: If person A ("that well-known drunkard") prefers x to y, then society should prefer y to x, and if A is indifferent, then so should be society. As a SWF this can be best described by a non-technical term, viz., wild, and in serious discussions it may be useful to restrict the class of SWFs (and of CCRs, in general) by eliminating possibilities like this. One way of doing it is to require that the SWF (or CCR) must satisfy certain conditions of "reasonableness." Since reasonableness is a matter of opinion, it is useful to impose only very mild conditions, and one might wonder whether one could really restrict the class of SWFs very much by such a set of mild conditions. Well, surprisingly the problem comes from the other end. In his "General Possibility Theorem" Arrow proved that a set of very mild looking conditions are altogether so restrictive that they rule out not some but *every possible* SWF. We now turn to this problem.[8]

---

[8] We follow here the second verson of Arrow's theorem, first put forward in Arrow (1952) and then in the second edition of his book, Arrow (1963), Chap. VIII. The original version presented in Arrow (1950), (1951), contained a small error in its formulation, which was corrected by Blau (1957). See also Inada (1955), (1964), and Murakami (1961) for other impossibility theorems related to Arrow's.

3.3. The General Possibility Theorem

The four conditions that Arrow uses in his theorem are informally discussed here, with emphasis on their rationale, and later presented formally in Chapter 3*.

First, as a method of going from individual preferences to social preference, the SWF must be wide enough in scope to work from any logically possible set of individual orderings. Consider, for example, the Pareto principle as a choice rule. It gives a perfectly fine social ordering if the individual preferences are unanimous in the sense described in the last chapter. But it will not yield a social ordering in other situations, in which it will yield incomplete preference relations, and hence it fails to satisfy this requirement of Arrow. Similarly, the method of majority decision may yield intransitivities unless the individual preference orderings satisfy certain patterns (discussed in Chapters 10 and 10*), and hence the MMD also fails this test. This requirement that the rule must work for every logically possible configuration of individual preference orderings we shall call the *condition of unrestricted domain*, or condition *U*, for short.

Second, the SWF must satisfy the Pareto principle in the weak form, i.e., if everyone prefers *x* to *y*, then society must also prefer *x* to *y*. We have already discussed this condition in Chapter 2. We shall call it the *weak Pareto principle*, or condition *P*.

Third, Arrow requires that social choice over a set of alternatives must depend on the orderings of the individuals only over *those* alternatives, and not on anything else, e.g., on rankings of "irrelevant" alternatives that are not involved in this choice. Suppose the choice is between *x* and *y*, and individual rankings of *x* and *y* remain the same, but the rankings of *x* vis-a-vis some other alternative *z* changes, or the rankings of *z* vis-a-vis another alternative *w* alters. What is required is that the social choice between *x* and *y* should still remain the same. To give an analogy, in an election involving Mr. *A* and Mr. *B*, the choice should depend on the voters' orderings of *A* vis-a-vis *B*, and not on how the voters rank Mr. *A* vis-a-vis Lincoln, or Lincoln vis-a-vis Lenin.[9] This

---

[9] Views on Lincoln or Lenin could enter the picture (indeed *must* do so) if and only if the voters' orderings of *A* vis-a-vis *B* should themselves change as a consequence of a revision of opinion on Lenin or Lincoln.

requirement is called the *condition of independence of irrelevant alternatives*, or condition *I*.

Finally, it is required that the SWF should not be dictatorial. That is, there should be no individual such that whenever he prefers x to y, society must prefer x to y, irrespective of the preference of everyone else. This is called the *condition of nondictatorship*, or condition *D*.

The rather stunning theorem that Arrow proved is that there is no SWF that can simultaneously satisfy all these four conditions, mild as they look. Each looks innocuous enough, but together they seem to produce a monster that gobbles up all the little SWFs in the world.

The theorem is proved in Chapter 3*. We turn now to a discussion of the significance of the result.

3.4.   A Comment on the Significance of Arrow's Results

It has been known for a long time that some methods of combining individual preferences into social preference lead to inconsistencies. Condorcet (1785) had noted intransitivities of majority decision almost two centuries ago. Analysis of inconsistencies of majority rule attracted such colorful thinkers as C. L. Dogson (1876), better remembered as Lewis Carroll. The most discussed case of such inconsistency, the so-called "paradox of voting," was presented by Nanson (1882). This example provides a very good introduction to the nature of the problem, and may be profitably stated here. Consider three individuals 1, 2 and 3, and three alternatives x, y and z. Let individual 1 prefer x to y, and y to z, and individual 2 prefer y to z, and z to x, and individual 3 prefer z to x and x to y. It is easily checked that x can defeat y by two votes to one, y can defeat z by the same margin, so that transitivity requires that x should defeat z in a vote too. But, in fact, z defeats x by two votes to one. Thus, the method of majority decisions leads to inconsistencies.

This is, in itself, a very interesting result, because the method of majority decision is a highly appealing CCR. In particular it can be easily checked that the MMD satisfies condition *P*, condition *I*, and condition *D*. But it fails to satisfy condition *U*, so that the MMD is not an acceptable SWF if these four tests are used. The importance of Arrow's theorem lies in the fact that it shows that this problem occurs not only for the method of majority decision, which is after all only one method of social choice, but for every method known or unknown that can be conceived of. There simply is no possibility of getting a SWF such that the four conditions stated can be simultaneously fulfilled.

It may be useful to illustrate this impossibility with some other well-known methods of social decision. A very old method is the so-called "rank order" method of voting. A certain number of marks are given to each alternative for being first in anyone's preference ordering, a smaller number for being second in someone's ordering, and so on; then the total number of marks received by each alternative is added up, and the one with the highest score wins. For example, in a three alternative case, let 3 be assigned for being first, 2 for being second, and 1 for being third. It is easily seen that this SWF is not dictatorial, so that it passes condition D. It conforms to the Pareto rule, thereby passing condition P. It also yields a complete social ordering starting from any set of individual orderings, and thus satisfies condition U. For example, note that in the case of Nanson's "paradox of voting" quoted earlier, x, y and z each receives six marks, and the outcome is not an inconsistency but a tie.

However, it does not pass condition I. Consider the following simple example: Let individual 1 prefer x to y and that to z, whereas individuals 2 and 3 prefer z to x and that to y. With the method of marking outlined, x receives 7 marks and so does z, and the outcome is a tie between the two. Now, consider a second case when everyone's ranking of x vis-a-vis z remains the same, but individual 1 changes his mind about an irrelevant alternative, viz., y, and decides that it is worse than both x and z. This change keeps the total score of x unchanged, but z gets one more mark, scoring 8, and now defeats x with its score of 7. While everyone's ordering of x and z are still the same, the social choice between x and z is not the same, and this of course violates condition I. So this SWF also fails to pass the test of the four conditions.

Next consider a somewhat odd CCR. Let the social preference be determined by an entirely specified traditional code implying a given ordering R^* of the social states. This satisfies condition U (trivially, since individual preferences do not really have any role), condition I (also trivially), and condition D (since no individual is a dictator and only a traditional code dictates). But this curious

SWF fails to pass the Pareto principle. Suppose the code requires that x be preferred to y. This remains so even if every person in the community prefers y to x, which violates condition P.

We can go on multiplying examples. The importance of the General Possibility Theorem lies in the fact that we can predict the result in each case, viz., that the specific example considered will not pass the four conditions, even without examining it. The theorem is completely general in its nihilism, and saves a long (and perhaps endless) search.

Chapter 3*

SOCIAL WELFARE FUNCTIONS

3*1. The Impossibility Theorem

A particular class of collective choice rules corresponds to Arrow's social welfare functions.

DEFINITION 3*1. *A social welfare function (henceforth, SWF) is a collective choice rule f, the range of which is restricted to the set of orderings over X. This restriction is to be called condition O on f.*

Arrow's general possibility theorem consists of imposing certain conditions on a social welfare function f and showing that these conditions are mutually incompatible. We state these conditions below.[1]

Condition U (unrestricted domain): The domain of the rule f must include all logically possible combinations of individual orderings.

Condition P (Pareto principle): For any pair, x, y in X, $[\forall i: x P_i y] \rightarrow x P y$.

Condition I (independence of irrelevant alternatives): Let R and R' be the social binary relations determined by f corresponding respectively to two sets of individual preferences, $(R_1, \ldots, R_n)$ and $(R'_1, \ldots, R'_n)$. If for all pairs of alternatives x, y in a subset S of X, $x R_i y \leftrightarrow x R'_i y$, for all i, then $C(S, R)$ and $C(S, R')$ are the same.

---

[1] We have used different labeling of the conditions from Arrow's own and used the first letter of the crucial word to facilitate recollection. We use the version in Arrow (1963).

	Arrow's		*Ours*
Condition 1'	no name	condition U	unrestricted domain
Condition P	Pareto principle	condition P	Pareto principle
Condition 3	independence of irrelevant alternatives	condition I	independence of irrelevant alternatives
Condition 5	nondictatorship	condition D	nondictatorship

Condition D (nondictatorship): There is no individual i such that for every element in the domain of rule f, $\forall x, y \in X: x P_i y \rightarrow x P y$.

Note that we have defined these conditions generally for any collective choice rule f (and not necessarily for a SWF), so that we can use these conditions later for exercises on rules other than SWF. Note also that with condition D we have included the bound "for every element in the domain of rule f." In the absence of such a universal bound, there is the logical danger of regarding a totally indifferent man as a dictator, since for him the antecedence $x P_i y$ is false for all x, y in X. Arrow's somewhat rough definition is open to this ambiguous interpretation, which would be far from Arrow's intention.

We assume throughout this book that there are at least two persons in the society and at least three alternative social states. There are few problems of collective choice in an one-man society, and transitivity is trivial if there are only two alternative social states. Arrow's "General Possibility Theorem" is the following. This is the later version of the theorem to be found in Arrow (1963).

THEOREM 3*1. *There is no SWF satisfying conditions U, P, I and D.*

We prove this theorem below via two definitions and a lemma.[2] The lemma may be recognized to be of importance in its own right quite aside from the importance of the General Possibility Theorem.

DEFINITION 3*2. *A set of individuals V is almost decisive for x against y if x P y whenever x P_i y for every i in V, and y P_i x for every i not in V.*

DEFINITION 3*3. *A set of individuals V is decisive for x against y if x P y when x P_i y for every i in V.*

Notationally, we separate out a certain individual J, and denote $D(x, y)$ to mean that J is almost decisive for x against y, and

---

[2] The proof of the theorem given here is logically equivalent to Arrow's own proof. Arrow's proof is somewhat opaque, particularly since the use of the crucial condition I (i.e., his Condition 3) is never clarified; in fact this condition is never even mentioned in the proof. What we have done is to reset Arrow's proof somewhat differently.

denote $\bar{D}(x, y)$ to mean that J is decisive for x against y.[3] Note that $\bar{D}(x, y) \rightarrow D(x, y)$.

LEMMA 3*a. *If there is some individual J who is almost decisive for any ordered pair of alternatives, then a SWF satisfying conditions U, P and I, implies that J must be a dictator.*

Proof. Suppose that person J is almost decisive for some x against some y, i.e., $\exists x, y \in X: D(x, y)$. Let z be another alternative, and let i refer to all individuals other than J. Assume $x P_J y$ & $y P_J z$, and that $y P_i x$ & $y P_i z$. Notice that we have not specified the preferences of persons other than J between x and z.

Now, $[D(x, y)$ & $x P_J y$ & $y P_i x] \rightarrow x P y$. Further, $[y P_J z$ & $y P_i z] \rightarrow y P z$ from condition P. But, $[x P y$ & $y P z] \rightarrow x P z$ by the transitivity of the strict social ordering relation P.

This result, $x P z$, is arrived at without any assumption about the preferences of individuals other than J regarding x and z. It is, of course, true that we have assumed $y P_i z$ and $y P_i x$. Now, if these rankings of x vis-a-vis y, and of y vis-a-vis z, have any effect on the social choice between x and z, we violate condition I (independence of irrelevant alternatives). Hence, $x P z$ must be independent of these particular assumptions. Hence it must be the consequence of $x P_J z$ alone irrespective of the other orderings. But this means that J is decisive for x against z.

$$D(x, y) \rightarrow \bar{D}(x, z) \qquad (1)$$

Now, suppose $z P_J x$ & $x P_J y$, while $z P_i x$ & $y P_i x$. By condition P, we must have $z P x$. And since $D(x, y)$ & $x P_J y$ & $y P_i x$, we conclude that $x P y$. By transitivity, $z P y$. And this with only $z P_J y$, without anything being specified about the preferences of the other individuals between y and z. Hence, J is decisive for z against y. The argument is exactly similar to that used in obtaining (1).

$$D(x, y) \rightarrow \bar{D}(z, y) \qquad (2)$$

---

[3] Roughly, a person is "almost decisive" if he wins if there is opposition, and he is "decisive" proper if he wins whether he is opposed or not. Note that if "positive association between individual and social values" (see Chapter 5) is assumed, then the two definitions will be equivalent. *Then* if a person is decisive in spite of opposition, he must be so when others do not oppose him. For Theorem 3*1, however, such a condition is not included. And in the absence of it, to be decisive is somewhat stronger than being almost decisive, for the former implies the latter but not vice versa.

Interchanging y and z in (2), we can similarly show

$$D(x, z) \rightarrow \bar{D}(y, z) \qquad (3)$$

By putting x in place of z, z in place of y, and y in place of x, we obtain from (1),

$$D(y, z) \rightarrow \bar{D}(y, x) \qquad (4)$$

Now,

$$D(x, y) \rightarrow \bar{D}(x, z) , \quad \text{from (1)}$$
$$\rightarrow D(x, z) , \quad \text{from Definitions 3*2 and 3*3}$$
$$\rightarrow \bar{D}(y, z) , \quad \text{from (3)}$$
$$\rightarrow D(y, z) ,$$
$$\rightarrow \bar{D}(y, x) , \quad \text{from (4)}$$

Therefore,

$$D(x, y) \rightarrow \bar{D}(y, x) \qquad (5)$$

By interchanging x and y in (1), (2) and (5), we get

$$D(y, x) \rightarrow [\bar{D}(y, z) \ \& \ \bar{D}(z, x) \ \& \ \bar{D}(x, y)] \qquad (6)$$

Now,

$$D(x, y) \rightarrow \bar{D}(y, x) , \quad \text{from (5)}$$
$$\rightarrow D(y, x)$$

Hence from (6), we have

$$D(x, y) \rightarrow [\bar{D}(y, z) \ \& \ \bar{D}(z, x) \ \& \ \bar{D}(x, y)] \qquad (7)$$

Combining (1), (2), (5) and (7), it is seen that $D(x, y)$ implies that individual J is decisive for every ordered pair of alternatives (six in all) from the set of three alternatives (x, y, z) given conditions U, P and I. Thus J is a dictator over any set of three alternatives containing x and y.

Now, consider a larger number of alternatives. Take any two alternatives u and v out of the entire set of alternatives. If u and v are so chosen that they are the same as x and y, then of course $\bar{D}(u, v)$ holds, as can be shown by taking a triple consisting of u, v and any other alternative z. If one of u and v is the same as one of x and y, say, u and x are the same but not v and y, then take the triple consisting of x (or u), y and v. Since $D(x, y)$ holds, it again follows that $\bar{D}(u, v)$, and also $\bar{D}(v, u)$.

Finally, let both u and v be different from x and y. Now, first take (x, y, u), and we get $\bar{D}(x, u)$, which implies of course $D(x, u)$. Now, take the triple (x, u, v). Since $D(x, u)$, it follows from previous reasoning that $\bar{D}(u, v)$, and also $\bar{D}(v, u)$. Thus $D(x, y)$ for some x and y, implies $\bar{D}(u, v)$ for all possible ordered pairs (u, v). Therefore, individual J is a dictator, and Lemma 3*a is proved.

Finally, Theorem 3*1 is proved by using Lemma 3*a.

Proof. We show that given conditions U, P and I, there must be an individual who is almost decisive over some ordered pair of alternatives. We make the contrary supposition and show that it leads to an inconsistency.

For any pair of alternatives, there is at least one decisive set, viz., the set of all individuals, thanks to condition P. Thus, for every pair of alternatives there is also at least one almost decisive set, since a decisive set is also almost decisive. Compare all the sets of individuals that are almost decisive for some pair-wise choice (not necessarily the same pair), and from them choose the smallest one (or one of the smallest ones). Let this set be called V, and let it be almost decisive for x against y.

If V contains only one individual, then we need not proceed further. If, however, it contains two or more individuals, we divide V into two parts, viz., V_1 containing a single individual, and V_2 containing the rest of V. All individuals not contained in V form the set V_3.

Due to condition U we can assume any logically possible combination of individual orderings. We pick the following:

(1) For all i in V_1, $x P_i y$ & $y P_i z$.
(2) For all j in V_2, $z P_j x$ & $x P_j y$.
(3) For all k in V_3, $y P_k z$ & $z P_k x$.

Since V is almost decisive for x against y, and since every individual in V prefers x to y, and every individual not in V does the opposite, we must have $x P y$. Between y and z, only V_2 members prefer z to y, and the rest prefer y to z, so that if $z P y$, then V_2 must be an almost decisive set. But V was chosen as the smallest almost decisive set, and V_2 is smaller than that (being a proper subset of it). Hence $\sim (z P y)$. Thus, for R to be complete as needed for condition U, $y R z$ must hold. But $x P y$ & $y R z \to x P z$. But only the individual in V_1 prefers x to z, the rest prefer z to x, so that a certain individual has turned out to be almost decisive. Hence there is a contradiction in the original supposition.

Note that this proof stands even if V_3 is empty, as will be the case if V contains all the individuals—a possibility that has not been ruled out.

The theorem now follows from Lemma 3*a since an individual almost decisive over some pair must be a complete dictator.

Chapter 4

CHOICE VERSUS ORDERINGS

4.1. Transitivity, Quasi-Transitivity, and Acyclicity

A SWF is a special type of a collective choice rule; it requires that all social preferences be orderings, i.e., social preferences must be reflexive, complete, and transitive. It was noted in Chapter 1 that if it is required that there be a best alternative in every subset (i.e., there be a "choice function"), reflexivity and completeness are not dispensable, but transitivity is not really necessary. Given reflexivity and completeness of a preference relation, the necessary and sufficient condition for the existence of a choice function is a condition that we called "acyclicity" in Chapter 1*. If x_1 is preferred to x_2, x_2 to x_3, and so on until x_n, then acyclicity requires that x_1 be regarded as at least as good as x_n. Obviously, this is a much weaker condition than transitivity, which would have required that x_1 be strictly preferred to x_n, and further would have required the transitivity of indifference.[1] Transitivity, incidentally, is essentially a condition on "triples," i.e., on sets of three alternatives. If for all triples transitivity holds, then it must hold for the entire set, no matter how long a sequence we take. This is not true of acyclicity. A preference relation may be acyclical over all triples and yet may violate acyclicity for the entire set, as was demonstrated in the penultimate paragraph of Section 1*5 in Chapter 1* (p. 16).

---

[1] Acyclicity is a close cousin of Houthakker's (1950) "semitransitivity," defined in the context of revealed preference theory, viz., if x_1 is revealed preferred to x_2, and so on until x_n, then x_n must not be revealed preferred to x_1. Given completeness, acyclicity and semitransitivity are equivalent except for the difference between being "preferred" and being "revealed preferred." The latter is, in one respect, *less* demanding, since in the context of demand theory alternatives are offered in specific sets ("budget sets"), and is, in another respect, *more* demanding since indifference is ruled out in most presentations of revealed preference theory.

The "impossibility" result of Arrow applies to SWFs. But if Arrow's objective is merely to ensure that "from any environment, there will be a chosen alternative,"[2] then that can be guaranteed by merely requiring acyclicity of social preference without requiring transitivity. We shall call collective choice rules which generate preference relations that are sufficient for the existence of choice functions, social decision functions (SDF).

Is the distinction between SWF and SDF significant, or is it hair splitting? It appears that it is somewhat significant. For one thing, the "impossibility" result of Arrow is valid for SWFs but not for SDFs, as shown in Sen (1969). There are collective choice rules which are sufficient for social choice and which satisfy all the four conditions of Arrow (Theorem 4*1). In fact, these conditions can be strengthened substantially (e.g., in ruling out local dictators as well as global dictators, in demanding the strong Pareto principle and not merely the weak Pareto principle as Arrow does), and still there is no inconsistency (Theorems 4*2 and 4*4). Arrow's impossibility theorem is precisely a result of demanding social orderings as opposed to choice functions.

An illustration would help. Consider a CCR which declares x to be socially better than y if it is Pareto-superior to y, and declares x to be socially at least as good as y if y is not Pareto-superior to x. Consider now the case of the "paradox of voting," discussed earlier, where person 1 prefers x to y and y to z, person 2 prefers y to z and z to x, and person 3 prefers z to x and x to y. The CCR specified will declare x, y and z to be all indifferent to each other. There is no problem in this case, and both acyclicity and transitivity hold. Next consider only persons 1 and 2 and let there be no person 3. By our CCR we now have y socially preferred to z, x and y indifferent, and x and z also indifferent. Transitivity does not hold, but acyclicity does, and there is a best alternative in every subset. This can be shown to be true for every configuration of individual preferences, so that condition U holds. This

---

[2] Arrow (1963), p. 120. Arrow also emphasizes the importance of "the independence of final choice from the path to it." When the choice set includes more than one alternative, this is never exactly true, in a strict sense, even with full transitivity, since which of the best alternatives will be chosen may depend on the path. However, it is guaranteed that one of the best alternatives will be chosen independently of the path, given transitivity. The same holds with acyclicity, provided indifference is followed by trying out *both* the indifferent alternatives against the remaing alternatives.

SDF also satisfies the Pareto principle, since it is based on it; satisfies the independence of irrelevant alternatives, since social preference between any x and any y depends only on individual preferences between x and y; and also meets the nondictatorship condition, since the CCR does not declare x to be socially better than y unless everyone regards x to be at least as good as y.

A weaker condition than transitivity but stronger than acyclicity is "quasi-transitivity," which is a condition that can be fully stated in terms of triples. If x is preferred to y, and y to z, then x should be preferred to z. This is somewhat like transitivity, but this does not require that indifference be transitive. The CCR described in the last paragraph yields quasi-transitive social preference relations, and is, thererore, fairly easy to analyse in terms of triples only. The difference between transitivity and quasi-transitivity, though apparently mild, is in fact sufficient to take us away from Arrow's impossibility result concerning social ordering to a straightforward possibility result concerning social choice.

4.2. Collective Choice and Arrow's Conditions

Does this mean that the Arrow problem is not really serious for social choice? I am afraid it does not. What all this really shows is how *economic* Arrow's impossibility theorem is. Relax any of his restrictions and the result collapses; if it had not we would have been able to strengthen Arrow's theorem immediately. The conditions that Arrow showed to be inconsistent are not conditions that he regarded as *sufficient* for a satisfactory system of collective choice, but what appeared to him to be plausible *necessary* conditions. That these conditions are not likely to be regarded as sufficient should be clear from the example in terms of which we showed the consistency of these conditions. It made all Pareto-optimal points indifferent, and this is unlikely to appeal to anyone who is worried by distributional considerations. While that was only one example, it is not at all clear that other examples will be more appealing.

In fact, it may be noted that Lemma 3*a, which says that any person who is decisive over a pair must be a dictator, still holds, for the proof does not use anything more than quasi-transitivity. Using this result, it can be proved[3] that all SDFs that satisfy con-

---

[3] Proved by A. Gibbard in 1969 in an unpublished paper.

ditions U, I, P and D, and yield quasi-transitive social preference must represent an "oligarchic" form of decision taking. There would be an identifiable and unique group of persons in the community such that if any one of them strictly prefers any x to any y, society must regard x to be at least as good as y; and if all members of the group strictly prefer x to y, then society must also prefer x to y. The example that we used corresponded to the case where the entire community belonged to this "oligarchy"; the other cases would appear to be, *prima facie*, less attractive.

Of course, even quasi-transitivity is not necessary for a SDF, since acyclicity is sufficient for choice functions. And it is possible to consider more complex but also more appealing examples with acyclicity. But the fact remains that the Arrow conditions must be recognized to be too weak rather than too demanding, as is usual to assume in the context of his "impossibility" result. A SDF can pass all the tests of Arrow and still look very unappetizing. In the next few chapters and notes, some other conditions on collective choice will be introduced and analyzed.

4.3. Rationality and Collective Choice

There is also a second reason for not jubilating at the formal absence of the Arrow impossibility for a social choice function. The fact that a best alternative exists in each subset is itself a sound basis for rational choice, but is it a completely satisfactory basis? Consider the case where x is preferred to y, y is preferred to z, and x and z are indifferent. A choice function exists, and in particular, for the choice over all the three alternatives x is the unique best alternative, being no worse than either of the other two. But consider the choice over x and z. There each is "best," since each is as good as the other. Would it be right to describe a choice process as "rational" if it can choose either x or z given the choice between the two, but must choose specifically x if the choice is over the triple x, y, z? This is a violation of property β (defined in Chapter 1*), which requires that if two alternatives are both best in a subset, then one of them should not be best in the whole set, without the other also being best in that set. The other rationality property, which we called property α, does not seem to cause much trouble. It requires that if x is best in a whole set, then it must be best in all its subsets also. This is satisfied by all

CCRs with which we have been concerned so far.   Is property α sufficient, or should we also require property β?

Various selection processes do not, in fact, satisfy property β. Two Australians may tie for the Australian championship in some game, neither being able to defeat the other, but it is perfectly possible for one of them to become the world champion alone, since he might be able to defeat all non-Australians, which the other Australian champion may not be able to do. Similarly, two poets or scientists could get the same national honors, with only one of them receiving some international honor such as the Nobel Prize, without this appearing as irrational in any significant sense.

Whether social choice functions should be required to satisfy property β, thus remains a somewhat problematic issue.   Given everything else, it would of course appear to be better that β be satisfied rather than that it be violated.   But there *is* a real conflict involved here, and other things are not necessarily the same.   We know that a relation generating a choice function that satisfies property β must be an ordering (Lemma 1*q). Hence a SDF that generates preference relations yielding choice functions satisfying β must be a SWF.   The Arrow impossibility theorem about SWFs will get readily transformed into an impossibility theorem about SDFs if property β is also imposed as a necessary condition of social choice (Theorem 4*5).   Then at least one of the four conditions of Arrow must be suppressed for the sake of consistency. The real question is, therefore, not whether property β is a good thing, but whether it is a better thing than any of the other four conditions in the context of a SDF.   Something has to give, and property β, while in itself attractive, may be thought to be more dispensable than the other possible candidates for elimination.

However, as was argued in the last section, the picture is really more complex than would appear from concentrating exclusively on the "impossibility theorem."   There are other conditions that must be considered in the context of choosing a satisfactory mechanism of collective choice.   In this field, there are many conflicts and many dilemmas, and since Arrow's is only one of them, it is not sufficient to try to solve only that particular problem.   In the chapters that follow Chapter 4*, we go into some of these problems, which should help us to take a more comprehensive view of the problem of collective choice.

Chapter 4*

SOCIAL DECISION FUNCTIONS

4*1. Possibility Theorems

A collective choice rule f that invariably specifies a social *ordering R* is a SWF. But as we noted in Chapter 1*, an ordering is neither a necessary nor a sufficient condition for the existence of a choice function. It is sufficient for finite sets but is not necessary even then. We may thus think about extending the range of the collective choice rule f to include those preference relations that are not orderings, but which nevertheless generate a choice function.

DEFINITION 4*1. *A social decision function (henceforth SDF) is a collective choice rule f, the range of which is restricted to those preference relations R, each of which generates a choice function $C(S, R)$ over the whole set of alternatives X. This restriction is to be called condition O* on f.*

It may be noted that if we consider infinite sets X, a SWF may not be a SDF, but with finite sets X, a SWF is always a SDF, but not the converse.

Does this extension of the range of a collective rule in the case of finite sets affect the impossibility result of Arrow? It certainly does as was noted in Chapter 4.[1]

THEOREM 4*1. *There is a SDF satisfying conditions U, P, I and D for any finite set X.*

Proof: An example will be sufficient for the proof. Define

$$x R y \leftrightarrow \sim [(\forall i: y R_i x) \ \& \ (\exists i: y P_i x)]$$

Clearly R is reflexive and complete. Further, the SDF satisfies conditions P, I and D. We show now that R is quasi-transitive for

---

[1] On this, see Sen (1969).

every logically possible combination of individual orderings.

$$[x\,P\,y \ \& \ y\,P\,z] \to [\{\forall i: x\,R_i\,y \ \& \ \exists i: x\,P_i\,y\} \ \& \ \forall i: y\,R_i\,z]$$
$$\to [\forall i: x\,R_i\,z \ \& \ \exists i: x\,P_i\,z]$$
$$\to x\,P\,z$$

Thus, R is quasi-transitive, and by Lemma 1*k, no restriction need be put on the domain of the SDF defined, i.e., condition U is also satisfied. This completes the proof.

Note that the social preference relation R generated by the SDF defined above is merely quasi-transitive, and is not fully transitive. Suppose there are two individuals 1 and 2 and three alternatives x, y, z, such that $x\,P_1\,y \ \& \ y\,P_1\,z$ and $z\,P_2\,x \ \& \ x\,P_2\,y$. We then have $x\,P\,y$, $y\,I\,z$ and $x\,I\,z$. This is clearly intransitive.[2] All that is guaranteed is that a "best" alternative will be present in every subset, i.e., a choice function will exist, no matter what the individual preferences are.

We can strengthen Theorem 4*1 by strengthening the Pareto rule and the nondictatorship condition. Define

Condition P* (strong Pareto rule): For any pair, x, y in X,

$$[\forall i: x\,R_i\,y \ \& \ \exists i: x\,P_i\,y] \to x\,P\,y$$

and

$$[\forall i: x\,I_i\,y] \to x\,I\,y$$

Condition D*: For no individual i does there exist a pair x, y in X such that for all $(R_1, \ldots, R_n)$ in the domain of f either of the following conditions holds:

(1) $x\,P_i\,y \to x\,P\,y$

or

(2) $x\,R_i\,y \to x\,R\,y$

Condition P^* is defined corresponding to $\bar{P}$ in Chapter 2*, Definition 2*3, and it is obviously a more demanding condition than condition P. Condition D^* is strengthened in two ways. First, while condition D rules out a global dictator, D^* rules out even a local dictator. No individual should be decisive over even a single pair. Second, it also rules out dictatorships of the kind that a

---

[2] Thus the SDF quoted is not a SWF with unrestricted domain, and this is not a counterexample to Arrow's General Possibility Theorem.

weak individual preference R_i could imply a weak social preference R over any pair of alternatives.

Clearly, condition P^* implies condition P, and condition D^* implies condition D, but not vice versa in either case. The following theorem does, however, hold:

THEOREM 4*2. *There is a SDF satisfying conditions U, P^*, I and D^* for any finite set X.*

The proof is provided by the same example as in the proof of Theorem 4*1. It would, thus, appear that the impossibility result of Arrow does not carry over to collective choice rules that are sufficient for choosing a best alternative in every subset, even though they may not be sufficient for generating an ordering.

This concerns the position with finite sets. With infinite sets such a SDF does not exist. Indeed the following result is then true:

THEOREM 4*3. *For an infinite set X, there is no SDF satisfying conditions U and P*

Proof: Let every individual have the same ordering with antisymmetry, i.e., a chain, such that $x_2 P_i x_1$, $x_3 P_i x_2$, ... By condition U such a set of individual preference orderings must be in the domain of f, and by condition P there can be no socially best element in the set X, which proves the theorem.

While superficially Theorem 4*3 looks like a disturbing theorem, in fact what it points out is that this way of posing the problem does not make much sense when the set of alternatives X is infinite. Since *individual* choice functions might not exist even if individual orderings exist over an infinite set, there is no point in invariably expecting the existence of a *social* choice function. Further, the following theorem holds:

THEOREM 4*4. *If at least one individual ordering R_i for each element in the domain of f generates a choice function over the set X, then there is a SDF satisfying conditions P, I and D^*, and condition U subject to the restriction noted.*

Proof: Choose the collective choice rule such that $x R y \leftrightarrow$ $\sim[\forall i: y P_i x]$, for all x and y. It is clear that $[x \in C(S, R_i)] \rightarrow$ $[x \in C(S, R)]$, for any x in any S, and any i. It follows that since at least one individual has a choice function, then so must society.

Fulfillment of conditions P, I and D^* can be easily shown.[3]

The complications raised by infinite sets do not, thus, appear to be particularly profound in this case. The real difficulty in seeking a solution of the "impossibility problem" in terms of the SDF (as opposed to SWF) resides in the relevance of property β as a rationality condition on choice. It was shown in Chapter 1* that while a choice function generated by a binary relation always satisfies property α, it satisfies property β if and only if R is an ordering. If property β is found to be an essential aspect of rational choice (we examined this question in Chapter 4), then the following theorem may be found to be disturbing:

THEOREM 4*5.   *There is no SDF satisfying conditions U, P, I and D, such that each R in the range of the SDF must generate a choice function that satisfies property β.*
The proof follows directly from Lemma 1*q and Theorem 3*1.

Theorem 4*5 represents the "impossibility problem" directly in terms of collective choice and its rationality, and clarifies one of the major issues involved. The question seems to turn on whether or not we impose the rationality condition β.[4]

---

[3] Note that condition P^* may be violated. It is not possible to strengthen Theorem 4*4 by replacing condition P by P^*, as the following counterexample shows. Let all individuals be indifferent between all alternatives, except one individual who has a chain with no best element. By condition P^*, society must then have the same chain with no best element.

[4] See also Chapters 5, 5*, 6, and 6*.

Chapter 5

VALUES AND CHOICE

5.1. Welfare Economics and Value Judgments

Welfare economics is concerned with policy recommendations. It explores the ways of arriving at such conclusions as "Given the choice between social states x and y, x should be chosen." It is obvious that welfare economics cannot be "value-free," for the recommendations it aims to arrive at are themselves value judgments. In view of this it must be regarded as somewhat of a mystery that so many notable economists have been involved in debating the prospects of finding value-free welfare economics.

The so-called "New Welfare Economics" (1939–1950) was much concerned with deriving policy judgments from purely factual premises.[1] To quote one of the most distinguished writers of the period:

> In fact, there is a simple way of overcoming this defeatism, a perfectly objective test which enables us to discriminate between those reorganizations which improve productive efficiency and those which do not. If A is made so much better off by the change that he could compensate B for his loss, and still have something left over, then the reorganization is an *unequivocal improvement*.[2]

This would seem to run counter to the widely held philosophical view asserting "the impossibility of deducing an 'ought'-proposition from a series of 'is'-propositions."[3] Recently a set of doubts have

---

[1] See the controversies involving Kaldor (1939), Hicks (1939a), (1941), Scitovsky (1941), Samuelson (1950), and Little (1949a), (1950). See also Graaff (1957) and Mishan (1960).

[2] Hicks (1941), p. 108; italics added.

[3] Hare (1961), p. 29. This is sometimes called "Hume's Law," after a statement made by him in the *Treatise*, III. I, i.

been raised about the validity of this "law"[4] and its logical compatibility with some other propositions in ethics.[5] But it would be a mistake to think that the search for value-free welfare economics that characterized the so-called New Welfare Economics had anything to do with these doubts.   For reasons that are somewhat obscure, being "value-free" or "ethics-free" has often been identified as being free from interpersonal conflict.   The implicit assumption seems to be that if everyone agrees on a value judgment, then it is not a value judgment at all, but is perfectly "objective."

It is for this reason that the Pareto principle has been often taken to be free from value judgments. On the negative side, Robbins' celebrated attack on the use of value judgments in economics concentrated exclusively on the difficulties of interpersonal comparisons (Robbins (1932)). The Hicksian comment on the "objectivity" of the compensation test quoted above is also based on the idea that if compensations are paid, everyone is better off, and there is no interpersonal conflict.[6] It is remarkable that even Samuelson concluded his definitive article on New Welfare Economics by asserting that "the only consistent and *ethics-free* definition of an increase in potential real income of a group is that based upon a uniform shift of the utility possibility function for the group."[7] We have chosen to comment on the stalwarts; other illustrations of the same assumption are easy to find throughout the literature on welfare economics.

While the view under discussion is analytically objectionable, its commonsense rationale is quite clear.   If everyone agrees on a certain value judgment, the fact that it cannot be verified may not cause any great commotion.   There is a clear difference between value judgments that everyone accepts and those that some do and some do not.   What is, however, odd in all this is the fact that people should be at all moved to look for "value-free" or "ethics-free" welfare criteria.[8] Unanimous value judgments may provide

---

[4] See, for example, Black (1964) and Searle (1964), (1969).

[5] See, for example, Sen (1966a).

[6] Hicks (1941), p. 109. However, to argue that it is an "unequivocal improvement" when compensations "could" be paid whether they are actually paid or not reintroduces the interpersonal conflict.

[7] Samuelson (1950), pp. 19–20; italics added. If real income comparisons are value judgments, then this is not an "ethics-free" definition. If, on the other hand, such comparisons are not value judgments, then this is not the *only* "ethics-free" consistent definition. See, however, Samuelson (1947), Chap. 8.

[8] For a critique of the economists' handling of the meaning and relevance of value judgments, see Little (1957). See also Streeton (1950) and Dobb (1969).

the basis of a great deal of welfare economics, but this is so not because these are not value judgments, but because these value judgments are acceptable to all. This banality would not be worth stating had the opposite not been asserted or implied in much of the literature.

5.2. Content of Welfare Economics: A Dilemma

Welfare economics is concerned with policy recommendations. A policy recommendation may be derived using (a) some factual premises, (b) some value judgments, and (c) some logic needed for the derivation. The first is the subject matter of "positive" economics and not of welfare economics. The second cannot be a subject, it is alleged, of scientific discussion, for one cannot argue on value judgments (as Robbins put it, "it is a case of thy blood or mine"[9]). The third, viz. logic, is a separate discipline altogether. What then can be the subject matter of welfare economics? Does it exist at all?

Though he does not quite hold it in this bald form, Graaff's (1957) masterly banishment of welfare economics is in similar spirit. In fact, nihilism has been the dominant note in a number of studies on welfare economics bearing, as Baumol puts it, "an ill-concealed resemblance to obituary notices."[10] If the subject matter of welfare economics is empty, as it might be thought to be on the reasoning outlined in the last paragraph, it is small wonder that nihilism should appeal. The trouble with that reasoning, however, is that it is grossly misleading, being based on very arbitrary definitions.

First of all, the logical exercises involved in deriving policy recommendations cannot be excluded from the body of welfare economics. In any discipline involving analytical reasoning, logic is involved, either as informal argumentation, or as formal logic, or as mathematical operations. Whether these exercises are classed as branches of logic, or of the discipline in question, is largely a matter of *convenience*. That it seems to be more convenient to permit economists to do the logical exercises needed for deriving policy recommendations in economics rather than leaving these for the logicians or mathematicians is, therefore, a fairly compelling

   [9] Robbins (1932), p. 132.
   [10] Baumol (1966), p. 2.

reason for regarding these to be part of the discipline of welfare economics. Indeed a variety of studies that are taken to be part of traditional economics, e.g., those dealing with the existence, efficiency, and stability, of competitive general equilibrium are almost exclusively logical exercises.

Secondly, value judgments are not always assumed to be simply "given" in exercises of policy recommendations. In fact the problem of the existence of the social welfare function (SWF) in the sense of Arrow is concerned with the question of getting a set of value judgments for the society as a whole (reflected by the social ordering) based on the orderings of the individuals. Again the exercises here take mainly a logical form, but the contours of the problem are defined by the question of moving from the preferences of the individuals to social values on the basis of which public choices are to be made. Much of the recent discussion on economic welfare has, naturally enough, been concerned with this basket of problems.

Finally, the dichotomy between facts and values implicit in the reasoning in the nihilistic argument seems to be doubtful. It is based on a reading of the nature of value judgments that is extremely limited. It can in fact be argued that controversies in welfare economics have often tended to be futile because of an inadequate recognition of the nature of value judgments.[11] We turn to this question in the next section.

5.3. Basic and Nonbasic Judgments

A partitioning of value judgments into two classes should be helpful for our purpose.[12] A value judgment can be called "basic" to a person if the judgment is supposed to apply under all conceivable circumstances, and it is "nonbasic" otherwise.[13] For example, a person may express the judgment, "A rise in national income measured both at base and final year prices indicates a better economic situation." We may ask him whether he will stick to this judgment under all factual circumstances and go on, enquiring, "Would you

---

[11] For a fine study of theories of value judgments, see Nowell-Smith (1954). A particularly interesting approach can be found in Hare (1960), (1963).

[12] This and other methods of partitioning value judgments are presented in Sen (1967).

[13] It is not asserted here that both the categories *must* be nonempty.

say the same if the circumstances were such and such (e.g., if the poor were much poorer)?"[14]   If it turns out that he will revise the judgment under certain circumstances, then the judgment can be taken to be nonbasic in his value system.   If, on the other hand, there is no situation when a certain person will, say, regard killing a human being to be justifiable, then "I should not kill a human being" is a basic value judgment in his system.

The distinction is a simple one and lies at the root of the relevance of factual considerations in ethical debates.   Roughly, it can be argued that in so far as a certain value judgment is basic to its author, one cannot really dispute it in the same way one disputes a factual or an analytical assertion, but if it is nonbasic, a dispute on it can take a factual or analytical form.

A few warnings may be worth recording to prevent a possible misunderstanding of the nature of the distinction.   First, the factual circumstances that are admissible are not necessarily probable ones. Note the following interchange:

> *A*:   Men and women should be allowed to dress as they like.
> *B*:   Even if it turned out that mini-skirts caused cancer in the eyes of the beholder?
> *A*:   Not in that case, of course.   But I don't think that situation very likely.

The judgment nevertheless is nonbasic, and a dispute on it can take a factual form, even though I doubt that the dispute on this one would be very fruitful.

Second, a value judgment may be made conditional on certain circumstances.   If the judgment is to be shown to be nonbasic, this will have to be done not by considering cases that violate those conditions, but by considering others that do not.   Suppose I express the judgment, "On rainy days, I should carry an umbrella." This is not shown to be nonbasic by demonstrating that I recommend a different course of action for a sunny day, but by showing that I may recommend something else even for a rainy day, if, say, an umbrella costs half one's annual income.

Third, a set of judgments that an individual holds might turn out

---

[14] An alternative line to take is to ask him what he would do if the criterion led to intransitivity of preference, as is indeed possible under some circumstances (see Gorman (1955), and also Chapter 2* above).

to be *logically* inconsistent, and if so, all of them cannot be basic. A man who judges that "consumption today should be maximized," and "consumption a year hence should also be maximized" is not involved in such a logical conflict, since the two judgments conflict only under specific (though plausible) factual circumstances. At least one of the two judgments must be nonbasic, but not for analytical reasons. In contrast, the kindly man who wishes everyone an income higher than the national average seems to have an analytical problem of some magnitude.

5.4. Facts and Values

If a person puts forward a value judgment and another person denies it, what, we might ask, can they argue about? They differ on what should be chosen given a choice between some alternatives. Given that the persons understand the meaning of the value judgment in the same way, what remains to be disputed? They can, of course, discuss the "reasons" for holding the value judgment or not holding it. But what, it might be asked, do we mean by "reasons"? How can there be a "reason" for accepting or denying a value judgment, as opposed to a factual or a logical statement?

The answer seems to be fairly clear. If the judgment is nonbasic, one "reason" for disputing it may be a doubt about its underlying factual or analytical assumption. Even when one accepts Hume's celebrated law that prescriptive conclusions cannot be derived from exclusively factual premises, there is no doubt that prescriptive conclusions can be drawn from factual premises *among others*. Therefore, someone disputing a value judgment put forward by another person can have a scientific discussion on the validity of the value judgment by examining the truth of the underlying factual premise or the logical derivation. Thus the "reasons" for recommending the rejection of a value judgment may be purely scientific.

Now, if the judgment expressed happens to be a "basic" one in the value system of the person expressing it, then and only then can it be claimed that there can be no factual or analytical method of disputing the judgment. That many of the value judgments we habitually express are not basic seems to be fairly easy to demonstrate.

From a nonbasic judgment dependent on a particular factual assumption, it is of course possible to move to another judgment independent of that factual assumption. Consider, for example, the value judgment, "The government should not raise the money supply more than in proportion to the real national output," based, let us assume, on a factual theory relating money supply and output to inflation. If this theory of inflation is disputed, which would be a legitimate reason against the value judgment in question, the person may move on to a more fundamental value judgment. "The government should not do anything that leads to inflation." If that too is based on some factual assumption, making it nonbasic, the process of moving backwards, as it were, may be repeated. From judgment J_0 based on factual assumptions F_1, one moves to a judgment (or a set of judgments) J_1 independent of F_1; if that is dependent on factual assumptions F_2, one moves to judgments J_2 independent of both F_1 and F_2. In this way one might hope to reach ultimately, in this person's value system, some basic value judgment J_n, though there is no guarantee that one would definitely get there.

Some generalizations about the futility of arguing on value judgments are based on considering the nature of *basic* value judgments, sometimes loosely called "ends." Indeed, this implicit concentration on basic value judgments, has had a pronounced and fundamental effect on the development of economics. Economists have been, with few exceptions, shy of having any dispute on value judgments as such, and the classic statement of the position was that by Robbins in his famous treatise on the nature and significance of economics, ". . . it does not seem logically possible to associate the two studies [ethics and economics] in any form but mere juxtaposition. Economics deals with ascertainable facts; ethics with valuation and obligations."[15] This contrast would hold if ethics dealt only with basic judgments. Robbins explains his position in the following manner:

> If we disagree about ends it is a case of thy
> blood or mine—or live or let live according to
> the importance of the difference, or the relative
> strength of our opponents. But, if we disagree
> about means, then scientific analysis can often
> help us to resolve our differences. If we disagree
> about the morality of the taking of interest (and

---

[15] Robbins (1932), p. 132.

we understand what we are talking about), then
there is no room for argument.[16]

The crucial difficulty with this approach is that it is not quite
clearly determinable whether a certain end, or the corresponding
value judgment stating the end, is basic or not. To take Robbins'
own example, why must both parties' judgments on the morality
of interests be necessarily basic?

Of course, we need not take such a simple view, and we may supplement the Robbinsian argument by some other test of basicness.
We may *ask* the person concerned whether a certain judgment is
basic in his value system. But since no one would have had occasion to consider all conceivable alternative factual circumstances
and to decide whether in any of the cases he would change the
judgment or not, his answer to the question may not be conclusive.
Another method is to ask the person concerned to think of a series
of suitable revisions of factual assumptions, and ask him whether
in any of the cases considered he will change the judgment. This
process never establishes basicness, though it can establish that the
judgment is not nonbasic in any obviously relevant way.

It is interesting to note that some value judgments are demonstrably nonbasic, but no value judgment is demonstrably basic. Of
course, it may be useful to *assume* that some value judgments, not
shown to be obviously nonbasic, *are* basic, until and unless a case
crops up when the supposition is shown to be wrong. In this respect there is an obvious analogy with the practice in epistemology
of accepting tentatively a factual hypothesis as true, until and unless
some new observations refute that hypothesis.

It may, incidentally, be noted that a basic value judgment need
not necessarily be an "ultimate" principle such as J_n defined above.
A suitable constraint might convert a nonbasic value judgment into
a basic judgment. An illustration may clarify this point. "A rise
in national income at every set of positive prices implies a better
economic situation" may be nonbasic, because the person expressing it may not hold this if he finds a "worsening" of income distribution.[17] From this, in getting a basic judgment, we can move in
either of two directions. Either we can enquire whether there is

---

[16] Robbins (1932), p. 134.
[17] Problems in distinguishing between the size of the national income and its
distribution are of course well-known. See especially, Samuelson (1950), Little
(1957) and Graaff (1957).

a more *fundamental* value judgment (e.g., aggregate utility maximization) to which a rise in national income corresponds, when the income distribution is no worse. Or, we can ask whether the person concerned will always accept the judgment that "a rise of national income indicates a better economic situation *if* the income distribution (measured, say, by the Gini-coefficient) is unchanged." If not, we can constrain the judgment further. So that even if there exist no "ultimate" value judgments that can be found out by the first method, there may be basic judgments that can be obtained by suitable constraining.

However, the difficulty of ascertaining basicness remains also with the second method, and even if we knew that some basic value judgments existed we might not be able to decide whether a certain judgment were one of those. The fundamental difficulty with the "emotivist" thesis of the impossibility of rational arguments on value judgments beyond a point, is this difficulty of decidability. It may be true that "in the end there must come a point where one gets no further answer, but only a repetition of the injunction: Value this because it is valuable,"[18] but there is no sure-fire test which tells us whether such an ultimate point has in fact arrived. From this we do not, unfortunately, get a rule to decide when rational disputation is potentially fruitful and when it is not. Non-basicness of a judgment in someone's value system can sometimes be conclusively established, but the opposite is not the case, and to take a given value judgment to be basic, is to give it, at best, the benefit of the doubt. It seems impossible to rule out the possibility of fruitful scientific discussion on value judgments.

5.5. Individual Orderings and Choice Rules

Consider the following problem: An individual A firmly prefers social state x to state y. But he knows that everyone else in the community prefers y to x. And further, individual A is strongly antidictatorial in his approach to collective choice. What should he do? If he recommends y, he will be running against his own preference. If he recommends x, he will be violating his antidictatorial values. There is clearly a conflict that he has to face.

In the models of collective choice, this conflict is an inescapable one. Individual values are relevant to the exercise in two ways:

---

[18] Ayer (1959), p. 244. See also Stevenson (1944), (1963).

(a) they affect individual preferences R_i, and (b) they are concerned with the choice of collective choice rules CCR. Values reflected in (a) and (b) could easily conflict, and both sets of judgments cannot be "basic."

One way of resolving the problem is to treat the judgments underlying the CCR to be basic in a sense that individual orderings R_i are not. The model may be one where individuals express their preferences and the CCR tries to give appropriate representation to these preferences, but once the CCR selects a social ordering, individuals feel obliged to accept that ordering as the right one, no matter what individual ordering they expressed earlier. An example of such a model can be found in professorial selection processes in some universities, where there are two rounds of voting. In the first the candidates are voted on, and once a decision is reached, everyone formally votes for the chosen man in the second round, thereby making his selection "unanimous."

However, this is not the only possible model. The opposite extreme will be a case where individuals are really completely committed to what they regard as the right preference R_i, and would reject a CCR that does not select that R_i for public policy. Individual attitudes to most actual collective choice mechanisms would tend to lie somewhere in between these extremes. One might not wish to raise a revolution every time one's preferences fail to get complete representation in collective choice, but then there are circumstances in which one would like to do precisely that and would try to change the mechanism of collective choice. Demands for liberty, equality and fraternity in the French Revolution were basically expressions of extreme dissatisfaction with the collective choice mechanism of the existing system. The prevalence of a CCR as an institutional feature in a society is no guarantee of its acceptance by all or even by many, since actually prevalent choice mechanisms reflect a balance of political and economic forces in the society, and is not necessarily based on unanimous or even wide approval.

The real conflict arises when a person really approves of a CCR and also wants his own ordering of social states to be chosen for public policy. He cannot really do both except in the special circumstances in which the CCR he approves of chooses the social ordering he recommends. In general, one or the other set of judgments must be nonbasic, possibly both.

Harsanyi (1955) has distinguished between an individual's "subjective preferences" and his "ethical preferences," and has given a specific interpretation to the distinction.   Harsanyi takes a person's actual preferences R_i as his subjective preferences, while he defines ethical preferences as those preferences that he would have if he thought that he had an "equal chance" of being in anyone's position.[19]   Harsanyi takes a set of axioms which ensure that each person will maximize expected utility.   This is a rather specific model, and while it is attractive, it is also open to some simple objections (see Chapter 9).

The distinction can be given a broader meaning in the context of a CCR.   A person may be required to choose between possible CCRs in terms of his moral values.   A CCR thus chosen can be called his ethical CCR.   A social preference relation yielded by such a person's ethical CCR, given an actual set of individual preferences, can be taken to be that person's ethical preferences. Harsanyi's definition corresponds to a particular procedure of aggregation and represents an important special case of this more general approach.[20]

I do not wish to enter into the suitability of the term "ethical" in this context.   Presumably the ethical values involved here are those relating to combining preferences, and one could have introduced other ethical values.   But it is important to distinguish between a person's preferences as they actually are and what he thinks he would accept as a basis of public policy given the preferences of others and given his values on collective choice procedures. Thus interpreted, there is no conflict between the two sets of preferences that he may entertain, since they are concerned with two different types of problems.   One might wish that others had the same ordering R_i as one had oneself (hence one's commitment to the R_i), but given the preferences of the others one might accept the social preference emerging from a particular CCR (hence one's

---

[19] In placing oneself in the position of another, as Harsanyi defines it, one is assumed to take on that person's subjective features (including his preferences), and not merely his objective circumstances.   Contrast Samuelson (1964) in extending a model of Lerner (1944) on "equal ignorance."   See Pattanaik (1968a) on Harsanyi.   See also Leibenstein (1965).

[20] This is not strictly right, since the Harsanyi procedure is based not on individual orderings but on individual utility functions.   The Harsanyi example is really a special case of an ethical "social welfare functional," to be defined in Chapter 8.

commitment to the CCR). This distinction will be found useful in discussing specific problems of collective choice.

5.6. Conditions on Choice Rules

There could be conflicts also between values that one would like to see reflected in the CCR. One such example is provided by Arrow's impossibility theorem. Conditions U, P, I and D, when imposed on a CCR subject to condition O (i.e., on a SWF), will conflict. Clearly, not all these values could be basic.

Of these conditions, condition U, which demands an "unrestricted domain," is in a somewhat different logical level from the rest. The other conditions specify or qualify what should be done given certain configurations of individual preferences. Condition U, on the other hand, asserts, that the CCR must work for all possible configurations of individual preferences. It is, of course, certainly possible to maintain that certain configurations of individual preferences would never occur.[21] If a person believed that some configurations could, in practice, be ruled out, he may have no reason to demand condition U for the CCR or the SWF.

There could be a more subtle conflict if a person believed that a CCR was a good one for most circumstances that are plausible, but was objectionable for certain configurations of preferences that might not be very plausible. The goodness of a CCR is not independent of the actual preference configurations, and in demanding that it works well in *all* circumstances one might be ruling out good rules that would have done nicely in most cases, but not in all. We shall go into this question further while discussing specific rules, e.g., the method of majority decision (Chapters 10 and 10*). In demanding condition U on top of others like conditions O, P or I, one is requiring that the transitivity of social preference, or the Pareto principle, or the independence of irrelevant alternatives, should not be violated by the CCR even for a single configuration of individual preferences, whether that configuration is plausible or not. This is what precipitates Arrow's impossibility result.

---

[21] The Marxist position that people's preferences depend on their class interests would immediately rule out certain logically possible configurations. In fact, any deterministic theory of individual preferences would tend to restrict the pattern of individual preferences somewhat, thereby reducing the need for the condition of unrestricted domain.

We can consider some other general conditions on CCRs. For CCRs that satisfy the independence of irrelevant alternatives, May (1952) has proposed a set of conditions. The condition of *anonymity* requires that if you have my preferences and I have yours, and so on, i.e., if a given set of preferences is permuted among the individuals, social preference should remain invariant. *Neutrality* requires that the rule of choice should not discriminate between alternatives, and whatever criterion permits us to say that x is socially as good as y should also be sufficient for declaring w to be as good as z, after replacing x and y by w and z, respectively, in the criterion.[22] *Positive responsiveness* requires that the relation between individual and social preferences must be positive, i.e., if x is considered as being socially as good as y in some situations and now x goes up in someone's preference vis-a-vis y and does not fall in anyone's preference, then x must now be regarded as socially strictly better than y.

These conditions look appealing, and May has proved that the only decisive CCR with an unrestricted domain, which is independent of irrelevant alternatives, and is also anonymous, neutral, and positively responsive, is the method of majority decision (see Theorem 5*1). If someone approves of all those conditions but is unwilling to accept the majority decision rule, then he has a problem, for at least one of these judgments must be rejected.

Further, for some configurations of individual preferences, majority decision yields social preferences that are intransitive and in fact even violate acyclicity (e.g., in the case of "the paradox of voting"). Hence, if we demand the conditions noted in the last paragraph, then we must reject not merely transitivity of social preference but also acyclicity (Theorem 5*2). If we like acyclicity, then at least one of the other conditions must be rejected. This is an impossibility result similar to Arrow's and it poses another problem of difficult choice.[23]

If instead of demanding positive responsiveness we demand *nonnegative responsiveness* (i.e., if x does not fall vis-a-vis y in anyone's ordering, then it must not fall in the social ordering vis-a-vis y),

[22] In the formal statement of this condition in Chapter 5*, "neutrality" is defined to incorporate "independence of irrelevant alternatives." This is true of May's formulation as well.

[23] Another interesting result due to Hansson (1969) shows that the independence of irrelevant alternatives, neutrality and anonymity when imposed on a SWF make all alternatives socially indifferent. The result does not, however, hold for SDFs as will be clear in Chapter 5*.

the picture changes somewhat. We now have some freedom and can satisfy acyclicity and even quasi-transitivity. Further, suppose we strengthen the Pareto principle by demanding that x be socially better than y if someone (not necessarily everyone) prefers x to y, and everyone regards x to be at least as good as y. Then it can be shown that the CCR must be the Pareto-extension rule which follows the Pareto rule and completes it arbitrarily by declaring all Pareto-incomparable pairs as socially indifferent (Theorem 5*3). We used such a CCR in proving Theorem 4*1, and earlier we discussed its relevance to theories of collective choice of Buchanan and Tullock (1962) and others (Chapter 2). Under this rule, if y is not Pareto-superior to x, then x is socially as good as y.

Many people will reject immediately the Pareto-extension rule with its complete avoidance of distributional judgments. But they may hesitate to reject any of the conditions such as quasi-transitivity, or anonymity, or independence of irrelevant alternatives, or unrestricted domain, or the Pareto principle, which together imply that the CCR chosen must be the Pareto-extension rule. This too is a dilemma belonging to a wide class of which Arrow's impossibility result is another example.

It may also be noted that the difference between the majority rule and the Pareto-extension rule, which are rules in two very different traditions, appears to be rather small in terms of the underlying conditions. The method of majority decision, like the Pareto-extension rule, satisfies the conditions of independence, anonymity, neutrality, nonnegative responsiveness, the strict Pareto principle, and unrestricted domain. The difference between the two is that the MMD satisfies positive responsiveness (and not merely nonnegative responsiveness), which the Pareto-extension rule does not; and the Pareto-extension rule satisfies quasi-transitivity of social preference, which the MMD does not. If one were to look at these conditions without knowing the relevant theorems, one need not have guessed how crucial these little variations in conditions might be. Arrow christens a condition as that of "positive association" which is even weaker than our condition of "nonnegative responsiveness,"[24] but a shift from May's "positive

---

[24] Arrow's "positive association" requires that if x does not fall vis-a-vis y in anyone's judgment, then if x was previously preferred to y, it must still be preferred. It does not say anything about the case where x was previously indifferent to y. Nonnegative responsiveness would have required that in this case too, x should not fall vis-a-vis y, i.e., x must remain at least as good as y.

responsiveness" to Arrow's "positive association" takes us almost all the way from the case of the majority rule to the very different case of the Pareto-extension rule.

The main moral is that these conditions are difficult to judge in isolation and must be viewed along with the other conditions with which they may be combined.   Judgments of this kind on the nature of the CCR tend to be nonbasic, and it is relevant for us to enquire into the precise circumstances in which these conditions might be used, before we put our signature on the dotted line. Some more conditions and some more conflicts are discussed in Chapters 6 and 6* to pursue further this line of reasoning.

Chapter 5*

ANONYMITY, NEUTRALITY AND RESPONSIVENESS

5*1. Conditions for Majority Rule

A set of conditions on collective choice rules may be satisfied by no rule (as with Arrow's four conditions for all rules satisfying condition O), or by many rules (as with the imposition of only the Pareto principle and nondictatorship on choice rules). In between lies the case in which the conditions can all be satisfied by one rule and one rule only. We shall illustrate this with a set of conditions that are necessary and sufficient for the method of majority decisions (see May (1952)), which we first define.

DEFINITION 5*1. *The method of majority decision holds if and only if*

$$\forall x, y \in X: \; x R y \leftrightarrow [N(x P y) \geq N(y P x)]$$

where for all a, b in X, N(a P b) is the number of people for whom a $P_i b$.

Note that since indifference will affect both sides, this is equivalent to defining $x R y \leftrightarrow [N(x R y) \geq N(y R x)]$, where N is the number of individuals i such that $x R_i y$ (see Arrow (1951)).

The method of majority decision (MMD) belongs to a class of collective choice rules such that the social preferences between x and y depend only on individual preferences between x and y. This is implied by condition I.

LEMMA 5*a. *For any decisive collective choice rule satisfying condition I, the social preference relation R over each pair x, y in X must be a function of individual preferences R_i only over x, y.*

The proof is immediate.

We shall now define three conditions on collective choice rules satisfying condition I.

DEFINITION 5*2.   *For all pairs* $(R_1, \ldots, R_n)$ *and* $(R'_1, \ldots, R'_n)$ *of n-tuples of individual orderings in the domain of a collective choice function* f, *which maps them respectively into* R *and* R',

(1)   *If* $(R_1, \ldots, R_n)$ *being a reordering of the components of* $(R'_1, \ldots, R'_n)$ *implies that* $\forall x, y \in X \colon x\,R\,y \leftrightarrow x\,R'\,y$, *then and only then anonymity (condition A) holds.*

(2)   *If* $\forall x, y, z, w \in X \colon [(\forall i \colon x\,R_i\,y \leftrightarrow z\,R'_i\,w)$ & $(\forall i \colon y\,R_i\,x \leftrightarrow w\,R'_i\,z)] \rightarrow [(x\,R\,y \leftrightarrow z\,R'\,w)$ & $(y\,R\,x \leftrightarrow w\,R'\,z)]$, *then and only then neutrality (condition N) holds.*

(3)   *If* $\forall x, y \in X \colon [\forall i \colon \{(x\,P_i\,y \rightarrow x\,P'_i\,y)$ & $(x\,I_i\,y \rightarrow x\,R'_i\,y)\}$ & $\exists k \colon \{(x\,I_k\,y$ & $x\,P'_k\,y) \lor (y\,P_k\,x$ & $x\,R'_k\,y)\}] \rightarrow (x\,R\,y \rightarrow x\,P'\,y)$, *then and only then positive responsiveness (condition S) holds.*

Anonymity requires that social preferences should be invariant with respect to permutations of individual preferences. Neutrality demands that if two alternatives x and y, respectively, have exactly the same relation to each other in each individual's preference in case 1 as z and w have in case 2, then the *social* preference between x and y in case 1 must be exactly the same as the social preference between z and w in case 2. Positive responsiveness requires that if some individual's preference shifts relatively in favor of x vis-a-vis y with everyone else's preference between x and y remaining the same, then social preference should shift positively in the direction of x, and if the society was previously indifferent, now it must strictly prefer x.

LEMMA 5*b.   *For any collective choice rule neutrality* (N) *implies independence of irrelevant alternatives* (I).

The proof follows directly from Definition 5*2 (2) if we put $x = z$ and $y = w$.

THEOREM 5*1.   *Conditions* U, A, N *and* S *are together necessary and sufficient for a decisive collective choice rule to be the method of majority decision.*[1]

Proof. It is clear from the definition of MMD that it satisfies all the four conditions mentioned, so we need concern ourselves only with the sufficiency part of the proof. By Lemma 5*b Condition I is satisfied and therefore we need look at R_i *only over* x and y for social preference over x and y. By anonymity (A), social prefer-

---

[1] This is a doctored version of May's (1952) theorem.

ence must depend only on the numbers of individuals preferring x to y, y to x, and being indifferent, respectively. By neutrality (N), if $N(x\,P\,y) = N(y\,P\,x)$, then $x\,I\,y$, as can be checked by assuming the contrary and then permuting x and y in each individual's preference ordering. Given that for x, y in X, $[N(x\,P\,y) = N(y\,P\,x)] \rightarrow x\,I\,y$, then by positive responsiveness, $[N(x\,P\,y) > N(y\,P\,x)] \rightarrow x\,P\,y$. But then this *is* the method of majority decision.

The following corollary of Theorem 5*1 poses a slight problem for collective choice:

COROLLARY 5*1.1. *No SWF can satisfy conditions U, A, N and S.*

The proof follows directly from Theorem 5*1 by noting that some configuration of individual preferences does yield an intransitive majority preference relation so that this choice rule will not be a SWF.

Corollary 5*1.1, is, however, weaker than Theorem 3*1 (the General Possibility Theorem) proved earlier and is implied by it. This is readily proved with the help of the two following lemmas:

LEMMA 5*c. *A collective choice rule that is anonymous must be nondictatorial.*

LEMMA 5*d. *A decisive collective choice rule that is neutral and positively responsive satisfies the strict Pareto principle.*

The proof of Lemma 5*c is immediate from the definitions. In proving Lemma 5*d, we note that by neutrality, $[\forall i: x\,I_i\,y] \rightarrow x\,I\,y$. Hence, by positive responsiveness, if $\exists i: x\,P_i\,y$ & $\forall i: x\,R_i\,y$, then $x\,P\,y$.

The strict Pareto principle (P^*) implies the weak Pareto principle (P), so that Corollary 5*1.1 follows directly from Theorem 3*1, and Lemmas 5*c and 5*d. The following is, however, a stronger result. The impossibility continues even if we impose the conditions on a SDF as opposed to a SWF.

THEOREM 5*2. *There is no SDF satisfying conditions U, A, N and S.*

The proof, in view of Theorem 5*1 and Lemmas 5*c and 5*d, consists of showing that for some configuration of individual preferences, the method of majority decision violates acyclicity, e.g., with three individuals 1, 2, 3, and three alternatives, x, y, z, let $x\,P_1\,y\,P_1\,z$, $y\,P_2\,z\,P_2\,x$, and $z\,P_3\,x\,P_3\,y$, so that $x\,P\,y$, $y\,P\,z$, $z\,P\,x$, by MMD.

Arrow's condition of "positive association between individual and social preferences" is somewhat in the same spirit as, though weaker than, condition S (positive responsiveness). We can make Arrow's condition stronger, but keeping it still weaker than condition S, and observe the implication of replacing condition S by this condition.[2]

Condition R (nonnegative responsiveness): For all pairs $(R_1, \ldots, R_n)$ and $(R'_1, \ldots, R'_n)$ of n-tuples of individual orderings in the domain of a collective choice function f, which maps them respectively into R and R', nonnegative responsiveness holds if and only if

$$\forall x, y \in X: [\forall i: (x P_i y \to x P'_i y) \ \& \ (x I_i y \to x R'_i y)]$$
$$\to [(x P y \to x P' y) \ \& \ (x I y \to x R' y)]$$

As long as x does not go down in anyone's preference ordering, it must not do so in the social ordering. Would a weakening of condition S into the weaker condition R make any significant difference? It indeed would, as we show in the next section.

5*2.   Pareto-Extension Rules

We define a pair of collective choice rules derived from converting Pareto incompleteness into Pareto indifference, as used in the proofs of Theorems 4*1 and 4*4, respectively,

DEFINITION 5*3.   (1)   *The weak Pareto-extension rule (henceforth, WPE), is a collective choice rule such that*

$$\forall x, y \in X: x R y \leftrightarrow \sim(y \bar{\bar{P}} x)$$

(2)   *The Pareto-extension rule (henceforth, PE) is a collective choice rule such that*

$$\forall x, y \in X: x R y \leftrightarrow \sim(y \bar{P} x)$$

Before proving a theorem on the necessary and sufficient conditions for a collective choice rule to be the Pareto-extension rule, two lemmas are noted.

LEMMA 5*e.   *If there is some individual J who is almost decisive for any ordered pair of alternatives, then a collective choice rule satisfying conditions U, P and I, and always yielding a quasi-transitive and*

---

[2] Cf. Murakami's (1968) "monotonicity."

complete social preference relation, implies that J must be a dictator.
Though this is a generalization of Lemma 3*a, the proof of
Lemma 3*a as given is sufficient in proving Lemma 5*e, since only
the quasi-transitivity property of R was used in the proof without
requiring full transitivity (see pp. 43-5).

If $x P_i y$ by some i implies $x R y$ and not necessarily $x P y$, then
individual i is decisive in a weaker sense.

DEFINITION 5*4. *A person J is semidecisive for x against y if $x R y$
whenever $x P_J y$. He is almost semidecisive for x against y if $x R y$
whenever $x P_J y$, and $y P_i x$ for all $i \neq J$.*

Notationally, $\bar{S}(x, y)$ and $S(x, y)$ will stand, respectively, for
person J being semidecisive and almost semidecisive.

LEMMA 5*f. *If there is some individual J who is almost semidecisive
for any ordered pair of alternatives, then a collective choice rule satisfying conditions U, P and I, and always yielding a quasi-transitive and
complete social preference relation, implies that J is semidecisive over
every ordered pair of alternatives.*

Proof. The proof is very similar to that of Lemma 3*a. Let
person J be almost semidecisive over some x against some y, i.e.,
$S(x, y)$. In the triple (x, y, z) let person J have the preference,
$x P_J y$ & $y P_J z$, and all other individuals i ($\neq J$) hold: $y P_i z$ &
$y P_i x$. By condition P, $y P z$. Since $S(x, y)$, clearly $x R y$. If
$z P x$, then $y P x$ (by quasi-transitivity), which is impossible.
Hence, by the completeness of R, $x R z$. But the preferences of
all $i \neq J$ are unspecified between x and z, and only J definitely
prefers x to z. Hence, J is semidecisive for x against z. Hence,
$S(x, y) \to \bar{S}(x, z)$.

By taking $z P_J x$ & $x P_J y$, and for all $i \neq J$, $z P_i x$ & $y P_i x$,
we can show similarly that $S(x, y) \to \bar{S}(z, y)$. By interchanging
y and z in this we obtain $S(x, z) \to \bar{S}(y, z)$. And by considering
a case where in the proof of $S(x, y) \to \bar{S}(x, z)$, x is replaced by y,
y by z, and z by x, we obtain $S(y, z) \to \bar{S}(y, x)$. Hence, $S(x, y) \to$
$\bar{S}(x, z) \to \bar{S}(y, z) \to \bar{S}(y, x)$. Hence, $S(x, y)$ alone implies all the
following three results: $\bar{S}(x, z)$, $\bar{S}(z, y)$ and $\bar{S}(y, x)$.

Now interchanging x and y, we would find that $S(y, x)$ implies
$\bar{S}(y, z)$, $\bar{S}(z, x)$ and $\bar{S}(x, y)$. But $S(x, y) \to \bar{S}(y, x)$. Hence $S(x, y)$
implies $\bar{S}(x, y)$, $\bar{S}(y, x)$, $\bar{S}(y, z)$, $\bar{S}(z, y)$, $\bar{S}(x, z)$, $\bar{S}(z, x)$, and J is
semidecisive for every pair in the triple (x, y, z).

The extension to any number of alternatives is exactly as in Lemma 3*a, and this, when spelt out, completes the proof of Lemma 5*f.

Finally, the determination of the Pareto-extension rule in terms of conditions on a CCR is given.

THEOREM 5*3. *For a CCR that always yields a quasi-transitive and complete social preference relation, conditions U, I, P* and A, are together necessary and sufficient for the CCR to be the Pareto-extension rule.*

Proof. As in the proof of Theorem 3*1, compare all the sets of individuals who are almost decisive for some pair-wise choice (not necessarily the same pair), and from these choose the smallest one (or any one of the smallest, if there is more than one smallest set). Let this set be called V, and let it be almost decisive for x against y. If V contains only one individual, then by anonymity every individual must be almost decisive for x against y, and by Lemma 5*e every individual must be a dictator, which is impossible. Hence V must have more than one individual.

Partition all the individuals in V into two groups with V_1 consisting of any one particular individual (say J) and V_2 consisting of all individuals who are not in V_1 but are in V, V_3 consists of all the others. Consider now the following configuration of individual preferences, exactly as in the proof of Theorem 3*1, over x, y and some z.

(1)   For all i in V_1, $x P_i y$ & $y P_i z$.
(2)   For all j in V_2, $z P_j x$ & $x P_j y$.
(3)   For all k in V_3, $y P_k z$ & $z P_k x$.

Since V is almost decisive for x against y, and everyone in V does prefer x to y, and everyone not in V prefers y to x, we have $x P y$. Since only those in V_2 prefer z to y, and all others prefer y to z, if we take $z P y$, then V_2 will turn out to be an almost decisive set, but this is impossible since V, of which V_2 is a proper subset, is the smallest almost decisive set. Hence, $y R z$. If we now take $z P x$, then by quasi-transitivity and by $x P y$, we must have $z P y$. But in fact $y R z$, so that we must conclude that $x R z$, by the completeness of R. But the single individual in V_1 is the only one who prefers x to z, and all others prefer z to x. Hence J is almost semidecisive for x against z. Hence, by Lemma 5*f, J is semi-decisive for every ordered pair of alternatives.

By anonymity, every individual must be semidecisive for every ordered pair of alternatives. Hence,

$$\forall i: [\forall x, y: (x P_i y \to x R y)]$$

This means that $\forall x, y: x P y \to \forall i: x R_i y$. But by the Pareto principle P^*, we know that

$$\forall x, y: [(\forall i: x R_i y \;\&\; \exists i: x P_i y) \to x P y]$$

and

$$\forall x, y: [\forall i: x I_i y \to x I y]$$

Hence, $\forall x, y: [(\forall i: x R_i y \;\&\; \exists i: x P_i y) \leftrightarrow x P y]$. Further, by the completeness of R,

$$\forall x, y: [x R y \leftrightarrow \sim(\forall i: y R_i x \;\&\; \exists i: y P_i x)]$$

But this *is* the Pareto-extension rule, and the proof of Theorem 5*3 is now complete.

It is easy to check that the Pareto-extension rule also satisfies neutrality (condition N) and nonnegative responsiveness (condition R). While the MMD satisfies conditions U, I, A, N, P^* and S, the Pareto-extension rule satisfies conditions U, I, A, N, P^* and R, and quasi-transitivity of social preference (see Theorems 5*1 and 5*3, and Lemma 5*d). A relaxation of responsiveness (from S to R) and a strengthening of properties of social preference (imposing quasi-transitivity) seem to transform the majority rule into the Pareto-extension rule.

Chapter 6

CONFLICTS AND DILEMMAS

6.1. Critique of Anonymity and Neutrality

The assumptions of anonymity and neutrality are quite powerful conditions when imposed on a social decision function, as we saw in Chapter 5*. How appealing are these conditions? It may first be noted that many actual collective decision procedures violate these conditions. Procedural matters may be decided by a simple majority vote in the United Nations' General Assembly, whereas matters of substance require a two-thirds majority. Hence collective choice, in this case, is not neutral. It is, however, anonymous, but things change if we move from the General Assembly to the Security Council, for only five particular countries have the right of the veto.

The free market allocation procedures, whether under capitalism or under market socialism (e.g., the Lange-Lerner system) are definitely nonneutral and nonanonymous. I choose my consumption basket and you choose yours, and a permutation of our preferences can result in a different social outcome even if the available social alternatives remain the same. This violates anonymity. Neutrality is violated too. Suppose that in one case I prefer having my walls blue rather than white with the rest of the social state being Ω, whereas you have the opposite preference. The market mechanism may guarantee that my walls will be blue. In another case I might prefer having your walls blue rather than white (the rest of the social state being $\hat{\Omega}$), while you have the opposite preference. This is simply a substitution of alternatives, but the market mechanism may make your walls white and not blue. This violates neutrality.

That the market mechanism may violate anonymity or neutrality is not a compelling argument against these principles. One could adhere to them and argue: "so much the worse for the market mechanism." Indeed the failure of the market mechanism to take note of "externalities" is one of the well-known deficiencies of the market system. However, values of individual freedom of choice are much deeper than the expression they find in the market mechanism; and they require a closer scrutiny.

6.2. Liberal Values and an Impossibility Result

It can be argued that certain social choices are purely personal, e.g., everything else in the society being Ω, Mr. A lies on his back when he sleeps (x), and eveything else being Ω, Mr. A lies on his belly when he sleeps (y). Suppose Mr. A prefers y to x, whereas many others may want the opposite. It is possible to argue that the social choice between x and y is a purely personal matter since Mr. A is the only one "really" involved, and the rest are just "nosey." It is also possible to choose a CCR such that in this purely "personal" choice Mr. A's preference should be precisely reflected by social preference.

A very weak form of asserting this condition of liberalism (condition L) is that each individual is entirely decisive in the social choice over at least one pair of alternatives, e.g., Mr. A being decisive between x and y. In general there could be more than one such pair, partly because (a) there are other examples of such personal choices, e.g., Mr. A doing a spot of yoga exercise before retiring (however revolting others might find the idea), and (b) even with the back-or-belly-sleep case there would be more than one such pair, since Ω could be different, e.g., if it is alright for Mr. A to sleep on his belly rather than on his back when Mr. B's kitchen walls are pink, it should be alright to do the same when Mr. B's kitchen walls are crimson. Thus condition L is really rather weak; while a liberal should accept condition L he must want something more.

A still weaker requirement than condition L is given by condition L^*, which demands that at least *two* individuals should have their personal preferences reflected in social preference over one pair of alternatives each. This condition is extremely mild and may be called the condition of "minimal liberalism," since cutting down any further the number of individuals with such freedom (i.e., cutting it down to one individual) would permit even a complete dictatorship, which is not very liberal.

Now the unfortunate fact is that this most mild condition L^* is inconsistent with conditions U (unrestricted domain) and P (weak Pareto principle) when imposed on a SDF, as shown in Sen (1970), and reproduced below in Theorem 6*1. This impossibility result can be contrasted with Arrow's impossibility theorem.

Condition L^* (minimal liberalism) is somewhat stronger than Arrow's condition D (nondictatorship), even though it seems to be much weaker than what "liberalism" requires. Conditions U and P are shared by Arrow's theorem and Theorem 6*1. Condition I (independence of irrelevant alternatives) is required in Arrow's theorem but not in Theorem 6*1. Further, the Arrow conditions apply to SWFs (i.e., condition O is imposed), whereas in this other theorem merely a SDF (i.e., condition O^*) is required, which does not require transitivity but only acyclicity of social preference. Acyclicity is, of course, strictly weaker than transitivity. Still the impossibility holds, and is, thus, rather disturbing.

An illustration could clarify the nature of the problem. Let the social choice be between three alternatives involving Mr. A reading a copy of *Lady Chatterly's Lover*, Mr. B reading it, or no one reading it. We name these alternatives a, b, and c, respectively. Mr. A, the prude, prefers most that no one reads it, next that he reads it, and last that "impressionable" Mr. B be exposed to it, i.e., he prefers c to a, and a to b. Mr. B, the lascivious, prefers that either of them should read it rather than neither, but further prefers that Mr. A should read it rather than he himself, for he wants Mr. A to be exposed to Lawrence's prose. Hence he prefers a to b, and b to c. A liberal argument can be made for the case that given the choice between Mr. A reading it and no one reading it, his own preference should be reflected by social preference. So that society should prefer that no one reads it, rather than having Mr. A read what he plainly regards as a dreadful book. Hence c is socially preferred to a. Similarly, a liberal argument exists in favor of reflecting Mr. B's preference in the social choice between Mr. B reading it and no one reading it. Thus b is preferred to c. Hence society should prefer Mr. B reading it to no one reading it, and the latter to Mr. A reading it. However, Mr. B reading it is Pareto-worse than Mr. A reading it, even in terms of the weak Pareto criterion, and if social preference honors that ranking, then a is preferred to b. Hence every alternative can be seen to be worse than some other. And there is thus no best alternative in this set and there is no optimal choice.

6.3. Critique of Acyclicity

It may be noted that there is no conflict between the Pareto principle and the condition of minimal liberalism over any particular pair of alternatives, even with unrestricted domain. The conflict arises when we put together more than one pair. One way out may be to reject pair-wise choice and not to generate a choice function out of a social preference relation. It is certainly possible to argue that a be choson in the choice between a and b, b be chosen given the choice between b and c, c be chosen in the choice between c and a, and, say, a be chosen in the choice between a, b and c. This will not be a collective choice rule, as we have defined it, since no social preference relation can represent this. In particular it will violate property α, since a is best in (a, b, c), but not so in (a, c).

An argument for dropping acyclicity is difficult to construct, but one possible line is precisely to refer to Theorem 6*1 and similar results. If neither condition P nor condition L^* may be relaxed, and if the choice mechanism should work for configurations of individual preference orderings noted in Theorem 6*1 (or in Section 6.2 above), then acyclicity must go. If P and L^* are "irresistible" forces, then acyclicity must be a moveable object.

But this is not really an attractive way out. First, a rejection of acyclicity in this case will mean that the choice function will not be based on a relation of pair-wise preference, and furthermore, even the rationality property α will be violated. Why select a in a choice between a, b and c, and reject it in a choice between a and c? Property α is a most appealing condition.

Second, avoiding the paradox by rejecting acyclicity is really cheating; it works only because conditions P and L^* are imposed here as conditions on pair-wise choice, whereas acyclicity makes social choice essentially non-pair-wise. Given acyclicity of social preference, it would be necessary to redefine conditions P and L^*. We might require (condition $\hat{P}$) that x should not be in the choice set $C(S)$ of the society if the set S contains some alternative y which is preferred by everyone to x. We also require (condition $\hat{L}^*$) that there are two pairs of alternatives (x and y, and z and w)

and two individuals 1 and 2 such that if individual 1 (respectively 2) prefer x to y (respectively z to w), then y (respectively w) should not be in the social choice set $C(S)$ if x (respectively z) is in the set S, and if individual 1 (respectively 2) prefers y to x (respectively w to z), then x (respectively z) should not be in the choice set $C(S)$ if y (respectively w) is in the set S.   Conditions $\hat{P}$ and $\hat{L}*$ merely restate the Pareto principle and the principle of minimal liberalism for a choice function that is not necessarily generated by a preference relation.   It is easy to show that conditions $\hat{P}$, $\hat{L}*$ and U are inconsistent when imposed on a collective choice mechanism (strictly not a CCR) that specifies a social choice function, given the set of individual preference orderings.   In fact the previous example with a, b and c, will suffice and it can be shown that by condition $\hat{P}$, the choice set for (a, b, c) must not include b, and by condition $\hat{L}*$, that choice set must not include a or c. Hence the choice set must be empty.   If we relax acyclicity, then the motivation of the conditions requires that the conditions be restated, and this brings back the impossibility.   Relaxing acyclicity is, thus, not a very promising way out.

6.4.   Critique of Liberal Values

It is, of course, possible to argue for the rejection of condition $L*$.   One argument may be the following: The idea that certain things are a person's "personal" affair is insupportable.   If the color of Mr. A's walls disturbs Mr. B, then it is Mr. B's business as well.   If it makes Mr. A unhappy that Mr. B should lie on his belly while asleep, or that he should read *Lady Chatterly's Lover* while awake, then Mr. A *is* a relevant party to the choice.

This is, undoubtedly, a possible point of view, and the popularity of rules such as a ban on smoking marijuana, or suppression of homosexual practices or of pornography, reflect, at least partly, such a point of view.   Public policy is often aimed at imposing on individuals the will of others even on matters that may directly concern only those individuals.   However, condition $L*$ is really extremely weak and a rejection of it is to deny such liberal considerations *altogether*.   Only one pair of alternatives per person is involved in condition $L*$ and that for only two persons.   My guess is that condition $L*$, in that very weak form, and even the somewhat stronger condition L, will find many champions.[1]   To deny condition L^* is not merely to violate liberalism, as usually understood, but to deny even the most limited expressions of individual freedom.   And also to deny privacy, since the choice between x and y may be that between being forced to confess on one's personal affairs (x) and not being so forced (y).   Thus support for L or L^* may come even from people who are not "liberals" in the usual sense.

6.5. Critique of the Pareto Principle

An alternative is to reject the Pareto principle.   It was pointed out in Chapter 2 that this principle, particularly in its "weak" form, is something of a sacred cow in the literature on social welfare.   But one can construct an argument against it based on examples of the type considered in Section 6.2 and Theorem 6*1. It may be argued that it is not merely important to know who prefers what, but also *why* he has this preference.   Mr. A does not wish to read the book himself if the choice is between his reading it and no one reading it, but he wants to deny Mr. B the advantage of reading it (an advantage that B values vis-a-vis not reading it).   This particular nature of A's preference ordering, it could be argued, distracts from the value of A's preference for his reading the book vis-a-vis B reading the book.   Preferences based on excessive nosiness about what is good for others, should be, it could be argued, ignored.

This line of reasoning, appealing or not, raises doubts also about things other than the Pareto principle.   First, if social choice were to depend not merely on individual preferences but also on other things, e.g., the causation of those preferences, then the concept of a collective choice rule (and therefore also of a SWF or a SDF) is itself in doubt.   Social preference would then no longer be a function of individual preferences only.

---

[1] The appeal of L or L^* would depend on the nature of the alternatives that are offered for choice.   If the choices are all nonpersonal, e.g., to outlaw untouchability or not, to declare war against another country or not, conditions L or L^* should not have much appeal.   However, in choices involving personal variations L or L^* would be appealing.   It is not being suggested that the conflict in question will be disturbing in every collective choice situation, but that there are many real choices where this conflict may raise serious difficulties.

Second, it may, however, be argued that the collective choice mechanism cannot really work on information of such a complicated nature as causation of (or reasoning behind) an individual ordering, and the only way it can take this consideration into account is by using preferences over other pairs of alternatives, as in the case noted above.   Mr. A's preference for his reading the book rather than Mr. B reading it could be thought to be rendered unimportant if it is noted that given the choice Mr. A would rather not read it at all.   If this approach is accepted, then we are confined to a CCR (and possibly a SWF or a SDF), but condition I (the independence of irrelevant alternatives) is violated.

In Theorems 6*1 and 6*2, condition I is not used as such, but the social decisions generated by the Pareto principle satisfy condition I and even this implicit use of the condition may be objectionable.[2]   If social preference between x and y should depend on individual preferences only between x and y, then the weak Pareto principle seems to be altogether compelling.   If, however, such an independence is not assumed, then it can be argued that the set of individual preferences between x and y is inadequate information for a social choice between x and y.   In this respect it seems slightly misleading to call the Pareto quasi-ordering "the unanimity quasi-ordering,"[3] since the unanimity in question is only over the particular pair.

If the Pareto principle is rejected, the consequence of that for collective choice in general and for welfare economics in particular must be immense.   Most of the usual political choice mechanisms are Pareto-inclusive.   While free market allocation does not necessarily achieve Pareto-optimality when externalities are present, Pareto-optimality is taken to be a goal that is regrettably missed. What seems to follow from the problem under discussion is that Pareto-optimality may not even be a desirable objective in the presence of externalities in the shape of "nosiness."[4]   The consequences of all this are far-reaching.

---

[2] The use of condition I in the proof of Arrow's General Possibility Theorem (Theorem 3*1) is, of course, much more direct and pervasive (see proof of Lemma 3*a).

[3] Arrow (1951) p. 36.

[4] Incidentally, in the example, the "liberal" solution, viz., b in (a, b, c), is not merely not Pareto-optimal, it is also a point of disequilibrium.   So the market will not achieve the Pareto-inoptimal "liberal" solution either.

Once again, the rejection of the Pareto principle cannot be a source of great joy. It is a highly appealing criterion and many would hesitate a lot to let it go. Bringing in "irrelevant" alternatives, as was done in the reasoning, is somewhat worrying, especially since the evidence of "nosiness," which may or may not be regarded as deplorable, is only indirect. Mr. A's reason for preferring to read the book himself rather than giving it to Mr. B may be based on A's expectation of B's social behavior after he reads that "dangerous" book. Merely by looking at A's preference ordering, no conclusive evidence for *genuine* nosiness can be found. While the Pareto principle seems to be open to doubt, a violation of it seems to require some caution.

6.6. Critique of Unrestricted Domain

The use of condition U in practically all impossibility theorems in collective choice tends to be important. For many configurations of individual preferences no conflict between conditions P and L^* (or L) will arise. If in reality actual preferences were all of such a benign type, then the problem under discussion may be shrugged off. We did, however, find examples that seemed plausible and which led to a conflict.

While the problem cannot be dismissed this way, it can certainly be argued that the eventual guarantee for individual freedom cannot be found in mechanisms of collective choice, but in developing values and preferences that respect each other's privacy and personal choices.

In the dilemmas and conflicts discussed in this chapter, a few lessons seem obvious. The Pareto principle does, of course, conflict with minimal liberalism unless individual preferences fall into certain specific patterns. This choice may cause no great confusion for a determined liberal.[5] The type of reasoning that justifies L^* seems to debunk a complete adherence to the Pareto principle P. There is no great tragedy even for the no-nonsense man who denies the notion of "nosiness" and takes A's interest in B's "personal" affairs as justification for regarding that to be A's affair also. He would very likely accept condition P and reject L^*.

---

[5] The term liberal is used in many senses, not all of which are consistent. Here, it is used to refer to a person who is deeply concerned with preserving individual freedom from interference by others.

The real dilemma is only for an intermediate observor, who finds the concept of nosiness meaningful and relevant, but does not want the Pareto principle to be rejected even when individual preferences are nosey.   This position is slightly schizophrenic, but that is no great consolation since a great many people *are* schizophrenic in this sense.

It is also possible to argue that whether a certain condition on a CCR such as the Pareto principle, or minimal liberalism, is a good condition or not might depend much on what patterns of individual preferences would actually hold, and not on what patterns are logically conceivable.   A condition may be fine for a CCR with a certain restricted domain and another may be alright for a CCR with a different restricted domain, and given a possible conflict between the two, we might choose with an eye to the likely sets of individual preferences.   It is possible to argue for a CCR that satisfies condition P over a domain Δ^1 and satisfies condition L^* over a domain Δ^2, with Δ^1 and Δ^2 having some, but not all, common elements.   This prospect may not make the air electric with expectations, but it is formally a possible way out of the disturbing dilemma.

Chapter 6*

THE LIBERAL PARADOX

6*1. Liberalism versus the Pareto Principle

Liberal values seem to require that there are choices that are personal and the relevant person should be free to do what he likes. It would be socially better, in these cases, to permit him to do what he wants, everything else remaining the same. We define the condition of liberalism in a very weak form.

Condition L (*liberalism*)*:* For each person i there is at least one pair of distinct alternatives (x, y) such that he is decisive in the social choice between them in either order, i.e., $x P_i y \to x P y$, and $y P_i x \to y P x$.

This condition can be weakened by requiring such limited decisiveness not for all persons, but for at least some. If we demand it for only one, then of course it is not a case of liberalism, since it will be consistent with dictatorship as well. So we must require it for at least two individuals.

*Condition L** (*minimal liberalism*)*:* There are at least two persons k and j and two pairs of distinct alternatives (x, y) and (z, w) such that k and j are decisive over (x, y) and (z, w), respectively, each pair taken in either order.

Obviously, $L \to L^*$, but not vice versa.

THEOREM 6*1. *There is no SDF satisfying conditions U, P and L*.*

Proof. If (x, y) and (z, w) are the same pair, then obviously condition L^* cannot hold. If the pairs have one of the elements in common, say $x = z$, then let $x P_k y$, $w P_j x$, and $\forall i: y P_i w$. By condition L^*, $x P y$ and $w P x$, and by condition P, $y P w$. This violates acyclicity and there is no best alternative.

Next, let all four of the alternatives be distinct. Assume now that $x P_k y$, $z P_j w$ and $\forall i:$ $(w P_i x$ & $y P_i z)$.[1]   By condition L^*, $x P y$ & $z P w$.   By condition P, $w P x$ & $y P z$.   But this too violates acyclicity.   Hence there is no SDF that will satisfy conditions L^* and P, given condition U, which completes the proof.

Note that the condition of the independence of irrelevant alternatives is not imposed.   Nor do we require social preference to be transitive, or even quasi-transitive, and all that is ruled out is acyclicity.   The theorem is disturbing, and even the corollary given below, which is much weaker, is disturbing.

COROLLARY 6*1.1.   *There is no SDF satisfying conditions U, P and L.*

6*2.   Extensions

A dilemma close to the one in Theorem 6*1 can be posed by relaxing the conditions that the two persons be decisive in either order, and requiring instead that they be decisive over two *ordered* pairs that are distinct in each element.

Condition L^{**}:   There are at least two persons k and j and two ordered pairs of alternatives (x, y) and (z, w), all four alternatives being distinct, such that $x P_k y \to x P y$, and $z P_j w \to z P w$.

THEOREM 6*2.   *There is no SDF satisfying conditions U, P and L^{**}.*

The proof is the same as in the second paragraph of the proof of Theorem 6*1.   Note, however, that neither does L^* imply L^{**}, nor does L^{**} imply L^*, so that the two theorems are independent.

Finally, we propose another condition L^{***}.

Condition L^{***}:   There are at least two persons k and j and two ordered pairs of alternatives (x, y) and (z, w), with $x \neq z$ and $y \neq w$, and such that $x P_k y \to x P y$, and $z P_j w \to z P w$.

THEOREM 6*3.   *There is no SDF satisfying conditions U, P and L^{***}.*

The proof, which is omitted here, is in the same line as that of Theorem 6*1.   Note that $L^{**} \to L^{***}$, and $L \to L^* \to L^{***}$, so that Theorem 6*3 subsumes Theorems 6*1 and 6*2, and Corollary 6*1.1, without being subsumed.   The logical gain is, however, not matched by a significant gain in relevance, so that in discussing the liberal dilemma, we could very well concentrate on Theorem 6*1, which is what we did in Chapter 6.

---

[1] Note that there are orderings *compatible* with each of the individual preference relations specified.

Chapter 7

INTERPERSONAL AGGREGATION
AND COMPARABILITY

7.1. Independence of Irrelevant Alternatives

It was noted in Chapter 3 that the rank-order method of voting is a SWF which satisfies conditions U, P and D, but not condition I. In Chapter 6 some arguments against the imposition of condition I were put forward in the specific context of the liberal paradox. Other reasons have also been noted in the literature (see Rothenberg (1961); also Wilson (1968)). It should, however, be observed that relaxing condition I opens up a number of possibilities, of which the rank-order method is only one. In fact, the classic approach of utilitarianism is ruled out by condition I, and if the condition of the independence of irrelevant alternatives is relaxed, that avenue may also be explored. However, it is not merely condition I that rules out aggregating individual utilities. The very definition of a collective choice rule outlaws it, since a CCR makes the social ordering a function of the set of individual orderings. Any change in utility measures without a change of the individual orderings R_i must leave the social ordering R generated by any CCR completely unchanged. This applies, naturally, also to such special cases of a CCR as a SWF and a SDF. But even if a CCR is redefined, so that the utility measures are admitted as arguments, the problem of condition I could remain.

It may not be obvious how condition I prevents the use of utilitarianism. The name "independence of irrelevant alternatives" is somewhat misleading. Two aspects of it must be distinguished. First, condition I is violated when in the social choice involving x and y, the individual rankings of a third alternative, say z, vis-a-vis either x or y or any other alternative, become a relevant factor, with an influence. This we can call the "irrelevance" aspect of the condition. Second, the condition, as stated, is violated if in the social choice involving x and y anything other than the individual *orderings* over x and y get a place, e.g., preference intensities. This may or may not include the placing of irrelevant alternatives in individual orderings. This we can call the "ordering" aspect of the condition. The "irrelevance" aspect is only a part of the "ordering" aspect, though in the naming of the condition, concentration seems to be only on the "irrelevance" aspect (see Rothenberg (1961) and Sen (1966b)).

An example will perhaps clarify the logical difference. Suppose each individual had a unique cardinal scale of utility and this for every one had been put together in a gigantic book, published in heaven. Suppose we wanted to use these cardinal utility indicators in a social choice involving two alternative social states, x and y. We would not have to look at any irrelevant alternative for the purpose of constructing a scale, since each individual's utility scale could be looked up on any weekday in any public library that has this precious book. Let us imagine that after adding up the differences in the utilities between x and y for the individuals, the sum came out positive, and using utilitarianism we declared x to be socially preferred to y. Meanwhile people started feeling a change in their utility scales. Shortly afterwards, let us further imagine, that it was announced in heaven that people's utility scales had changed, and a new edition of the book was being made available presently. It turned out on inspection that everyone's ordering of x and y, and indeed of all other certain alternatives, had remained the same, but the cardinal gaps between them had changed. After adding up the differences in the utilities between x and y for all individuals, this time it turned out that the sum was negative, and so y was declared socially peferred to x. This involved a violation of Arrow's condition of the independence of irrelevant alternatives. But no irrelevant alternative had ever entered the picture. This is a case of violation of the "ordering" aspect of the condition without involving the "irrelevance" aspect of it.

In practice, however, this may not make much actual difference, in spite of the analytical differences involved. Individual utilities are not found in natural cardinal units, and cardinalization follows experimental observations, yielding a set of numbers that are unique *but for* an increasing linear transformation. Since the utility scale has to be fixed by specifying the utility value of two points on it, implicitly or explicitly, the other alternatives come into this valuation.[1] In trying to achieve an interpersonal correspondence, for the sake of social aggregation, this has to be done, and then any use of preference intensity violates not only the "ordering" aspect of the condition, but also its "irrelevance" aspect.

An illustration might help to clarify the point. Let us imagine that there are only three alternatives relevant for our consideration, viz., x, y and z. Let individual 1 rank them in the order stated. Some experiment also reveals the following utility numbers for the three: 200, 110, and 100, respectively, but the numbers are unique *up to* a linear transformation. There is, thus, no natural correspondence between the utility numbers of the different individuals. A common convention is to attach the value 0 to the worst alternative, and the value 1 to the best. A linear transformation of the original set of numbers, therefore, yields 1 for x, 0.1 for y, and 0 for z. By a similar method of normalization let the utility numbers of two other individuals turn out to be exactly the same, in particular, 1 for y, 0.6 for x, and 0 for z. If the community consists of these three, x wins over y, for the aggregate utility from x is 2.2, and that from y is 2.1. Next imagine that individuals 2 and 3 revise their opinion of z, an irrelevant alternative in the choice between x and y. They now regard z to be just as good as x. While everyone's attitude to x and y has remained the same, nevertheless the utility numbers of x and y will change for persons 2 and 3. For them, x will now have value 0, while y will continue to get 1. Now y will win over x, y having an aggregate utility of 2.1 as opposed to x's 1. The social ordering between x and y is reversed by a change in the position of an irrelevant alternative, z.[2]

Note that the result is not due to the particular method of normalization used. For example, if we follow the rule of taking the worst alternatives as 0, and the aggregate of utilities from all the social states[3] as 1, the same problem can occur. It does occur, as it happens, in the numerical example discussed above. In the initial situation, with this method of numbering, individual 1 gets

---

[1] This will be so even if the utility numbers were unique up to a proportional transformation, for the "units" will still be arbitrary.

[2] The particular example discussed here is a slight variation of the one discussed by Arrow (1963), p. 32.

[3] The number of social states considered must be the same for all individuals.

(10/11) unit of utility from x, (1/11) from y, and 0 from z, while individuals 2 and 3 get (5/8) from y, (3/8) from x, and 0 from z. Here, x yields more aggregate utility than y. Now if z moves up to be indifferent to x for individuals 2 and 3, the numbers become (0, 1, 0) for (x, y, z), respectively, for individuals 2 and 3. Now, y yields more aggregate utility than x, reversing the social choice between x and y, as a consequence of a change in the ordering involving an irrelevant alternative. The problem is indeed perfectly general, and arises entirely because of the fact that the utility scales have arbitrary "units."[4]

7.2. Comparability, Cardinality and Discrimination

The question of arbitrariness of individual utility units is largely a reflection of the problem of interpersonal comparability. If utility scales of different persons are calculated separately, as in experimental methods involving, say, the von Neumann-Morgenstern approach, then interpersonal correspondences are left completely undefined. It is possible to, say, double the units of one individual, leaving it the same for others, and this will immediately alter the interpersonal trade-offs.

In our fancy example in the last section, involving the big book, this problem was avoided because the utility measures came for everyone in a one-to-one correspondence. Behavioristic measures of utility in terms of people's expressions include an interpersonally comparable element. It may be possible to say that person A is happier than person B by looking at delighted Mr. A and morose Mr. B. It may also be possible to make marginal comparisons. This approach to objective interpersonal comparability has been most elegantly put forward by Little (1950).[5]

In Chapter 7* an approach will be developed which permits interpersonal variability of any degree, from infinite variability to none. Meanwhile, however, we must be clear about the distinction between (a) getting a cardinal measure of individual welfare,

---

[4] Being unique only up to a linear transformation, they also have arbitrary "origins," but that is not crucial for utilitarianism, since it makes use only of utility differences between x and y.

[5] Little points out that even though interpersonal comparisons may be, in this approach, perfectly objective, the goal of maximizing aggregate utility for the society is based on a value judgement, and one that may not be easy to accept.

and (b) getting some rules for interpersonal comparisons, and review the main theories in the light of these two questions.

One attempt at cardinalization of individual utility has been based on the assumption that the individuals cannot really make very fine comparisons, so that each person only has a finite number of "levels of discrimination." The difference between one discrimination level and the next is the minimum utility difference that is noticeable to the individual. The individual is "indifferent" between all alternatives that belong to the same discrimination level and we can get a cardinal measure of the utility difference between any two alternatives by checking how many discrimination levels separate them. The cardinal scale thus obtained is, of course, unique up to a positive linear transformation, and subject to the choice of an origin and a unit, a unique cardinal utility function is obtained. Based on this approach originally touched on by Borda (1781) and Edgeworth (1881), the problem of cardinalization has been explored by Armstrong (1951), Goodman and Markowitz (1952), and Rothenberg (1961), among others.

Regarding interpersonal comparability, Goodman and Markowitz make the normative assumption that the ethical significance of a movement from one discrimination level to the next is the same for each individual, and it is independent of the level from which this change is made. The calculation becomes very simple with this assumption. If alternative x is to be compared with alternative y, check by how many discrimination levels does x exceed (or fall short of) y in each individual's scale; and then simply add the differences in levels, with appropriate signs.

The difficulties with this approach are reasonably clear. The practical problems in the use of this method in real life need not be emphasized here (they are, in any case, clear enough), but there are analytical difficulties also. First, as Goodman and Markowitz themselves point out, it is not possible to observe all the discrimination levels of an individual, given a fixed set of alternatives. Thus the numbering system depends on the actual availability of the alternatives. Suppose a new commodity becomes available, and this expands the set of feasible alternatives for the individual; it is now perfectly possible for new discrimination levels to emerge, which lie in between the old discrimination levels. This will alter the utility numbering system used for the individual. Thus the social evaluation between two alternatives x and y will not be independent of what other alternatives are available.

A second difficulty lies in the ethical assumption that the significance for social welfare of a change from one discrimination level to the next is the same for all individuals. Not only is this an arbitrary assumption, it is eminently objectionable when dealing with individuals who appear to differ in the sensitivity of their perception. Someone may have a small number of discrimination levels but feel very strongly about the difference between one level and another, and another may have a large number of discrimination levels but regard the difference between the one and the next to be not worth worrying about. In this case the Goodman-Markowitz system will be very partial.[6] Indeed, there are individuals who tend to be extremists and find things either "magnificent" or "horrible," while others finely differentiate between such things as "excellent," "good," "mediocre," "poor" and "awful." It seems manifestly unfair to make the ethical assumption that the welfare significance of moving the first individual from what he regards as "horrible" to what he finds as "magnificent" is no more than moving the second individual from what he finds "poor" and what strikes him as "mediocre." What is particularly objectionable about this particular mechanism is not that it violates condition I, which of course it does, but that it implies an ethical assumption that will appear to be arbitrary and objectionable.

7.3.   Uses of von Neumann-Morgenstern Cardinalization

The behavior of a rational individual in a market involving no risks can be, in general, explained entirely in terms of ordinal utility.[7] If we try to derive a utility scale for an individual in terms of his behavior under perfect certainty, without making some very special assumptions of "independence" of commodity

---

[6] In fact Arrow (1963) shows (pp. 117–118) that with the Goodman-Markowitz system a slight difference in the sensitivity of the two persons can make complete inequality (with no income going to the less sensitive individual and all to the other) the socially "optimum" outcome in a problem of distribution.

[7] In fact, even the assumption of the existence of an ordinal utility is too demanding. With a lexicographic ordering, the alternatives may be completely ordered without there being a utility scale (even ordinal) that can be fitted to it. See Chapter 3.

groups (or more generally, of action sets),[8] the utility numbers will be unique only up to a monotonic transformation. However, the situation changes radically when we consider rational behavior in risky situations. As demonstrated by von Neumann and Morgenstern (1947), provided a person's behavior satisfies a set of clearly definable postulates, we can find a set of utility numbers for him corresponding to the set of alternatives, such that his behavior can be taken to be an attempt at the maximization of the mathematical expectation of these utility numbers.[9] These numbers can be shown to be unique up to a positive linear transformation.

A set of postulates sufficient for this was put forward by von Neumann and Morgenstern (1947), and other sets have been presented by Marschak (1950), and others. They have much in common, but the Marschak postulates are simpler to follow.

There are four postulates in the Marschak system: (a) the postulate of *complete ordering*, i.e., the relation of preference establishes a weak ordering among all prospects; (b) the postulate of *continuity*, i.e., if prospect x is preferred to prospect y and y in its turn is preferred to prospect z, then there is a probability mixture of x and z (a "lottery" involving the two) that makes the individual indifferent between that mixture and the certainty of y; (c) the postulate of the number of nonindifferent prospects being *sufficient*, viz., there must be at least four mutually nonindifferent prospects; and (d) the postulate of the *equivalence of the mixture of equivalent prospects*, i.e., if prospect x and prospect x^* are indifferent, then for any prospect y, a given probability mixture of x and y must be indifferent to a similar mixture of x^* and y.[10]

We cannot possibly go into a detailed evaluation of this approach here. We should, however, note a few of the simpler problems of using this approach. First, it is clear that the postulates imply the following "monotonicity" property: "If one alternative is better than another increase the probability of the former at the

---

[8] See Samuelson (1947), Leontief (1947), (1947a), Debreu (1960), Koopmans (1966), Gorman (1968).

[9] The mathematical expectation of utility is the same thing as the "moral expectation" of Bernoulli (1730). The utility from each alternative is weighted by its probability. See also Ramsey (1931).

[10] There are three different versions of postulate (c) discussed by Marschak. We have chosen the one which is easiest to comprehend. Samuelson (1952) calls postulate (d) "the strong independence assumption." It is also called "the sure-thing principle" especially in the literature of game theory.

expense of the latter.   If opportunities are unlimited, choose the prospect that promises the best history with 100% probability."[11] But, as Marschak points out, a mountain climber with the "love of danger" (or of gambling) may prefer a survival chance of 95% to that of, say, 80%, but also to one of 100%.   For him monotonicity will not do.

A second reservation concerns the postulate of continuity.   A person who regards gambling or taking chances as "sinful" may prefer a very poor life with taking no chances (x) to gambling with a good prospect to win a fortune (y), and that to gambling with no prospect to win (z).   But there may not be any mixture of x and z that will make him indifferent to y, for once he takes a chance on x, i.e., a chance on "a very poor life with taking no chances," he is in the sinful quota anyway, and then might sensibly prefer gambling with a good prospect to win (y) to all combinations of x and z.   For him the preference for x against y lies in its purity, which is destroyed with a gamble involving x and z. This is a violation of postulate (b).

Postulate (d) is also open to doubt.   It does not, of course, rule out people enjoying "taking a chance" or hating it, as von Neumann and Morgenstern correctly point out.[12]   But a person may get his thrill from the *number* of lotteries that he takes part in, and not only on the overall probabilities.   It is a fair bet that a gambler may prefer to have several goes at the wheel to having one simple turn representing the probabilities of the whole series for the evening compounded into one.

What is, however, certainly true is that the postulates do not rule out people having simple attitudes towards gambling as such, viz., liking it or not liking it, as long as this is related only to the overall probability distribution, simple or compound.   The utility numbers take the attitude to risk into account, and this is indeed one of the sources of objection to the use of these utilities for social choice.   Arrow has pointed out that the von Neumann-Morgenstern utility indicators may not be the appropriate scale to

---

[11] Marschak (1950), p. 138. (The result follows from Theorem 6 of Marschak.) The word "history" is used in a somewhat special sense here, meaning the prospects over "future time intervals, up to a certain time point called horizon," defined by Marschak as "future history" (p. 113).

[12] See von Neumann and Morgenstern (1947), p. 28, in the context of their postulate C. See also Marschak (1950), p. 139.

use for social choice, i.e., "if we are interested primarily in making a social choice among alternative policies in which no random elements enter.   To say otherwise would be to assert that the distribution of the social income is to be governed by the tastes of the individuals for gambling."[13]

This objection, in spite of its faintly priggish air, is a strong one, and relates to the general problem of arbitrariness of *any* cardinal scale in choices over certain alternatives.   This arbitrariness applies to other methods of cardinalization, such as the approach of assuming the independence of action sets.[14]   For example, a person may happen to satisfy independence in choosing between social states on earth given hypothetical states in heaven and vice versa, and this could help the cardinalization of his utilities on earth. Should this cardinal element be relevant for social choices here and now?   This is not at all obvious.   Further, the independence assumption needed in this case is stronger than that required for von Neumann-Morgenstern cardinalization (viz., postulate (d) of Marschak discussed above), since the latter does not deny complementarity in the usual sense, as the former does.[15]

All this is somewhat discouraging, but not decisively so.   First, any particular cardinal scale is "arbitrary" only in the sense that in choices over the set of certain alternatives (or over a relevant subset of it) individual behavior is consistent with other methods of scaling as well.   But in an ethical argument one may wish to choose some particular scaling in spite of this "arbitrariness," on some *other* grounds that may be additionally specified.   Second, as Harsanyi (1953), (1955), has argued, we may be interested in individual preferences over social states with an as-if element of uncertainty deliberately built into it, as was noted in Chapter 5. People's "ethical judgments" may be defined as judgments they would subscribe to if they had an equal chance of being in anyone's shoes.   With this interpretation, individual preferences will be choices over risky alternatives, and people's "attitude to gambling" may indeed be an appropriate element in social choice. Thus there are frameworks of collective choice for which the von

[13] Arrow (1951), p. 10.

[14] See Samuelson (1947), Leontief (1947), (1947a), Debreu (1960), Koopmans (1966) and Gorman (1968).   See also Luce and Tukey (1964) and Luce (1966).

[15] See Samuelson (1952), Manne (1952), Malinvaud (1952), and others in the same number of *Econometrica*, **20**, 1952.

Neumann-Morgenstern cardinalization *is* the relevant one.

Third, all is not lost if more than one method of cardinalization are found to be relevant. Procedures of aggregation can still be used to obtain quasi-orderings that rank some social states vis-a-vis each other, though not necessarily all of them (see Chapter 7*, especially Section 7*4). We can use each measure and take the common rankings, which will thus be noncontroversial. This problem will be discussed in Sections 7.5 and 7*4.

Cardinal measurability is only a part of the problem of using utilitarianism;[16] another is interpersonal aggregation. With von Neumann-Morgenstern cardinalization, this difficulty is as serious as in any other system, since the measures are entirely personal. Any method of interpersonal normalization is open to criticisms. It may be argued that some systems, e.g., assigning in each person's scale the value 0 to the worst alternative and the value 1 to his best alternative, are interpersonally "fair," but such an argument is dubious. First, there are other systems with comparable symmetry, e.g., the system we discussed earlier of assigning 0 to the worst alternative and the value 1 to the *sum* of utilities from all alternatives. Neither system is noticeably less fair than the other (one assumes equal maximal utility for all and the other assumes equal average utility for all), but they will yield different bases of social choice.[17] Second, in comparing the utility measures of different persons, one may wish deliberately to take account of interpersonal variability of capacity for satisfaction, e.g., one may wish to give special consideration to handicapped people whose enjoyment measure may be thought to be uniformly lower.[18]

---

[16] This expression "utilitarianism" is being used very broadly here as the approach of maximizing aggregate individual welfares. In fact, "utilitarianism" corresponds to that special case where individual welfare is identified with individual "utility" defined as the person's psychological feeling of satisfaction. It has now become conventional in economics and in some other social sciences to define utility as any measure of individual welfare, not necessarily a measure of "pleasure" in the sense of Bentham. We follow this practice, even though it is a somewhat doubtful procedure. Contrast Little (1950).

[17] In an important contribution, Hildreth (1953) considers two specially defined social states X and Y such that everyone prefers X to Y, and assigns two fixed real values a and b to them, respectively, in everyone's utility scale (p. 87). This too, given the assumption, is a possible method of interpersonal normalization.

[18] This is not easy to do in the utilitalian framework, but is important in other approaches, e.g., in Rawls' theory of justice (Chapter 9).

Again, the situation is not really quite hopeless, though the problems are serious. One way of facing the problem is to use a number of alternative schemes of interpersonal normalization and select those pair-wise rankings which are invariant with respect to the choice of any of these schemes. We discuss this approach of "partial comparability" in the next section, or more formally in Chapter 7*.

7.4. Partial Comparability

Suppose we are debating the consequence on the aggregate welfare of Romans of the act of Rome being burnt while Nero played his fiddle. We recognize that Nero was delighted while the other Romans suffered, but suppose we still say that the sum total of welfare went down as a consequence. What type of interpersonal comparability are we assuming? If there is no comparability at all, we can change the utility units of different individuals differently, and by multiplying Nero's utility measures by a suitably large number, it should be possible to make Nero's gain larger in size than the loss of others. Hence we are not assuming noncomparability. But are we assuming that every Roman's welfare units can be put into one-to-one correspondence with the welfare units of every other Roman? Not necessarily. We might not be sure what precise correspondence to take, and we might admit some possible variability, but we could still be able to assert that no matter which of the various possible combinations we take, the sum total went down in any case. This is a case intermediate between noncomparability and full comparability of units.

To take another example, suppose we denounce the existing inequality in the distribution of money income, and assert that this amounts to a lower aggregate of individual welfare. Are we assuming that we can put everyone's welfare units into one-to-one correspondence? We do not have to. We may be somewhat uncertain about the precise welfare functions of the different individuals and the precise correspondence between the respective welfare units, but we could quite reasonably still assert that in every possible case within the permitted variations the sum-total is less than what could happen with a more equal distribution. The attack of Robbins (1932) and others on interpersonal comparability does not distinguish between *some* comparability and *total* comparability of units, and the consequence has been the virtual elimination of distributional questions from the formal literature on welfare economics. (Among the exceptions are Lerner (1944), Dobb (1955), (1969), Fisher (1956), Mishan (1960), and a few others.)

What we may wish to do is to introduce some limited variability in the relative welfare units of different individuals, and deal not with one-to-one correspondences but with many-to-many correspondences. The general framework is developed in Chapter 7* but here we can illustrate the approach in terms of a simple example.

Consider the following case: There are three individuals A, B and C, and three alternatives x, y and z. As arbitrators we are trying to figure out which alternative is socially most desirable in terms of aggregate welfare. We first obtain the cardinal welfare functions of the three; each of these are of course unique only up to an increasing linear transformation. We reflect on the correspondences between the welfare units of the three individuals, but cannot decide completely. We may be inclined to use, say, the familiar normalization procedure of setting the welfare from the worst alternative as 0 and that from the best alternative as 1 for each individual, even though we may not be really convinced that this is exactly right. Suppose that this yields Table 7.1.

Table 7.1. Tentative Welfare Indicators

Individuals	Alternatives		
	x	y	z
A	1	0.90	0
B	1	0.88	0
C	0	0.95	1

In terms of welfare sum the tentative ordering is y, x, z, in decreasing order. What other criterion can we use? Note that no alternative in this collection is Pareto-superior to any other. In terms of majority decision, we get a consistent social ordering, with x being socially preferred to y and that being preferred to z, but it raises some doubts. It would appear that C's preference for y over x is very sharp, while the preference of A or B for x

over y is rather mild. But this comparison of "sharpness" or "mildness" depends on our assumptions about interpersonal comparisons. If, for example, we blow up the welfare levels of A ten times, by choosing correspondingly smaller units for A, then A's welfare from x, y and z will respectively be equal to 10, 9 and 0. Then A's preference for x over y (measured by 1) will look even sharper than C's preference for y over x (measured by 0.95).

Is a ten-fold blow-up for A legitimate? Our value judgments may be imprecise and we may be agreeable to accept some variability, but we might nevertheless feel that a ten-fold blow-up is too large a variation. We may set the limit as raising or lowering the welfare units of any person by a factor of, say, 2 either way. If any alternative has at least as large a welfare sum as any other unit for every possible combination within these limits the former can be said to have at least as large an aggregate welfare as the latter. To check this we obtain the welfare differences in our first estimate (Table 7.2).

Table 7.2. Tentative Welfare Differences

Individuals	Between		
	x and y	y and z	z and x
A	0.10	0.90	-1.00
B	0.12	0.88	-1.00
C	-0.95	-0.05	1.00

We first take x and y for comparison. Under the first estimate the sum of the welfare difference of the three individuals between x and y is -0.73, so that y seems to be favored. We can, however, change these welfare difference measures. The most favorable combination for x against y is to double A's and B's measures and to halve C's measures. This yields a net gap of -0.035, so that y still has a larger welfare sum than x. Hence y can be declared to be better than x, according to the aggregation criterion with the specified degree of variability.

Coming to y and z, the most favorable combination for z is to halve the welfare measures of A and B and to double it for C, but still the welfare sum for y is larger than that for z by 0.79. Hence y is better than z.

However, the comparison of z and x is inconclusive. As they stand in Tables 7.1 and 7.2, x has a larger welfare sum, but if we halve A's and B's welfare measures and double C's, we get a difference in favor of z and not x. Hence the aggregation relation must be declared to be incomplete over this pair. But as it happens, this does not affect the choice between x, y and z, since y is noted to be better than both x and z. There is a unique best element.

This is a very simple example; the general framework is analyzed in Chapter 7*. The example considered here is a special case of what is called "strong symmetry" in that chapter. "Strong symmetry" is a special case of "weak symmetry," which is itself a special case of "regularity." There will be no attempt here to summarize the results of Chapter 7* besides noting that (a) under every assumption of comparability, however partial, the aggregation relation R^a is always reflexive and transitive; (b) R^a always subsumes the Pareto quasi-ordering and coincides with it under noncomparability; (c) under "regularity," if the extent of partial comparability is made more strict, then the aggregation relation gets extended monotonically; (d) under "weak symmetry" we can find a measure of the degree d of partial comparability between 0 and 1, such that $d = 0$ implies noncomparability, $d = 1$ implies complete comparability of units, and $d^1 > d^2$ implies that the aggregation quasi-ordering under the latter will be a subrelation of that under the former. Thus, under some relatively mild assumptions, we would find a very well-behaved sequence of quasi-orderings, each a subrelation of the next, starting with the Pareto quasi-ordering under noncomparability and ending up with a complete ordering under full comparability of units ("unit comparability"). A complete ordering can, of course, be reached for degrees of comparability less than 1, and it is possible that a "best" element may emerge for even lower degrees partial comparability. Incidentally, in the example quoted, we had $d = 0.25$, and even with such a low degree of comparability a best alternative was seen to emerge. With a degree of comparability of 0.71 or more, a complete ordering would have been reached in that example. Complete comparability is not merely a doubtful assumption, it is also quite unnecessary.

7.5. Adding Ordinal-Type Welfare

Just as haziness of values may exist about interpersonal comparisons, there might be some haziness even in measuring individual utility. As was noted before, more than one system of cardinalization is possible, and ethically it may be difficult to establish the superiority of one system over the others. If all these systems are admitted, then each individual will be associated with a set of utility functions, not all linear transformations of each other, unlike the case of cardinality. They will, of course, all be positive monotonic transformations of each other. But, unlike the case of strict ordinality, not every monotonic transformation will be necessarily included. We shall call this case that of "ordinal-type" welfare. One extreme case of this is strict ordinality, when the set includes all positive monotonic transformations, while the other extreme is strict cardinality when only positive *linear* transformations are included.

With ordinal-type utility and partial comparability, it is possible to obtain a quasi-ordering of aggregation using the rule that if x has at least as large a welfare sum as y under every measure of individual utilities (given by the measurability assumptions) and under every interpersonal correspondence (given by the comparability assumptions), then and only then is x at least as good as y. Irrespective of the particular measurability and comparability assumptions chosen, an aggregation relation thus defined will be a quasi-ordering (i.e., will be transitive and reflexive), and will incorporate at least the Pareto quasi-ordering. The stricter the measurability and comparability assumptions, the more extensive will be the quasi-ordering. It is of course, possible to obtain a complete ordering even with less than strict cardinality and less than full comparability.

The formal analysis is presented in Section 7*4. The important point to note here is that cardinality and full interpersonal comparability of individual welfare units are *sufficient but not necessary* assumptions for rational choice under aggregate welfare maximization. Hence the rejection of these assumptions does not render the approach impotent, in contrast with what seems to be frequently held. The wide appeal of aggregate welfare maximization as an approach to the analysis of collective choice, of which classic utilitarianism is a special case, is based on an implicit use of a framework wider than that permitted by complete comparability and cardinality. Such a general framework, which is defined and analyzed in Chapter 7*, does lack the sure-fire effectiveness of classical utilitarianism, which is one of its very special cases, but it also avoids the cocksure character of utilitarianism as well as its unrestrained arbitrariness.

Chapter 7*

AGGREGATION QUASI-ORDERINGS[1]

7*1. Comparability and Aggregation

Let X be the set of alternative social states, x. Every individual i has a set L_i of real-valued welfare functions, W_i, each defined over X. If individual welfare is "ordinally measurable," then every element of L_i is a positive monotonic transformation of every other element and furthermore, every positive monotonic transformation of any element of L_i belongs to L_i. If, on the other hand, individual welfare is "cardinally measurable," then every element of L_i is a positive linear transformation of every other element, and every positive linear transformation of any element of L_i belongs to L_i.[2] In this section and in the two following, cardinal measurability of individual welfare will be assumed. In Section 7*4, aggregation with noncardinal utility will be studied.

To sum the levels of individual welfare, we have to choose one element from every L_i. We shall call any such n-tuple of individual welfare functions a functional combination.

DEFINITION 7*1. *A functional combination, W, is any element of the Cartesian product $\prod_{i=1}^{n} L_i$, denoted L.*

For the purpose of comparison of aggregate welfare of alternative social states in X, we define a subset $\bar{L}$ of L, and sum the individual welfare differences between any pair x, y in X for every element of $\bar{L}$. The specification of $\bar{L}$ reflects our assumptions of interpersonal comparability. We denote $x R^a y$ for x having at

---

[1] This chapter is closely related to Sen (1970a).

[2] By a positive linear transformation, mappings of the following kind are meant: $U^1 = a + bU^2$, where a and b are constants, and $b > 0$. Strictly speaking, these are "affine transformations," and not linear transformations, a term that algebraists would reserve for homogeneous transformations of the type $U^1 = bU^2$.

least as much aggregate welfare as y.

DEFINITION 7*2.   *A comparison set $\bar{L}$ is any specified subset of L, such that we declare that x has at least as much aggregate welfare as y, for any pair x, y, if and only if the sum of the individual welfare differences between x and y is nonnegative for every element W of $\bar{L}$, i.e.,*

$$\forall x, y \in X: [x\, R^a\, y \leftrightarrow \forall W \in \bar{L}: \sum_i \{W_i(x) - W_i(y)\} \geqq 0]$$

We define $x\, P^a\, y$ as $x\, R^a\, y$ and $\sim(y\, R^a\, x)$, and $x\, I^a\, y$ as $x\, R^a\, y$ and $y\, R^a\, x$.

Certain distinguished cases of interpersonal comparability deserve special mention, and should help to illustrate the relation between interpersonal comparability and the comparison set. (We refer to the ith element of any W as W_i; it is the welfare level of person i.)

DEFINITION 7*3.   (1) *Noncomparability holds if and only if $L = \bar{L}$.*

(2)   *Full comparability holds if and only if $\bar{W}$ being any element of $\bar{L}$ implies that $\bar{L}$ includes only and all functional combinations W such that for all i,*

$$W_i = a + b\,\bar{W}_i$$

where a, and $b > 0$, are constants, invariant with i.

(3)   *Unit comparability holds if and only if $\bar{W}$ being any element of $\bar{L}$ implies that $\bar{L}$ includes only and all functional combinations W such that for all i,*

$$W_i = a_i + b\,\bar{W}_i$$

where a_i can vary with i but $b > 0$ must be invariant with respect to i.

In the case of noncomparability the set L of functional combinations is not restricted in any way to arrive at the comparison set $\bar{L}$.   In the case of full comparability a particular one-to-one correspondence is established between the welfare functions of different individuals.   In the case of unit comparability if the welfare function of one individual is specified, it specifies a one-parameter family of welfare functions for every other individual, each member of the family differing from any other by a constant (positive or negative).   It may be noted that with unit comparability the absolute levels of individual welfare are not comparable (e.g., it makes no sense to say that person A is better off than person B), but welfare differences *are* comparable (e.g., it does make sense to say that person A gains more than B in the choice of social state x rather than y). In this case, welfare units are comparable (there is a one-to-one correspondence of welfare units), though the origins are arbitrary.

The following results concerning the binary relation of aggregation R^a are important. $\bar{R}$ and $\bar{P}$ are the Pareto preference relations as defined in Definition 2*2.

THEOREM 7*1.   *With cardinally measurable individual welfares*

(1)   *For any $\bar{L}$, i.e., for every possible assumption of interpersonal comparability, R^a is a quasi-ordering.*

(2)   *For any $\bar{L}$, i.e., for every possible assumption of interpersonal comparability, $\bar{R}$ is a subrelation of R^a, i.e., $\forall x, y \in X: [x \bar{R} y \rightarrow x R^a y]$ and $[x \bar{P} y \rightarrow x P^a y]$.*

(3)   *With noncomparability, $R^a = \bar{R}$.*

(4)   *With unit comparability, or with full comparability, R^a is a complete ordering.*

Proof: (1) Reflexivity of R^a follows directly from each W_i being an order-preserving transformation of R_i for every element of L. Transitivity of R^a is also immediate:

$$[x R^a y \ \& \ y R^a z] \rightarrow \sum_i [W_i(x) - W_i(y)] \geq 0 \qquad \text{and}$$

$$\sum_i [W_i(y) - W_i(z)] \geq 0 \qquad \text{for all } W \in \bar{L}$$

$$\rightarrow \sum_i [W_i(x) - W_i(z)] \geq 0 \qquad \text{for all } W \in \bar{L}$$

$$\rightarrow x R^a z$$

(2)   For any $x, y \in X$:

$$x \bar{R} y \rightarrow \forall i: [W_i(x) - W_i(y)] \geq 0 \qquad \text{for every } W \in L$$

$$\rightarrow x R^a y$$

since $\bar{L} \subset L$.   Further,

$$x \bar{P} y \rightarrow [\exists i: x P_i y \ \& \ \forall i: x R_i y]$$

$$\rightarrow \exists i: [W_i(x) - W_i(y)] > 0 \ \&$$

$$\forall i: [W_i(x) - W_i(y)] \geq 0 \qquad \text{for every } W \in L$$

$$\rightarrow x P^a y$$

since $\bar{L} \subset L$.

(3) In view of (2) all we need show is $x R^a y \rightarrow x \bar{R} y$. For any x, y in X, $\sim(x \bar{R} y) \rightarrow \exists j: y P_j x \rightarrow \exists j: [W_j(y) - W_j(x)] > 0$, for every $W \in L$. For each W, define $\alpha_1(W) = W_j(y) - W_j(x)$, and $\alpha_2(W) = \sum_{i, i \neq j} [W_i(x) - W_i(y)]$. Take any arbitrary $W^* \in L$. If $\alpha_1(W^*) > \alpha_2(W^*)$, then clearly $\sim(x R^a y)$. Suppose, however, that $\alpha_1(W^*) \leq \alpha_2(W^*)$. Consider now $W^{**} \in L$ such that $W_i^{**} = W_i^*$ for all $i \neq j$, and $W_j^{**} = n W_j^*$, where n is any real number greater than $\alpha_2(W^*)/\alpha_1(W^*)$. Clearly, $\alpha_1(W^{**}) > \alpha_2(W^{**})$, and $W^{**} \in L$. Since $\bar{L} = L$, given noncomparability, we have $\sim(x R^a y)$, which completes the proof.

(4) In view of (1) all we need show is the completeness of R^a. First assume unit comparability. Take any $W^* \in \bar{L}$, and any $x, y \in X$. Obviously, $\sum_i [W_i^*(x) - W_i^*(y)] \geq 0$, or ≤ 0. Since for every $W \in \bar{L}$, for each i, $W_i = a_i + b W_i^*$, for some $b > 0$, we must have $\sum_i [W_i(x) - W_i(y)]$ either nonnegative for each $W \in \bar{L}$, or nonpositive for each $W \in \bar{L}$. Hence, R^a must be complete. Since full comparability implies that $\bar{L}$ is even more restricted, clearly R^a must also be complete in this case.

7*2. Partial Comparability

Partial comparability is the term used for all cases of interpersonal comparability lying in between unit comparability and noncomparability. Let $\bar{L}(0)$ and $\bar{L}(1)$ stand respectively for $\bar{L}$ under noncomparability and unit comparability.

DEFINITION 7*4. *If $\bar{L}$ is a subset of $\bar{L}(0)$ and a superset of $\bar{L}(1)$, then partial comparability holds. We shall refer to $\bar{L}$ under partial comparability as $\bar{L}(p)$.*

We know from Theorem 7*1 that the aggregation relation R^a is a quasi-ordering under every case of partial comparability. Since for the purpose of aggregation we are really interested in the welfare *units* and not in the respective *origins*, it is convenient to specify the set of vectors b of coefficients of individual welfare measures with respect to any comparison set $\bar{L}(p)$. The set of b must obviously be defined with respect to some particular $W^* \in L$ chosen for normalization, which we may call the reference element. Since the choice of W^* is quite arbitrary, the properties of the set of b that we would be concerned with should be independent of the particular W^* chosen. We denote the ith element of b as b_i.

DEFINITION 7*5. *The set of all vectors b such that some $W \in \bar{L}(p)$ can be expressed for some vector a, as $(W_1, \ldots, W_n)$, where*

$$W_i = a_i + b_i W_i^*$$

is called the coefficient set of $\bar{L}$ with respect to W^*, and will be denoted $B(W^*, \bar{L})$. When there is no possibility of ambiguity we shall refer to $B(W^*, \bar{L})$ as B.

A representation of B may be helpful. Consider the n-dimensional Euclidean space E^n, n being the number of individuals. With unit comparability, B is an open half-line with origin 0, but excluding 0.[3] If some element b of the coefficient set B is revealed, the rest can be obtained simply by scalar multiplication by $t > 0$. The precise specification of the half-line from origin 0 will depend on the element W^* chosen for the representation; the important point is that in this case B will simply be one ray from the origin. Incidentally if W^* is chosen from $\bar{L}$, then for all i, j, we must have $b_i = b_j$ for all b.

On the other hand, with noncomparability, B will equal the positive orthant of E^n, i.e., the entire nonnegative orthant except the boundary.[4] Any strictly positive vector can be chosen as b.

Given the set of social states X and the set of individual utility functions defined over X, we might wonder what the relation would be between the size of B and the aggregation quasi-ordering generated in each case. We first obtain the following elementary result with R^1 and R^2 being two aggregation quasi-orderings with respect to B^1 and B^2, respectively.

LEMMA 7*a. *If $B^2 \subset B^1$, then for all $x, y \in X$: $x R^1 y \rightarrow x R^2 y$.*
The proof is obvious. It may be remarked that it does not follow that $x P^1 y \rightarrow x P^2 y$, so that R^1 need not be a subrelation of R^2 whenever $B^2 \subset B^1$. An illustration will suffice. In a two-person world, take $W^* \in \bar{L}$ as the reference element. Compare a case of unit (or full) comparability requiring $b_1 = b_2$ for each W in $\bar{L}$, with a case of strictly partial comparability, where we can choose b_1/b_2 from the closed interval $(1, 2)$. Assume further that

$$[W_1^*(x) - W_1^*(y)] = [W_2^*(y) - W_2^*(x)] > 0$$

---

[3] It is necessary to exclude 0 since only *positive* linear transformations are permitted.

[4] The boundary is excluded since only *positive* linear transformations are allowed.

Clearly, $x I^1 y$ in the first case and $x P^2 y$ in the second. Hence R^1 is not a subrelation of R^2.

We have defined partial comparability so generally that any B from a half-line to the entire positive orthant falls in this category. It would be reasonable to expect, however, that B under partial comparability will satisfy certain regularity conditions. First, the coefficients should be scale-independent. If $b \in B$, then for all $\lambda > 0$, $(\lambda b) \in B$, i.e., B should include all points on the half-line $0, b$, except 0 itself. For example, if $(1, 2, 3)$ is a possible b, then so should be, say, $(2, 4, 6)$, for nothing essential depends on the scale of representation. This implies that B will be a cone with vertex 0 but excluding 0 itself, i.e., it is the complement of 0 in a cone with vertex 0.

Second, it seems reasonable to assume the convexity of B. For example, given a coefficient of 1 for individual 1, if we are ready to apply both the coefficients 1 and 2 to individual 2's welfare units, then we should be ready to apply 1.5 as well. More generally, if b^1 and b^2 are two elements of B, then so is $tb^1 + (1 - t)b^2$ for any $t : 0 < t < 1$. Since with the exception of 0, B is a cone, this is equivalent to the convexity of the cone.

AXIOM 7*1. *Scale-independence and convexity: If $b^1, b^2 \in B$, then for all $t^1, t^2 \geq 0$, except for $t^1 = t^2 = 0$, it can be concluded that $(t^1 b^1 + t^2 b^2) \in B$.*

This axiom is more or less unexceptionable. In the next section we introduce a series of increasingly stronger requirements.

7*3. Regularity and Symmetry

We introduce now an axiom of regularity.

AXIOM 7*2. *Regularity: For every possible partition of the set of individuals into two subsets (V^1 and V^2), if B^2 is a proper subset of B^1, then*

$$\exists (b^1 \in B^1 \ \& \ b^2 \in B^2): [\{\forall i \in V^1: b_i^2 < b_i^1\} \ \& \ \{\forall i \in V^2: b_i^2 > b_i^1\}]$$

THEOREM 7*2. *With cardinal individual welfares, given Axiom 7*2, $B^2 \subset B^1$ implies that R^1 is a subrelation of R^2.*

Proof: If $B^1 = B^2$, then clearly $R^1 = R^2$, so that we can concentrate on the case when B^2 is a proper subset of B^1. In view of Lemma 7*a all that need be proved is that $x P^1 y \rightarrow x P^2 y$, for all

$x, y \in X$. Suppose, to the contrary, that for some $x, y \in X$, we have $x \, P^1 \, y$ & $\sim (x \, P^2 \, y)$. In view of Lemma 7*a this implies that $x \, P^1 \, y$, $x \, R^2 \, y$ and $y \, R^2 \, x$. Since $x \, I^2 \, y$, we must have $\forall b^2 \in B^2$: $\sum_i [W_i^*(x) - W_i^*(y)] b_i^2 = 0$. Partition the individuals into two groups J and K such that $i \in J$ if and only if $x \, P_i \, y$, and $i \in K$ otherwise. By Axiom 7*2, we can assert that $\exists b^1 \in B^1$: $\sum_i [W_i^*(x) - W_i^*(y)] b_i^1 < 0$, or $\forall i$: $x \, I_i \, y$. But neither of the alternatives could be true, since $x \, P^1 \, y$, and this contradiction establishes the theorem.

It may be noted that Axiom 7*1 is not necessary for Theorem 7*2. However, this fact may not be very important from a practical point of view, since convexity and scale-independence appear to make Axiom 7*2 less objectionable.

How demanding a condition is the regularity axiom? Consider B^1 and B^2 as two convex cones (excluding the vertex). What the regularity axiom asserts is that if B^2 is a proper subset of B^1, then there is at least one half-line in B^2 that is an interior ray[5] of B^1. All that this excludes is the possibility that the relaxation of comparability is so biased that all permitted cases in the smaller set are simply boundary positions in the larger set. This is, in any case, impossible if the linear dimension of the cone representing B^2 is n, when n is the number of individuals. Further, even if the linear dimension of B^2 is less than n, the regularity axiom will hold unless the move from B^2 to B^1 is severely biased.

A somewhat stronger requirement than regularity is the requirement of what we call "weak symmetry."

AXIOM 7*3. *Weak symmetry: For every pair of coefficient sets B^1 and B^2, we have*

$$\left[\exists i, j: \sup_{b1 \in B^1} \left(\frac{b_i^1}{b_j^1} \right) > \sup_{b2 \in B^2} \left(\frac{b_i^2}{b_j^2} \right) \right] \to \left[\forall i, j: \sup_{b1 \in B^1} \left(\frac{b_i^1}{b_j^1} \right) > \sup_{b2 \in B^2} \left(\frac{b_i^2}{b_j^2} \right) \right]$$

This is a much stronger requirement than the regularity axiom. With the latter it is sufficient that one ray in $B^2 \subset B^1$ be an interior ray of B^1, whereas with weak symmetry every ray in B^2 has to be interior in B^1, if B^2 is a proper subset of B^1. When the extent of comparability is relaxed between any pair of individuals, it has to be relaxed for every pair of individuals in the case of weak sym-

---

[5] An interior ray of a cone C is a ray (r) such that C contains an ε neighborhood of (r) for some $\varepsilon > 0$. For this we have to define a metric on rays related to the usual topology of E^n. This can be done in many ways which are essentially similar. See Dunford and Schwartz (1958), Vol. I, or Fenchel (1953).

metry. However, the precise extent of the relaxation may vary from pair to pair (hence it is "weak," to be contrasted with "strong symmetry" later). It also imposes a directional symmetry between each individual in a pair. If the least upper bound on the ratio of coefficients goes up between i and j, then the greatest lower bound of the ratio must go down (i.e., the least upper bound of the ratio between j and i must go up). The motivation of Axiom 7*3 is to rule out directional bias in alternative cases of partial comparability. This yields the following important result:

LEMMA 7*b. *With cardinal individual welfares, given Axioms 7*1 and 7*3, the binary relation of set inclusion defines an ordering over the class of all coefficient sets.*

Proof: Since $B \subset B$ for all B, and $B^3 \subset B^2$ & $B^2 \subset B^1 \rightarrow B^3 \subset B^1$, for all B^1, B^2 and B^3, we know that $\subset$ must be reflexive and transitive. If $B^1 \neq B^2$, then given convexity, for some i, j, $\sup_{b^1 \in B^1} (b_i^1/b_j^1)$ is either strictly greater or strictly less than $\sup_{b^2 \in B^2} (b_i^2/b_j^2)$. Without loss of generality, let it be strictly greater. Then by the weak symmetry axiom, we have for all i, j, $\sup_{b^1 \in B^1} (b_i^1/b_j^1) > \sup_{b^2 \in B^2} (b_i^2/b_j^2)$. Since B^1 and B^2 are convex cones (excluding the vertex), this implies that $B^2 \subset B^1$.

In view of Theorem 7*2 and Lemma 7*b, we obtain immediately the following result, noting the fact that Axiom 7*3 implies Axiom 7*2:

THEOREM 7*3. *For cardinal individual welfares, if R^1 and R^2 are two aggregation quasi-orderings generated by two cases of partial comparability, then given Axioms 7*1 and 7*3, either R^1 is a subrelation of R^2, or R^2 is a subrelation of R^1, and the binary relation between quasi-orderings of "being a subrelation of" defines a complete ordering over all possible aggregation quasi-orderings under partial comparability.*

We have thus a sequence of aggregation quasi-orderings, each a subrelation of the next starting from the Pareto quasi-ordering, which is yielded by noncomparability, and ending up with a complete ordering, which is yielded by unit comparability. In between lie all cases of partial comparability, and as the extent of partial comparability is raised, i.e., as B is shrunk, the aggregation quasi-ordering gets extended (if it changes at all), without ever contradicting an earlier quasi-ordering obtained for a lower extent of partial comparability.

A measure of the degree of partial comparability may be useful in this case. Define for every ordered pair of individuals i, j, the following ratio, which we shall call the comparability ratio:

$$c_{ij} = \inf_{b \in B} (b_i/b_j)/\sup_{b \in B} (b_i/b_j)$$

We can define the degree of partial comparability as the arithmetic mean of the comparability ratios for every ordered pair of individuals.

DEFINITION 7*6. *Given Axioms 7*1 and 7*3, the degree of partial comparability $d(B)$ will be measured by the arithmetic mean of c_{ij} for all ordered pairs i, j.*

Since each c_{ij} must lie within the closed interval $[0, 1]$ the degree of partial comparability is also defined over this interval. Further, the following theorem holds:

THEOREM 7*4. *For cardinal individual welfares, given Axioms 7*1 and 7*3, $d(B) = 0$ implies that the aggregation quasi-ordering will be the same as the Pareto quasi-ordering R, and $d(B) = 1$ implies that it will be an ordering. Further, if $d(B^2) > d(B^1)$, the aggregation quasi-ordering R^1 will be a subrelation of the aggregation quasi-ordering R^2.*

Proof: If $d(B) = 1$, clearly $c_{ij} = 1$ for each ordered pair i, j. In this case B will consist of only one ray through the origin, and unit comparability will hold. We know from Theorem 7*1 that in this case R^a will be a complete ordering. If, on the other hand, $d(b) = 0$, each c_{ij} must equal zero, so that the ratio b_i/b_j can be varied without bound (except those already implied in each b_i being a positive number) for every i, j. This implies that noncomparability holds, and from Theorem 7*1 we know that $R = \bar{R}$.

If $d(B^2) > d(B^1)$, then for some i, j, $c_{ij}^1 < c_{ij}^2$. This implies that for some pair i, j, either $\sup (b_i^1/b_j^1) > \sup (b_i^2/b_j^2)$, or $\inf (b_i^1/b_j^1) < \inf (b_i^2/b_j^2)$. If the former, then it follows from Axiom 7*3 that B^2 is a proper subset of B^1. If the latter, then $\sup (b_j^1/b_i^1) > \sup (b_j^2/b_i^2)$, and once again B^2 must be a proper subset of B^1. Now, since weak symmetry implies regularity, it follows from Theorem 7*2 that R^1 must be a subrelation of R^2.

It is clear from Theorem 7*4 that if weak symmetry holds in addition to the relatively harmless assumptions of convexity and scale-independence, then all cases of partial comparability can be measured by a precise degree, $d(B) = q$, of partial comparability, with interesting properties. It is a real number q lying in the closed interval $[0, 1]$, and the corresponding quasi-ordering R^q is a subrelation of all quasi-orderings obtained with all higher degrees of partial comparability $(d > q)$, while all quasi-orderings with lower degrees of partial comparability $(d < q)$ are subrelations of R^q. This monotonicity property in the relation between the continuum of degrees of comparability in the interval $[0, 1]$ and the sequence of aggregation quasi-orderings from the Pareto quasi-ordering to a complete ordering is a phenomenon of some importance.

It should also be noted that it is not *necessary* to assume $d(B) = 1$ for a complete ordering to be generated, though it is sufficient. Even with $d(B) < 1$, completeness may be achieved. The necessary degree will depend on the precise configuration of individual welfare functions.

A more restrictive case than weak symmetry is that of "strong symmetry," which is defined below.

AXIOM 7*4. *Strong symmetry: There exists some functional combination $W^* \in \bar{L}(p)$ such that for each $B(W^*, \bar{L})$, $\sup_{b \in B} (b_i/b_j)$ is exactly the same for all ordered pairs i, j.*

Obviously strong symmetry implies weak symmetry, but not vice versa. Further, under strong symmetry c_{ij} is the same for all i, j. We can express the degree of partial comparability simply as any c_{ij}. It is to be noted that the property of having the same upper bound is one that depends on which W^* we choose as the reference point; W^* is thus no longer inconsequential. The strong symmetry axiom asserts that for *some* W^* this set of equalities holds, but not, of course, for every arbitrary choice of W^*.

An example of strong symmetry, related to a case discussed in Chapter 7 is the following: Consider the restriction that for some real number p, $0 < p < 1$, for all i, j we must have $p < (b_i/b_j) < 1/p$. The degree of comparability will be given by p. [0, 1], and as p would be increased from 0 to 1, we would move monotonically from noncomparability to unit comparability.

With strong symmetry a sufficient degree of partial comparability that will guarantee the completeness of the aggregation quasi-ordering is easy to specify. For any pair of alternatives x, y in X, partition the individuals into two classes, viz., J consisting of all those who prefer x to y, and K consisting of all those who regard y to be at least as good as x.

Define

$$m(x, y) = \sum_{i \in J} [W_i^*(x) - W_i^*(y)]$$

and

$$m(y, x) = \sum_{i \in K} [W_i^*(y) - W_i^*(x)]$$

Now define $a(x, y)$ as the following:

$$a(x, y) = \frac{\min [m(x, y), m(y, x)]}{\max [m(x, y), m(y, x)]}$$

THEOREM 7*5. *For cardinal individual welfares, with convexity, scale-independence and strong symmetry, the aggregation quasi-ordering will be complete if the degree of partial comparability is greater than or equal to* a^*, *where* $a^* = \sup_{x,y \in X} a(x, y)$.

Proof: For any pair x, y, completeness can fail to be fulfilled if and only if $\sum_i [W_i(x) - W_i(y)] > 0$ for some $W \in \bar{L}$, and < 0 for some other $W \in \bar{L}$. First consider W^*. Without loss of generality, let $\sum_i [W_i^*(x) - W_i^*(y)] > 0$, i.e., $m(x, y) > m(y, x)$. We have to show that the sum of welfare differences between x and y is nonnegative for all $W \in \bar{L}$. Assume the degree of partial comparability to be d, so that the welfare units of each individual can be raised at most by a ratio $p = d^{1/2}$, and can be reduced at most by a ratio $1/p$. If contrary to the theorem, the sum of welfare differences between x and y is negative for any $W \in \bar{L}$, then, $[pm(x, y) - (1/p) m(y, x)] < 0$. Hence, $p < [m(y, x)/m(x, y)]^{1/2}$. But this is impossible, since $p^2 = \sup_{x,y \in X} a(x, y)$. This contradiction proves that the aggregation quasi-ordering must be complete.

It is clear that unit comparability is an unnecessarily demanding assumption, and some degree of strict partial comparability, i.e., $d < 1$, may yield a complete ordering—precisely the same ordering as one would get under unit comparability (or full comparability).

7*4. Addition of Noncardinal Welfare

It has been assumed so far that each element of L_i is a positive linear transformation of every other element, i.e., individual welfare is cardinally measurable. This is an unnecessarily strong assumption for exercises in partial comparability. In what follows this restriction is relaxed, and L_i can include elements which are not linear transformations of each other, though each must be a positive monotonic transformation. However, not every positive monotonic transformation need be included. We can, thus, have cases that are more restricted than cardinal measurability and less so than ordinal measurability.

DEFINITION 7*7. *If, for each i, each element of L_i is a positive monotonic transformation of every other element of L_i, and every positive linear transformation of any element of L_i is in L_i, then individual welfare is ordinal-type.*

It may be remarked that the welfare measure being strictly ordinal (including *all* positive monotonic transformations) and being strictly cardinal (including *only* positive linear transformations) are both special cases of welfare being of the ordinal-type. Ordinal-type is, in fact, a very general class of measurability.

We define L as before, viz., as the Cartesian product of L_i for all i, and $\bar{L}$ as any subset of it, as before, in the context of the aggregation relation R^a, as in Definition 7*2. The definition of noncomparability remains unchanged, viz., $L = \bar{L}$. The following theorem is a generalization of three of the four statements in Theorem 7*1:

THEOREM 7*6. *With ordinal-type individual welfares*
(1) *For any $\bar{L}$, R^a is a quasi-ordering.*
(2) *For any $\bar{L}$, R^a is a subrelation of $\bar{R}$, i.e.,*

$$\forall x, y \in X: [\{x \, \bar{R} \, y \to x \, R^a \, y\} \, \& \, \{x \, \bar{P} \, y \to x \, P^a \, y\}].$$

(3) *With noncomparability, $R^a = \bar{R}$.*
The proofs are exactly as in Theorem 7*1, for the property of cardinality is not used in the proofs.
Next, consider a choice over precisely one pair x ~~~~ Y. ~~~

be a real number such that

$$g_i^* \, \hat{b}_i = [W_i(x) - W_i(y)] = g_i$$

Consider now the n-tuple $(\hat{b}_1, \ldots, \hat{b}_n)$, denoted $\hat{b}$.

DEFINITION 7*8. *For any specified pair $x, y \in X$, the set of all $\hat{b}$ such that $g_i = g_i^* \hat{b}_i$, for all i for some W in $\bar{L}$, is called the coefficient set of $\bar{L}$ with respect to W^*, and is denoted $\hat{B}(W^*, \bar{L})$.*

It is easily checked that if cardinality holds, then the coefficient set $\hat{B}$ will be the same no matter which pair x, y we take, and further it will be the same as the coefficient set B as defined in Definition 7*5. It is now easily checked that Lemmas 7*a and 7*b, and Theorems 7*2, 7*3 and 7*4, are all valid with ordinal-type welfare, if we consider only one pair of alternatives x, y, after replacing B with $\hat{B}$ in all the axioms. Each of the axioms is now defined for each pair x, y.

Further, we know from Theorem 7*6 that R^a under ordinal-type individual welfare must be a quasi-ordering irrespective of the number of alternatives involved. This permits us to establish the following theorems immediately:

THEOREM 7*7. *For ordinal-type individual welfares, if Axiom 7*2 holds for each pair $x, y \in X$, then $\bar{L}^2 \subset \bar{L}^1$ implies that R^1 is a sub-relation of R^2.*

THEOREM 7*8. *For ordinal-type individual welfares, given Axioms 7*1 and 7*3 holding for each pair $x, y \in X$, if R^1 and R^2 are two aggregation quasi-orderings, then either R^1 is a subrelation of R^2, or R^2 is a subrelation of R^1.*

THEOREM 7*9. *For ordinal-type individual welfares, given Axioms 7*1 and 7*3 holding for each pair $x, y \in X$,*

$$[\forall x, y \colon d(\hat{B}) = 0] \to R^a = \bar{R}$$
$$[\forall x, y \colon d(\hat{B}) = 1] \to R^a \quad \text{is an ordering}$$

and

$$[\forall x, y \colon d(\hat{B}^2) > d(\hat{B}^1)] \to R^1 \quad \text{is a subrelation of } R^2.[6]$$

The theorems are easily established by using Theorem 7*6, and Theorems 7*2, 7*3 and 7*4.

---

[6] Note that $d(\hat{B})$ is now defined separately for each pair $x, y \in X$.

Chapter 8

CARDINALITY WITH OR WITHOUT COMPARABILITY

8.1. Bargaining Advantages and Collective Choice

In using individual welfares functions for collective choice, there are at least three separate (but interdependent) problems, viz., (a) measurability of individual welfare, (b) interpersonal comparability of individual welfare, and (c) the form of a function which will specify a social preference relation given individual welfare functions and the comparability assumptions. In Chapters 7 and 7*, while a number of alternative assumptions about (a) and (b) were considered, the operation on individual welfare measures was simply one of addition. It is, of course, possible to combine them in other ways.

In his solution to the "bargaining problem," Nash (1950) takes the *product* (and not the *sum*) of individual welfares after a suitable choice of origins. The model is one of two persons, though it is possible to generalize it. There is a certain social state $\tilde{x}$ (the "status quo") which will be the outcome if the two persons fail to strike a bargain. If $\tilde{x}$ is regarded by both as being at least as good as every alternative that can be achieved through bargaining, then the problem will be trivial, since the absence of a bargaining contract cannot possibly hurt anyone. If, on the other hand, there are cooperative outcomes that both prefer to $\tilde{x}$, then the problem may be interesting. It will, however, once again be rendered

less with those. This is what the bargain is about.

Nash specifies assumptions about individual behavior under uncertainty that permit a cardinal representation of individual preferences.   He proposes a solution that is given by maximizing the product of the differences between the utility from a cooperative outcome x (Pareto-superior to $\tilde{x}$) and the status quo outcome $\tilde{x}$ for the two, i.e., maximizing $[U_1(x) - U_1(\tilde{x})][U_2(x) - U_2(\tilde{x})]$. This amounts to maximizing the product of utilities after a suitable choice of origin.[1]

It is readily apparent that the Nash solution has the property of being invariant with respect to the changes of origins and units of individual utility functions.   The origins get subtracted out, and the units simply change the scale of the product without changing the *ordering* of the outcomes by the value of the product.   This is where the absence of interpersonal comparability is absorbed, since any individual's utility units and origin can be shifted without any regard to the origin and the units of the other person's utility.

While this invariance with respect to the choice of origin and unit of individual utility function can be preserved by other functional forms as well,[2] the simple product formulation satisfies also the requirement, which Nash imposes, of "symmetry" in the treatment of the two individuals.[3]   The exact axioms and the proof that the Nash solution is the only one to satisfy them are presented in Chapter 8*.

Whether we add individual utilities, or multiply them, or play with them in some other way, the variability of units or origins of individual utilities poses a problem.   It is instructive to contrast the way this problem is tackled in the two approaches we have considered so far.   In the aggregation approach of Chapters 7 and

---

[1] It may be tempting to think of this operation as *addition* in disguise, since maximizing the product is equivalent to maximizing the sum of the logarithms of the numbers.   All that is needed, it might be thought, is the interpretation of the logarithmic transformation of a utility function as a utility function itself.   However, this is illegitimate since cardinality, as used by Nash (and indeed others), permits only linear transformations, which rule out a logarithmic transformation.   Further, what would be needed is a mixture, viz., first some transformation to get $U_i(\tilde{x}) = 0$, and *then* a logarithmic shift.   It is not at all obvious what precise properties of preference will be preserved by such hybrid changes.

[2] For example, we can take $[U_1(x) - U_1(\tilde{x})]^\alpha[U_2(x) - U_2(\tilde{x})]^\beta$, with α and β as two positive real numbers.

[3] We can, of course, get this in the example given in footnote 2 by taking $\alpha = \beta$, but then the social *ordering* generated will be exactly the same as in the Nash system of comparing simple products.

7*, origins are irrelevant since only *differences* in utility between x and y are added for all individuals to generate a social ordering. The units are crucial, but if variations in units for one individual are systematically related to variations in units of others, then the ranking of social states may not be very sensitive to these variations. The systematic relation may vary from a one-to-one correspondence (in the case of complete unit comparability) yielding a complete ordering, to none at all (noncomparability) when only Pareto preferences and indifferences are reflected in social choice. In between lies a variety of possibilities with quasi-orderings of varying extent of completeness. In contrast, in the Nash approach no such comparability is introduced, but the origins are knocked out through the use of the status quo and the units are rendered irrelevant through the multiplicative form. This makes the collective solution crucially dependent on the status quo point. Given everything else, a different status quo point will usually generate a different Nash solution.

Is this dependence on a precisely defined noncooperative outcome justifiable? The answer to this question seems to depend a great deal on the objective of the exercise. In *predicting* the actual outcome of a bargaining battle, the status quo is clearly relevant, for it defines what will happen in the absence of the parties agreeing to a cooperative solution. There is always the threat that this outcome, which is inferior for both, will emerge as the actual outcome.[4] In splitting the gains from an agreement, state $\tilde{x}$ is clearly relevant. Indeed, as Harsanyi has noted, there is a process of making and accepting concessions that was originally put forward by Zeuthen (1930) and which is not implausible, which will indeed yield precisely the Nash outcome.

---

[4] The analysis can be extened by admitting specific "threats" that the players may put forward as what they would do should there be no cooperative agreement. By threatening the other party with policies that will yield dire consequences to that party, a player may try to strengthen his own bargaining ...

... once the bargaining is dead. The theory of threats has to cope with this problem.

This does not, however, mean that the Nash solution is an ethically attractive outcome and that we should recommend a collective choice mechanism that incorporates it. A best prediction is not necessarily a fair, or a just, outcome. In a labor market with unemployment, workers may be agreeable to accept subhuman wages and poor terms of employment, since in the absence of a contract they may starve ($\tilde{x}$), but this does not make that solution a desirable outcome in any sence. Indeed, compared with $\tilde{x}$, while a particular solution may be symmetric in distributing utility gains from the bargain between workers and capitalists, we could still maintain that the workers were exploited because their bargaining power was poor.

It may be useful to clarify the contrast by taking Harsanyi's (1955) model of "ethical judgments," even though it is only one possible model. What someone would *recommend* as a solution if he thought that he had an equal chance of being in either party's position, will yield, in that model, an "ethical" recommendation. On the other hand, what he will *predict* as the likely outcome, taking the parties as they are, is a different thing altogether. The Nash "bargaining solution" seems to be rather uninteresting from the former point of view, and might represent the latter if it represents anything at all. Whether or not the Nash solution is predictive (for doubts on this see Luce and Raiffa (1957)), its ethical relevance does seem to be very little.

This contrast is a very general one and can be brought out with ethical models different from Harsanyi's, e.g., with models of aggregate welfare maximization with partial comparability, or with models of fairness and justice of Rawls (1958), (1967), or with Suppes' (1966) "grading principles," or with such collective choice mechanisms as the method of majority decision.

It is worth noting that many supposedly ethical solutions are similar in spirit to Nash's solution. For example, Braithwaite's (1955) interesting use of game theory as "a tool for the moral philosopher" seems to be based on an identification of these two questions. In Braithwaite's example a certain Luke likes playing the piano in his room, and a certain Matthew likes improvising jazz on the trumpet in the adjacent room, with imperfect sound-proofing between the rooms. They disturb each other if they play together, but as might be expected, the trumpeter makes a bigger mess for the pianist than the pianist can for the trumpeter. The final solution that Braithwaite recommends divides up the time giving substantially more time to the trumpeter than to the pianist. As Braithwaite ((1955), p. 37) puts it, "Matthew's advantage arises purely from the fact that Matthew, the trumpeter, prefers both of them playing at once to neither of them playing, whereas Luke, the pianist, prefers silence to cacophony." Matthew has the threat advantage in the absence of a contract, and it is indeed possible that Braithwaite's solution may well emerge should Luke and Matthew actually bargain.[5] But in what sense does this solution "obtain maximum production of satisfaction compatible with fair distribution"?[6] An unbiased judge may well decide that the fact that Matthew can threaten Luke more effectively (and more noisily) than Luke can threaten Matthew does not entitle him to a bigger share of playing time. Matthew himself might concede that if he did not know whether he was going to be Luke or Matthew before deciding on a system of distribution of time he might well have ignored the threat advantage and recommended a more equal sharing of time. A solution based on the threat advantages of the two parties may indeed be manifestly unfair.

We should, however, note that it is possible to take the stand of a "hard-headed realist" that all ethical discussions are pointless and what is really interesting is the prediction of an outcome. What is the point of discussing what *should* happen if it will not? This point of view, which is of respectable antiquity, is not a very useful one to take for a theory of collective choice. First, part of the object of the study of collective choice is social criticism. In making use of certain widely held value judgments, particular collective choice mechanisms may be meaningfully criticized, which might in the long run help the development of a more appropriate choice mechanism. Second, bargaining power of different groups is itself a function of the appreciation of the nature of the society and its choice mechanisms. The feeling of injustice to a certain group (e.g., the workers) may itself contribute to bringing about institutions (e.g., trade unions) that alter the relative bargaining power of different groups. Rousseau's analysis of "injustice" and Marx's theory of "exploitation," to take two obvious examples, have had a bigger impact on the shape of the world than would

---

[5] See, however, Luce and Raiffa (1957), pp. 145-150. See also Raiffa (1953), for an alternative approach, and Luce and Raiffa (1958), pp. 143-145.

[6] Braithwaite (1955), p. 9. See also Lucas (1959).

have been predicted by the "hard-headed realist."[7]   Third, there is often a conflict between the general principles that people swear by and the courses of action they choose.   These principles may take the form of conditions on collective choice, and the analysis of their logical implications is an interesting and useful basis for discussion and argumentation on social decisions.   It is useful also to examine the existing mechanisms of collective choice in the light of the general principles widely accepted in the society to check the consistency of theory and practice.

To conclude this section, the solutions put forward by Nash, Braithwaite, and others in similar models, might be relevant for predicting certain outcomes of bargains and negotiations, but they seem to be very unattractive solutions in terms of widely held value judgments about principles of collective choice.   The special importance attached to the status quo point and to threat advantages, and the complete avoidance of interpersonal comparisons, seem to rule out a whole class of ethical judgments that are relevant to collective choice.

8.2.   Cardinality and Impossibility

It may be noted that the dependence of social choice on attitudes to the status quo point ($\bar{x}$) is a violation of the "independence of irrelevant alternatives" when it has been redefined to apply to social preference being a function of individual welfare functions (as opposed to being a function of individual orderings).   In fact, if on top of the Nash conditions, we also demand that social choice between any two cooperative outcomes x and y must depend only on the welfare numbers for x and y of the two individuals, then an impossibility theorem would readily result.

This problem applies not merely to the Nash approach but to all uses of cardinality in the absence of any interpersonal comparability (i.e., assuming invariance of social choice with respect to positive linear transformations of individual utility functions). Indeed the Arrow impossibility result can be readily extended to the use of individual cardinal utility functions (rather than individual orderings) as the arguments of collective choice rules.   A social welfare functional (SWFL) is a mechanism that specifies one

---

[7] Lenin could finish writing only six chapters of his *The State and Revolution* because the October Revolution intervened.

and only one social ordering given a set of individual welfare functions, one function for each individual. Noncomparability requires that any transformation (permitted by the measurability assumption) of any individual's welfare function leaves the social ordering unchanged. Cardinality requires that all positive linear transformations of any utility function attributed to any individual are permitted. Given these, we may require the Arrow conditions, suitably modified to apply to a SWFL, viz., unrestricted domain, weak Pareto principle, nondictatorship, and the independence of irrelevant alternatives. The first three are straightforward to redefine, while the last is redefined by making the social preference between x and y invariant as long as each individual's utility measure for x and y remain invariant. When these conditions are put together, what we get is another impossibility (Theorem 8*2), in the line of Arrow's general possibility theorem, but now applying to SWFLs with cardinal individual utility functions.[8]

It may be instructive to compare this impossibility result with the aggregation quasi-orderings that were obtained in Chapters 7 and 7*. That relation was based on invariance not with respect to every possible linear transformation of individual utility functions, but only with respect to some (those in L, a specified subset of L), reflecting our assumptions about interpersonal comparability. With unit comparability and cardinality, the aggregation rule is a SWFL with an unrestricted domain, satisfying the Pareto principle, nondictatorship, and independence of irrelevant alternatives. The crucial difference lies in introducing comparability. It was noted before that if noncomparability is assumed, the aggregation quasi-ordering will coincide with the Pareto quasi-ordering (Theorem 7*1). What Theorem 8*2 shows is that not merely aggregation, but all Pareto-inclusive, nondictatorial, irrelevant-alternative-independent rules of going from individual welfare functions to a social ordering will fail to generate a social ordering if cardinality is combined with noncomparability.

This is, of course, not surprising. Given noncomparability,

---

[8] This confirms Samuelson's (1967) conjecture on this. Samuelson does not mention the requirement of noncomparability, but it is implied by his earlier discussion of invariance with respect to transformations of units and origin. Incidentally, in Sen (1966b), which Samuelson refers to in this context, the proposal was not to introduce cardinality alone, but in conjunction with comparability.

the relative preference intensities of individuals over any pair can be varied in any way we like except for reversing the sign, i.e., without reversing the ordering, so that cardinality is not much of an advance over individual orderings when combined with non-comparability.   To give some bite to cardinality we have to relax one of the other conditions.   The Nash procedure violates the condition of the independence of irrelevant alternatives by making the choice set dependent on the status quo $\bar{x}$, whereas the aggregation procedure does it through permitting interpersonal comparability fully or partly.   Cardinality alone seems to kill no dragons, and our little St. George must be sought elsewhere.

Chapter 8*

BARGAINS AND SOCIAL WELFARE
FUNCTIONALS

8*1. The Bargaining Problem of Nash

It is instructive to consider Nash's model of bargaining as an exercise in going from individual welfare functions to a social ordering assuming cardinality of individual welfare but no interpersonal comparability.[1] The solution depends on a distinguished social state $\tilde{x}$, which we may call the status quo point and which represents what would happen if there is no cooperation between bargainers. Here, X represents all social states that are available if the two parties cooperate. It is assumed that there are points in X that both prefer to the status quo $\tilde{x}$. Further, Nash's bargaining problem is concerned with a two-person society. While a natural extension of this to n-person cases exists, we shall let follow Nash's own formulation.

Each point x in X maps into a pair of utility numbers representing the welfare of the two individuals respectively, for any given W. The set of such pairs of utility numbers corresponding to the set of all elements in X for any W will be called $U(X, W)$, or U for short. It can be viewed as a subset of the two-dimensional Euclidean space. We shall, following Nash, assume U to be compact and convex.

Our presentation will, however, differ somewhat from Nash's own, but our five axioms will be essentially equivalent to Nash's eight-axiom presentation. We use Definition 7*1 of a functional combination W, as any element of the Cartesian product $\prod_{i=1}^{n} L_i$ of individual sets of welfare functions.

---

[1] See Nash (1950). For an excellent exposition and a critical evaluation see Luce and Raiffa (1957). See also Nash (1953), and Harsanyi (1956), (1966).

DEFINITION 8*1.   *A bargaining solution function (hereafter, BSF) is a functional relation that chooses one and only one social state $\bar{x} \in X$ for any specified functional combination $W \in L$, given the distinguished social state $\tilde{x} \in X$ representing the status quo.*

We shall use the following set of axioms:

AXIOM 8*1.   *Well-behaved cardinal utility: For each i, every element of L_i is a positive linear trasformation of every other element, and every positive linear transformation of any element of L_i belongs to L_i. Further, each W_i is continuous on X, and for any $W \in L$, U is compact and convex.*

AXIOM 8*2.   *Noncomparability: The value of the BSF is invariant with respect to the choice of W in L.*

AXIOM 8*3.   *Weak Pareto optimality: The range of the BSF is confined to only those elements $x \in X$ such that $\sim[\exists y \in X: y \; \bar{\bar{P}} \; x]$*

AXIOM 8*4.   *Property α: If $\bar{x}$ is the solution given by the BSF when X is the set of social states and $\bar{x} \in S \subset X$, then $\bar{x}$ is the solution given by the BSF for S.*[2]

AXIOM 8*5.   *Symmetry: If for some $W^* \in L$, $W_1^*(\tilde{x}) = W_2^*(\tilde{x})$, and for that $W^* \in L$, U is symmetric,*[3] *then $W_1^*(\bar{x}) = W_2^*(\bar{x})$.*

THEOREM 8*1.   *For any X, a BSF satisfying Axioms 8*1–8*5 must yield that $x^0 \in X$ such that $x^0 \in X$, $x^0 \; \bar{\bar{P}} \; \tilde{x}$, and for any $W \in L$*

$$x^0 = x \left| \begin{array}{l} \max\,[W_1(x) - W_1(\tilde{x})][W_2(x) - W_2(\tilde{x})] \\ x \in X \\ x \; \bar{\bar{P}} \; \tilde{x} \end{array} \right.$$

Proof.   Obviously, point x^0 as described exists and is unique by the compactness and convexity of U. Further, it is obviously invariant with respect to the choice of $W \in L$ thanks to cardinality. Consider now that $W^* \in L$ such that $W_1^*(\tilde{x}) = W_2^*(\tilde{x}) = 0$, and $W_1^*(x^0) = W_2^*(x^0) = 1$; such a $W^* \in L$ exists by cardinality.   By the choice of x^0, there is no $x \in X: W_1^*(x) \cdot W_2^*(x) > 1$.   Hence,

---

[2] This is called the independence of irrelevant alternatives by Luce and Raiffa (1957).   It is, however, not to be confused with Arrow's condition of the same name.   We discuss the corresponding condition to that of Arrow later; see Axiom 8*6.   See Chapter 1* on property α.

[3] That is, if $(a, b) \in U$, then $(b, a) \in U$.

there is no $x \in X$: $[W_1^*(x) + W_2^*(x)] > 2$, for if such an x existed, then a convex combination (W_1^*, W_2^*) of $(W_1^*(x), W_2^*(x))$ and $(1, 1)$ will yield $W_1^* W_2^* > 1$, and further, by convexity, (W_1^*, W_2^*) will belong to U. It is now easy to construct a symmetric set U^* on the utility space corresponding to X^*, which includes all $(W_1^*(x), W_2^*(x))$ for all $x \in X$, i.e., $X \subset X^*$, and no x such that $W_1^*(x) \geqq 1$, and $W_2^*(x) \geqq 1$, except $x = x^0$. By Axioms 8*3 (weak Pareto optimality) and 8*5 (symmetry), x^0 is yielded by the BSF for X^*, given $W^* \in L$. By Axiom 8*4 (property α), x^0 is yielded by the BSF for $X \subset X^*$, given $W^* \in L$. By Axiom 8*2 (noncomparability), x^0 is yielded by the BSF for X, given any $W \in L$. The proof is completed by checking that x^0 always satisfies Axioms 8*1–8*5.

While Nash's solution satisfies property α, which has been described as a condition of independence of irrelevant alternatives by Radner and Marschack (1954), Luce and Raiffa (1958), and others, it violates the cardinal equivalent of Arrow's independence of irrelevant alternatives. Here we define Arrow's condition in a very weak form appropriately for a BSF as opposed to a collective choice rule. Consider that x^0 is chosen and x^1 is rejected by the BSF from x, given some status quo $\tilde{x}$, so that x^0 is socially preferred to x^1. Assume now that $\tilde{x}$ changes, but everything else remains the same, including $W_i(x^0)$ and $W_i(x^1)$ for each i. If the choice between x^0 and x^1 should be independent of irrelevant alternatives, then clearly the BSF should not now choose x^1 and reject x^0.

AXIOM 8*6.   *Independence: For some $W \in L$ and $\hat{W} \in \hat{L}$, each defined over X, if for all x, $\forall i$: $W_i(x) = \hat{W}_i(x)$, then the BSF must yield the same solution for $W \in L$ as for $\hat{W} \in \hat{L}$.*

It is obvious that the following result is true:

COROLLARY 8*1.1.   *There is no BSF satisfying Axioms 8*1–8*6.*

The proof is immediate since the Nash solution is sensitive to $\tilde{x}$.[4] This property of the Nash solution is not necessarily objectionable in the context of a positive model of bargaining solutions, but its ethical limitations are important and were discussed in Chapter 8.

8*2.   Social Welfare Functional

We can now turn to a more general formulation of the problem

---

[4] There is, in fact, some redundancy in this, as will be clear from Section 8*2.

of using cardinality with noncomparability.   In line with a SWF we define a social welfare functional.

DEFINITION 8*2.   *A social welfare functional (SWFL) is a functional relation that specifies one and only one social ordering R over X, for any W, i.e., for any n-tuple of individual welfare functions, $W_1, \ldots, W_n$, each defined over X.*

Note that a SWF is a special case of a SWFL, in which only the individual ordering properties are used.   It may also be remarked that while the aggregation relation for any $W \in L$ is a SWFL, in Chapter 7* the aggregation relation was made a function of $\bar{L} \subset L$ and not necessarily of an individual element $W \in L$.

Corresponding to Arrow's conditions on a SWF, similar conditions are imposed on a SWFL.

Condition $\bar{U}$ (unrestricted domain):   The domain of the SWFL includes all logically possible W, viz., all possible n-tuples of individual welfare functions defined over X.

Condition $\bar{I}$ (independence of irrelevant alternatives):   If for all i, $W_i(x) = \hat{W}_i(x)$ and $W_i(y) = \hat{W}_i(y)$, for some pair $x, y \in X$, for some pair of welfare combinations W and $\hat{W}$, then $x R y \leftrightarrow x \hat{R} y$, where R and $\hat{R}$ are the social orderings corresponding to W and $\hat{W}$.

Condition $\bar{D}$ (nondictatorship):   There is no i such that for all elements in the domain of the SWFL, $x P_i y \rightarrow x P y$.

Condition $\bar{P}$ (weak Pareto principle):   If for all i, $x P_i y$, then for all elements in the domain of the SWFL, consistent with this, we have $x P y$.

Condition $\bar{C}$ (cardinality):[5]   For each i, every positive linear transformation of any element of L_i belongs to L_i.

Condition $\bar{M}$ (noncomparability):   For any L, the social ordering R yielded by the SWFL for each $W \in L$ must be the same.

THEOREM 8*2.   *There is no SWFL satisfying conditions $\bar{U}$, $\bar{I}$, $\bar{D}$, $\bar{P}$, $\bar{C}$ and $\bar{M}$.*

Proof.   Consider a pair $x, y \in X$.   For $W \in L$, we have $W_i(x)$ and $W_i(y)$ for all i.   Consider now a change in the individual welfare

---

[5] We do not require that *all* elements of L_i are linear transformations of each. We can, however, add this without affecting the result.   Incidentally, Condition $\bar{C}$ binds a SWFL only in conjunction with Condition $\bar{M}$.

functions, keeping the individual orderings the same, let L get transformed to $\hat{L}$. Clearly, by condition $\bar{C}$, which gives us two degrees of freedom for the welfare measure for each person, we can find a $\hat{W} \in \hat{L}$, such that $W_i(x) = \hat{W}_i(x)$ and $W_i(y) = \hat{W}_i(y)$. By condition $\bar{I}$, $x \, R \, y \leftrightarrow x \, \hat{R} \, y$, where R and $\hat{R}$ are social orderings corresponding to W and $\hat{W}$. Hence, by $\bar{M}$, the social ordering must be same for the elements of L as for those of $\hat{L}$. Thus, the only possible SWFLs satisfying conditions $\bar{I}$ and $\bar{C}$ are all SWFs, with R a function merely of the n-tuples of individual orderings $(R_1, \ldots, R_n)$.[6] But we know from Theorem 3*1 that no SWF satisfies conditions U, I, D and P, which conditions are implied by conditions $\bar{U}$, $\bar{I}$, $\bar{D}$ and $\bar{P}$, for SWFL. The proof is, thus, complete.

This problem did not arise for aggregation in Chapter 7*, since the collective choice criterion was defined there in terms of invariance for each W in a specified $\bar{L} \subset L$, without demanding invariance with respect to the choice of all W from L. The choice of $\bar{L}$ reflected our assumption about interpersonal comparability. Theorem 8*2 confirms the suspicion that mere cardinality without any comparability may not be helpful.

---

[6] In fact, R over each pair of social states is a function of the n-tuple of R_i over *that* pair only.

Chapter 9

EQUITY AND JUSTICE

9.1. Universalization and Equity

One method of making interpersonal comparisons is to try to put
oneself in the position of another. The approach, not surprisingly,
has cropped up in various forms in different cultures almost throughout recorded history, though the use to which the approach has
been put has varied a great deal from society to society.

The so-called Golden Rule of the gospel is an expression—a rather
narrow one—of this approach: "Do unto others as ye would that
others should do unto you." Kant's study of the "moral law" is
closely related to this approach of placing oneself in the position
of others, as is his general rule: "Act always on such a maxim
as thou canst at the same time will to be a universal law."[1]
Sidgwick's principle of "equity" or "fairness" is a particularly useful expression of this approach:[2]

> ...whatever action any of us judges to be right
> for himself, he implicitly judges to be right for
> all similar persons in similar circumstances. Or,
> as we may otherwise put it, 'if a kind of conduct
> that is right (or wrong) for me is not right (or
> wrong) for some one else, it must be on the
> ground of some difference between the two cases,
> other than the fact that I and he are different
> persons.' A corresponding position may be

---

[1] See Kant (1785). In Abbott's translation, Kant (1907), p. 66.

[2] Sidgwick (1907), Book III, Chap. XIII, p. 379. Sidgwick attributed this to
Kant: "That whatever is right for me must be right for all persons in similar
circumstances—which was the form in which I accepted the Kantian maxim—
seemed to me certainly fundamental, certainly true, and not without practical
importance" (p. xvii). For a survey of the generalization argument, see Singer
(1961).

stated with equal truth in respect of what ought
to be done *to*—and not *by*—different individuals.[3]

A relatively recent extension of this approach is to be found in
Hare (1952), (1963). Hare relates the question of "equity," in the
sense of Sidgwick, to the property of "universalizability" of value
judgments in general (viz., in exactly similar circumstances exactly
similar judgments would have to be made), and makes this a matter
of *meaning* rather than a moral principle that we might wish value
judgments should satisfy. A quotation from Hare ((1961), pp. 176–
177) might help to exemplify his interpretation.

> Suppose that I say to someone "You ought not
> to smoke in this compartment," and there are
> children in the compartment. The person ad-
> dressed is likely, if he wonders why I have said
> that he ought not to smoke, to look around,
> notice the children, and so understand the reason.
> But suppose that, having ascertained about the
> compartment, he then says "All right; I'll go next
> door: there's another compartment there just as
> good; in fact it is exactly like this one, and there
> are children in it too." I should think if he said
> this that he did not understand the function of
> the word "ought", for "ought" always refers to
> some general principle; and if the next compart-
> ment is really exactly like this one, every princi-
> ple that is applicable to this one must be appli-
> cable to the other. I might therefore reply: "But
> look here, if you ought not to smoke in this com-
> partment, and the other compartment is just like
> this one, has the same sort of occupants, the

---

[3] The celebrated epitaph of Martin Engelbrodde has been quoted by Arrow
(1963) as an example of this approach of "extended sympathy."

> Here lies Martin Engelbrodde,
> Ha'e mercy on my soul, Lord God,
> As I would do were I Lord God,
> And Thou wert Martin Engelbrodde.

The interesting question as to whether Lord God should be obliged to have
mercy on Engelbrodde's soul under Sidgwick's principle of equity is left as an
exercise to the reader. (Hint: Contrast "as I would do" with "as Thou
wouldst want"!)

same notices on the windows, &c., then obviously you oughtn't to smoke in that one either."

Similarity of circumstances is interpreted by Hare (like Sidgwick)
to include *as if* interpersonal permutations everything else remaining the same.   If a white South African claims that apartheid is
good, but concedes that his judgment would have been different if
he were himself black, then in Hare's system he would reveal an
ignorance of "the way in which the word 'good' functions."   In
contrast, if the criterion was taken as a moral principle and not as
a matter of meaning, then the white South African in question
could be called, in some sense, *immoral*, but not, in any sense,
ignorant (of the language of morals).

In all this, two different questions must be clearly distinguished:
(a) the question of universalizability of value judgments, and (b)
the question whether *as if* interpersonal permutations given other
things should be taken as "exactly similar" circumstances.   We
take up question (a) first.

Universalizability is indeed a widely accepted criterion, and as
Arrow has argued in another context, "value judgments may equate
empirically distinguishable phenomena, but they cannot differentiate empirically indistinguishable states."[4]   The use of universalizability does, however, raise at least two difficult problems.   First,
taking universalizability as a logical necessity rather than as a moral
principle implies a violation of the so-called "Hume's law," which
asserts that no value judgment can be deduced from exclusively
factual premises.   Normative value, in this view, must be a function defined over factual states, and while there is no compulsion
to accept any particular form for the function on factual grounds
(as there may be in the classic "naturalist" position), two identical
factual states must be required to have the same normative value.
If this is taken as a logical necessity, two states being factually
exactly the same (a fact) seems to imply that they are equally good
(a value judgment).[5]   This need not disturb anyone, except those
committed totally to Hume's law, which, however, does include

---

[4] Arrow (1963), p. 112.
[5] See Sen (1966a).   In terms of the theory of identity, if $x = y$, then $f(x) = f(y)$,
for all f.   This is so even if f is a moral function.   The former statement is
factual and the latter is moral.

Hare himself.[6]

A more important difficulty for universalizability than fidelity towards Hume's doctrine concerns the *scope* of the principle irrespective of whether it is interpreted as a logical necessity or as a normative rule. *Can* two situations really be exactly alike? If not, then universalizability is empty of content. If two situations are not exactly similar, they could, of course, be claimed to be "relevantly similar," e.g., buying a car with a certain number on it and buying another car physically identical to it except for the number. The concept of relevant similarity, which itself involves a value judgment, is not easy to define, but one possible line is the following: If x and y are exactly similar except in some respects, and if a person's judgments in question involving x and y are independent of those respects, then x and y are relevantly similar in that person's system. In this extended form, universalizability will require that a person's judgments be exactly similar for x and y when the two alternatives are relevantly similar. There are problems with this extension, but they would seem to be less serious than the possibly vacuous nature of universalizability in its unadulterated form.

We now turn to the second question. Do interpersonal permutations, everything else unchanged, preserve "similarity"? If it is so taken, as Hare does, then Sidgwick's principle of equity is a direct consequence of universalizability. If not, then the question of relevant similarity arises, and we have to face the problem of the white South African referred to earlier who might claim that whether he is white or black *is* a relevant difference in his system. Hare would rule this out, but it seems to be possible to take the view that such a judgment, while "wicked," is not impossible by virtue of the discipline of the language of morals.

There is a further difficulty with Hare's use of interpersonal permutations to develop a criterion for moral judgments. It is, in fact, possible that no judgment might pass such a test, and questions might be asked about a case when an individual cannot honestly say that he will hold on to exactly the same judgments under every conceivable interpersonal permutation. Insofar as Hare is right in believing that the discipline of the moral language already in

---

[6] "I have been in the past, and still am, a stout defender of Hume's doctrine that one cannot deduce moral judgments from non-moral statements of fact" (Hare (1963), p. 186). See also Hare (1961), pp. 29–31, 79–93.

operation does require universalizability in this demanding sense, and insofar as this language is meaningfully used by people, it can be claimed that the criterion does not, by and large, define an empty set of value judgments. There is no doubt, however, that this is a hard requirement, especially since it is supposed to apply to every kind of moral judgment.[7]

A somewhat less demanding set of rules have been put forward by a number of writers in the specific context of judgments about "fairness," "justice" and "ethical (as opposed to subjective) preferences." These requirements are less stringent for two reasons. First, they are intended to apply to some limited categories of moral virtues (like fairness or justice). Second, and perhaps more importantly, the condition of making the same judgment under every conceivable permutation of personal positions is replaced by the requirement that the judgment be made in a situation where the individual is unaware of the exact position that he is to hold in any of the social states considered. Some of these approaches will now be examined.

9.2. Fairness and Maximin Justice

Rawls' analysis of the concept of fairness makes use of a hypothetical situation (the "original position") where individuals choose "principles" in a state of primordial equality without knowing their own placing in social states resulting from it, being ignorant even of their personal features in addition to social positions. In such a situation the principles that would be generally accepted would satisfy the criterion of "fairness," being the result of a fair agreement with no vested interests. (See Rawls (1958), (1963), (1963a), (1967), and (1968)).

Rawls derives his principles of "justice" from his criterion of fairness. His concept of "justice as fairness" expresses the idea that the principles of justice are those that would be chosen in an initial situation that is fair. Unlike in the model of Hare, it is not required that a moral judgment be held from *every* position that a

---

[7] There has been considerable discussion among philosophers on the validity and usefulness of Hare's approach, touching on several issues. See, for example, Madell (1965), Montague (1965), Gauthier (1968), to quote just a few of these contributions. Hare himself outlines some problems, including that of the "weakness of will," and the problem of the "fanatic;" see Hare (1960), (1963).

person can occupy through interpersonal permutations. Instead, the principles of justice are those which would be accepted in a fair situation in the "original position."

A certain similarity of this view of justice with Rousseau's analysis of the "general will" and of a hypothetical "social contract" has been noted.[8] Principles of justice can be viewed as solutions of cooperative games in the "original position." However, Rawls' approach differs essentially from those of Nash (1950), (1953), Raiffa (1953), and Braithwaite (1955) in that the notions of "fairness" and "justice" are not related to cooperative solutions of bargaining problems in *actual* situations with given interpersonal inequalities (e.g., of economic wealth, political power, and similar contingencies), but with cooperative solutions in a state of primordial equality. Our reservations (see Chapters 8 and 8*) about the former as interpretations of fairness and justice do not, therefore, apply to Rawls.

Having thus established a framework for fairness, Rawls argues that the two following principles of justice would have been chosen in the "original position": (a) "each person participating in a practice, or affected by it, has an equal right to the most extensive liberty compatible with a like liberty for all"; and (b) "inequalities are arbitrary unless it is reasonable to expect that they will work out for everyone's advantage, and provided that the positions and offices to which they attach, or from which they may be gained, are open to all" (Rawls (1958)).

The meaning of these principles is not altogether obvious, but on Rawls' analysis it turns out that the proper maximand is the welfare of the worst-off individual (Rawls (1963)). The first principle recommends the extension of liberty of each as long as similar liberty is extended to all. Interpersonal conflicts is the subject matter of the second principle, which is interpreted to require that "social inequalities be arranged to make the worst-off best-off," i.e., the welfare level of the worst-off individual be made as high as possible.

This last is a well-defined criterion when ordinal interpersonal comparisons can be made to discover who is the worst-off person. It is essentially a "maximin" criterion, and the minimal element

---

[8] Runciman and Sen (1965) provide a game-theoretic interpretation of Rousseau's "general will" and of Rawls' "original position."

in the set of individual welfares is maximized.[9]   Rawls' main focus is on the type of institutions to be chosen, but the maximin principle can be used also to order social states based on individual orderings. For any social state, we order the individuals in terms of their welfare and pick on the worst-off individual.   His welfare level is noted for comparison with the welfare of the worst-off individual in another social state.   As long as each individual has a complete ordering and some method exists to order the well-being of different individuals, i.e., to make interpersonal comparisons of levels of welfare, we can obtain a complete social ordering.

Is this maximin procedure a SWF in the sense of Arrow?   It is not, for the Arrow SWF is a function that specifies one and only one social ordering for any given collection of individual orderings. Suppose every individual's ordering remains the same but the welfare level of individual i, who was previously the worst-off person in social state x, goes up for every alternative, making him no longer the worst-off man in situation x.   Now the social ordering involving x, being based on a different individual's welfare, can be different.   This would not be permitted by a SWF.

There is another way of looking at the contrast.   A SWF, or more generally a CCR, specifies a social preference relation based on the set of individual orderings of actual social states.   For the Rawls type of comparison, what is needed is not an ordering merely of social states viewed from one's own position, but a ranking of social states with interpersonal permutations.   The statement that individual i has a higher welfare level in state x than individual j has in state y can be translated as: it is better to be person i in state x than to be person j in state y.   If there are m states and n individuals, what is involved is an ordering $\tilde{R}$ of mn alternatives. Given such an ordering, the Rawlsian maximin ordering of the m social states is immediately obtained.[10]   A CCR (or a SWF) would have, on the other hand, made the social ordering dependent on n orderings, each defined over m social states.   A CCR is thus based on n orderings of m elements, whereas a Rawlsian maximin choice mechanism is based on one ordering of mn elements.

---

[9] For the use of the Rawls criterion of justice, measurability of individual welfare is not really necessary, not even in the ordinal sense.   The criterion can be presented in terms of orderings (Chapter 9*), and discussions on it can take place perfectly well without bringing in welfare measures at all.

[10] Strictly, an ordering is not needed, since the non-worst-off positions can be ranked in any manner and may not even be ranked vis-a-vis each other.

This extended ordering over *mn* positions may reflect one individual's assessment, or may even represent the unanimous views of all. Unanimity is not absurd to assume here since everyone orders the positions, bearing in mind that being person *i* in state *x* means not merely to have the social position of *i* but also his precise subjective features.[11] However, differences in judgment between persons can still arise, and if they do, a problem similar to that faced with a CCR, or a SWF, will be faced here as well. For the moment we assume unanimity in ordering "positions," or assume that all the exercise is done by some consistent observer.

But how appealing is the maximin criterion as a social decision rule? It certainly does involve a number of problems when viewed as a formal criterion, of which the following may be important:

(1) While it satisfies the weaker version of the Pareto rule (condition *P*), it may violate its stronger version. Consider two situations *x* and *y* with the following welfare levels of two individuals *A* and *B*:

	Welfare of *A*	Welfare of *B*
state *x*	10	1
state *y*	20	1

The maximin rule will make *x* and *y* indifferent, while *y* is Pareto-wise superior to *x*. Since the accentuation of inequality is not to "everyone's advantage," and the worst-off individual is no better off under *y* than under *x*, *y* is not socially judged better than *x*.[12]

---

[11] This identity of orderings of positions should not be confused with the identity of judgments about social states required in Hare's model. A person with a given ordering of positions could, nevertheless, recommend different choices, depending on which position he himself holds.

[12] We can avoid this problem by defining a lexicographic ordering in the following form, without losing the essence of the maximin rule, for a community of *n* individuals:

(1) Maximize the welfare of the worst-off individual.
(2) For equal welfare of the worst-off individuals, maximize the welfare of the second worst-off individual.

$\vdots$

(*n*) For equal welfare of the worst-off individuals, the second worst-off individuals, ..., the (*n* − 1)th worst-off individuals, maximize the welfare of the best-off individual.

In the example in the text, *y* is obviously preferred to *x* under this rule, which we can call the lexicographic maximin rule.

(2)   Our values about inequality cannot be adequately reflected in the maximin rule, because an exclusive concern with the well-being of the worst-off individual, or the worst-off group of individuals, hides various other issues related to equality.   Consider the following alternative states:

	Welfare of A	Welfare of B	Welfare of C
state x	100	80	60
state y	100	61	61

The maximin rule will indicate that y is preferred to x.   However, while the gap between B and C is reduced, that between A and B is accentuated.   There are no simple measures of inequality for a group and our values also tend to be too complicated to be caught by a simple rule like "make the worst-off best-off."

While this criticism is valid, its importance is not quite obvious. If the institutional features are such that a reduction of the gap between the average and the minimum can be achieved only through a reduction of inequality as measured by other indices, it will be somewhat pointless to lose much sleep on this question.   Judgments of this kind tend to be nonbasic and the factual background is important.   Rawls' argumentation is based on a certain institutional framework, and to assess the effectiveness of his criterion we have to bear this in mind.   However, it is likely that the difficulty will be more serious in the choice between social states in general, which is our problem, than in the choice between certain institutions, which is Rawls' focus of attention.

(3)   Because of the purely ordinal nature of it, the maximin criterion is not sensitive to magnitudes of gains and losses.   There is no such thing here as a slight gain of the worst-off person being wiped out from a social point of view by big gains (as big as we dare to postulate) of the others.   There is *no* trade-off.

(4)   For Rawls, the justification of the maximin rule lies in its relationship with the principle of "fairness," and the above arguments may be irrelevant in that context.   There is little doubt that the requirement of "fairness" is highly appealing.   If people choose a system while totally ignorant of their personal attributes, it certainly does satisfy an important value in our moral system.   The link between the concept of "fairness" and the two principles of "justice" that identify the maximin rule lies in the belief that in

a "fair" agreement these two principles will be chosen.   Is this argument acceptable?

The theory of decision-taking under uncertainty does not yield very definite conclusions on problems of this kind.   Certainly with a predominantly pessimistic outlook the maximin rule will be the only one to choose.   There are other arguments also, which Rawls (1967), (1968) specifies.   The rule is clear and is relatively easy to handle.   Unlike the approach of utilitarianism it is not blind to distributions of utility over the individuals.   In its application to institutional choices it will militate against persecution, religious or otherwise, since the sufferings of the man under an inquisition will never be washed out by the gain, however large, of the inquisitor.   In several institutional questions the appeal of the maximin approach is well demonstrated by Rawls.   Nevertheless, the fact remains that Rawls' maximin solution is a very special one and the assertion that it *must* be chosen in the original position is not altogether convincing.   Even if one rejects the criterion of maximizing expected utility, which we discuss in the next section, there are other criteria that must be considered.[13]   The pessimism-optimism index of Hurwicz (1951), of which the maximin rule is an extreme case (corresponding to a degree of pessimism equal to 1), is a possibility that can be explored, after suitable generalization. To choose one particular decision rule, viz., maximin, out of many may be appropriate some time, but to claim that it must be chosen by rational individuals in the "original position" seems to be a rather severe assumption.

It is not our purpose here to evaluate Rawls' highly original and valuable contribution to the notions of fairness and justice.   His main interest is not so much in the ordering of social states, which is our concern, but with finding just institutions as opposed to unjust ones, which is a somewhat different problem.   Rawls' approach to the latter problem is relevant to the former question also, but it is not a complete picture in that context.

Finally, it is worth noting that Rawls' principle of fairness is more fundamental than his principles of justice, which he derives from the former.   And it is possible to accept Rawls' criteria of fairness without committing oneself fully to his identification of

---

[13] For a lucid introduction to various decision criteria, see Luce and Raiffa (1957), Chapter 13, and Raiffa (1968).

justice.[14]   Indeed the idea of morally recommending a collective choice mechanism can be given considerable content in terms of the notion of an *as if* uncertainty as outlined by Rawls.

9.3.   Impersonality and Expected Utility Maximization

Harsanyi (1955) considers two sets of preferences for each individual.   Their "subjective preferences" are their preferences as "they actually are."[15]   Their "ethical preferences" must satisfy the characteristic of being "impersonal."

> An individual's preference satisfy this requirement of impersonality if they indicate what social situation he would choose if he did not know what his personal position would be in the new situation chosen (and in any of its alternatives) but rather had an equal *chance* of obtaining any of the social positions existing in this situation, from the highest down to the lowest.[16]

This concept of "impersonality" is very closely related to notions of "universalizability" and "fairness" discussed in the last two sections.   Hare's "universalizability" is the most demanding of the three conditions.   To satisfy it a person's judgment must remain the same no matter whose shoes one is in.   Rawls' "fairness"

---

[14] A half-jocular, half-serious objection to the criteria of fairness of Rawls and others runs like this: Why confine placing oneself in the position of other human beings only, why not other animals also?   Is the biological line so sharply drawn?   What this line of attack misses is the fact that Rawls is crystallizing an idea of fairness that our value system does seem to have, rather than constructing a rule of fairness in vacuum based on some notions of biological symmetry.   Revolutions do take place demanding equitable treatment of human beings in a manner they do not demanding equality for animals.   "If I were in his shoes" is relevant to a moral argument in a manner that "if I were in its paws" is not.   Our ethical systems may have, as is sometimes claimed, had a biological origin, but what is involved here is the *use* of these systems and not a *manufacture* of it on some kind of a biological logic.   The jest half of the objection is, thus, more interesting than the serious half.

[15] These personal utility functions, of course, do not rule out interdependence between the individuals' utilities, and correspond to what Arrow calls "values" rather than "tastes" (Arrow (1963), p. 18; Harsanyi (1955), p. 315).

[16] Harsanyi (1955), p. 316.   See also Vickrey (1945), p. 329.   Also Harsanyi (1953), Leibenstein (1965), and Pattanaik (1968a).

requires acceptance in the "original position" without knowing in whose shoes one would be. Harsanyi's "impersonality" requires acceptance under the assumption of equiprobability. Similarities between Rawls' and Harsanyi's concepts are striking, and would be even more so if the "principle of insufficient reason" could be used to convert Rawls' "ignorance" into Harsanyi's "equiprobability." Rawls rejects this and chooses the nonprobabilistic maximin criterion. Harsanyi, however, defines his "impersonality" directly in terms of *as if* equiprobability, and assumes further that individuals will satisfy the von Neumann-Morgenstern (or Marschak) postulates of rational behavior under risk. (See Chapter 7 for a statement of the postulates.) Ethical preferences are, therefore, determined by expected utility maximization, and under the equiprobability assumption this boils down simply to maximizing the sum of utilities of all. Utilitarianism is, thus, vindicated on grounds of "impersonality," and the relevant utilities are of the von Neumann-Morgenstern type, thereby easing the problem of cardinalization which we discussed in Chapter 7.

Aside from this direct approach to ethical preferences, Harsanyi also explores a more general approach to social choice. He proves the following theorem: If social preferences as well as all individual preferences satisfy the Marschak (or von Neumann-Morgenstern) postulates, and if everyone being indifferent implies social indifference, then social welfare must be a weighted sum of individual utilities.[17]   There are various ways of using this theorem (see Pattanaik (1968a)). Harsanyi takes social preferences to be the "social welfare function of a given individual,"[18] and this provides a background to his notion of "ethical preferences" which are a type of "social preferences" in this sense. Under the equiprobability assumption, the ethical preferences are those social preferences which use the unweighted (i.e., equiweighted) sum of utilities.

How satisfactory is the test of impersonality? The following difficulties seem to be relatively serious.

(1)   Consider a slave society with 99 free men and 1 slave. The latter serves the former to their convenience and to his great discomfort. Given an equal chance of being in anyone's position it is possible that someone might be ready to take a 1% chance of

---

[17] Theorem V in Harsanyi (1955), p. 314. See also Fleming (1952).
[18] Harsanyi (1955), p. 315.

being a slave, since the 99% chance of being a free man served by a slave might tickle his fancy. Would a slave society be then morally supportable? Many people will not accept this test.

It might incidentally be noted that in this case the Rawlsian model of "justice" will tend to give different judgments from that derived from "impersonality." Since the maximin notion fixes on the welfare of the worst-off individual, problems of this kind cannot appear in the use of that criterion. Similarly, to claim that slavery or apartheid was "just" with Hare's requirement of "universalizability" would demand much more than the test used here. The author of the judgment will have to maintain this not merely under the equiprobability assumption of impersonality, but when imaging himself occupying (with certainty) every relevant position in that social situation.

(2) Consider now a somewhat different problem. Let there be two alternative social states represented by x and y with a two-person welfare situation as given below:

	Welfare of 1	Welfare of 2
state x	1	0
state y	$\frac{1}{2}$	$\frac{1}{2}$

In terms of expected utility, the assumption of impersonality will make each of them indifferent between x and y, since both have an expected value of $\frac{1}{2}$. Are they equally appealing? If someone values equality as such (and not for such derived reasons that equality maximizes the aggregate of individual welfares[19]), he may categorically prefer state y to x. It would appear that in social choices we are interested not only in the mathematical expectation of welfare with impersonality, but also with the exact distribution of that welfare over the individuals.

In an interesting and important note, Diamond (1967) has argued that the "strong independence assumption" (or the "sure thing principle;" see Section 7.3, p. 95) is the guilty party in the Harsanyi framework of social preference.[20] This assumption is included in the set of Marschak postulates accepted by Harsanyi.

---

[19] Note that the units in the above table are of individual welfare and not of income or output.

[20] See also Strotz (1958), (1961), and Fisher and Rothenberg (1961), (1962).

	0.5 probability	0.5 probability
lottery I	$U_A = 1$, $U_B = 0$	$U_A = 0$, $U_B = 1$
lottery II	$U_A = 1$, $U_B = 0$	$U_A = 1$, $U_B = 0$

Diamond considers a case of two individuals (say, A and B) and two alternative "lotteries" (say, I and II). If II is chosen, it is certain that individual A will have a unit of utility while B will have none. With I there is a probability of 0.5 that A will have one unit of utility and B none, while there is also a probability of 0.5 that B will have one unit of utility and A none.

In terms of aggregate expected utility maximization, I and II are equally good, having an expected aggregate value of 1. It seems reasonable to be indifferent between the second prize of I and that of II because they seem very much the same except for the substitution of name tags A and B. But the first prize of both the lotteries is the same, so that "the sure thing principle" (or "the strong independence assumption") would make us indifferent between I and II. But lottery II seems so unfair to individual B, while lottery I "gives B a fair shake." Hence Diamond's rejection of "the sure thing principle" as applied to social choice.

It should, however, be noted that the Diamond argument depends crucially on the individual welfare levels (and thus also "origins") being comparable—an assumption that is not needed for Harsanyi's model of aggregate welfare or, for that matter, in any model of aggregate welfare. Suppose we add 1 to individual B's welfare function, keeping A's welfare function unchanged. In the utility space the two lotteries get transformed to the following:

	0.5 probability	0.5 probability
lottery I	$U_A = 1$, $U_B = 1$	$U_A = 0$, $U_B = 2$
lottery II	$U_A = 1$, $U_B = 1$	$U_A = 1$, $U_B = 1$

It will now be easy to build an argument in favor of II against I on much the same grounds ("a fair shake") as Diamond's reason for preferring I to II. And this is brought about by a mere change in the origin of one individual's welfare function, which leaves the ordering of aggregate welfare completely unchanged. Clearly the type of comparability that Harsanyi needs is in this respect less demanding than what Diamond needs for criticizing Harsanyi. Since neither Harsanyi nor Diamond states his assumptions of interpersonal comparability explicitly, the debate is not easy to evaluate. In our terminology (Chapters 7 and 7*), Harsanyi needs "unit comparability" for the aggregation exercise, whereas Diamond needs "full comparability" to be able to make his point.

If can also be asked whether the strong independence assumption is really guilty *even if* full comparability is assumed. Someone could argue that *after* the lottery takes place the end result will be that one person will have one unit of utility and the other none in the case of each lottery. So in terms of *actual* utility distribution rather than *anticipated* utility distribution, lottery I is no more egalitarian (and thus may really be no more attractive) than lottery II. Why should the process of lottery matter since the ultimate result is a 1–0 distribution anyway? This is a possible position to take, though there are people who would find much fairness in having the intermediate phase of randomization.[21]

Whether we accept strong independence or not, the attractiveness of expected utility maximization is in doubt. The example given in the table on p. 143 applies to expected utility maximization in general. And the argument for choosing $(\frac{1}{2}, \frac{1}{2})$ rather than $(1, 0)$ would appear to be rather strong, if full comparability is assumed. While utilitarianism in general and Harsanyi's criterion in particular would be indifferent between the two, the maximin rule would have favored the egalitarian distribution.[22] The crucial question is that of comparability, since unit comparability will rule out any possible consideration of equality in utility distributions without affecting utilitarianism and Harsanyi's criterion.

It should also be added that just as we introduced "partial comparability" of *units* in Chapters 7 and 7*, we can use partial comparability of utility *origins* (and more generally of *absolute levels* of welfare, cardinal or not) of different persons. The formal framework will be in the same lines as the framework of partial comparability of units, and we resist the temptation here to charge full steam into this area. The interested reader can try it out.

---

[21] In a seminar run jointly by Arrow, Rawls and myself, at Harvard in the fall of 1968, the participants (about thirty in all) were found to be roughly equally divided on this.

[22] This being a two-person case, some of the difficulties with Rawls' rather extreme criterion which we discussed in the last section could not possibly arise here.

It is interesting to contrast the formal requirements of the maximin criterion with the utilitarian principle. The former requires comparability of levels of welfare, which the latter does not. On the other hand, the latter can be taken to be a sure-fire principle of social ordering in every possible case only if cardinality and unit comparability are assumed, while the maximin criterion works perfectly well with ordinality and even with orderings with no possible numerical representation. These technical considerations are not, of course, ethically decisive, but they certainly are relevant. Utilitarianism may be accepted with enthusiasm if we can compare differences of welfare for different persons, but not levels. On the other hand, if we cannot compare units, or if we can compare levels, the enthusiasm may be limited. In evaluating these principles for our own social judgments we can do worse than considering the types of interpersonal comparisons we tend to make.

9.4. Grading Principles of Justice

While both the maximin criterion and the utility principle yield complete social orderings given their respective measurability and comparability assumptions, Suppes' (1966) model of "grading principles" yields only partial orderings. On the basis of these grading principles, Suppes devises simple ethical rules of behavior in two-person games. Given the state of nature and the decisions or acts chosen by the two persons, the set of consequences on each can be found out. With S being the set of states of nature, D_1 and D_2 the respective sets of decisions or acts available to the two persons, and C_1 and C_2 the respective sets of consequences for the two persons. Suppes' "social decision function"[23] specifies values of C_1 and C_2 for each combination of S, D_1 and D_2. The object is to find a partial ordering of the pairs of consequences on the two.

Let $(x, 1)$ and $(x, 2)$ be the consequences on the two individuals 1 and 2, respectively, in some two-person decision situation that has to be compared with another when the consequences on the two, respectively, are $(y, 1)$ and $(y, 2)$. The point is to compare x with y in terms of "extended sympathy." We know that x will be Pareto-superior to y, if individual 1 regards $(x, 1)$ to be at least as good as $(y, 1)$, individual 2 regards $(x, 2)$ to be at least as good as

---

[23] Not to be confused with SDF defined in this work (see Definition 4*1).

(y, 2), and at least one of them strictly prefers the respective component of x to that of y.   The ranking *more just than* is, however, done for each individual separately in terms of his own tastes.   The essence of the approach is to use the individual's ordering over the set of individual consequences, i.e., over (x, 1), (x, 2), (y, 1), (y, 2), etc., to obtain the required justice relation over the set of social states, i.e, over x, y, etc.   If individual 1 finds that he prefers (x, 1) to (y, 1) and regards (x, 2) to be at least as good as (y, 2), then he judges x to be more just than y.   He makes the same judgment if he prefers (x, 2) to (y, 2) and finds (x, 1) at least as good as (y, 1).

So far this is simply a Pareto-like judgment, done in terms of the individual's own preferences.   But now he might reverse the actual interpersonal distribution of consequences.   Suppose he finds that the above requirements are not satisfied, but the following set is.   He strictly prefers (x, 1) to (y, 2) and regards (x, 2) to be at least as good as (y, 1).   That is, he prefers to be himself in situation x than be in individual 2's shoes in situation y, and he likes being in individual 2's shoes in situation x at least as much as being himself in situation y.   He might once again decide that x is more just than y.   Exactly similarly, if he strictly prefers (x, 2) to (y, 1), and regards (x, 1) to be at least as good as (y, 2), he may again regard x to be more just than y.

The conditions outlined in the last two paragraphs indicate the basis of Suppes's "grading principle of justice" for each individual, defining a partial strict ordering over the pairs of consequences. Since the principle of comparison may appear to be slightly difficult, being unfamiliar and novel (a tribute to the originality of Suppes), the condition may be stated slightly differently (making it somewhat weaker), requiring strict preference for both the comparisons.   The Suppes' rule says that x is more just than y according to individual i, if either (a) he prefers to be himself at x rather than at y, and also prefers to be the other individual at x rather than at y, *or* (b) he prefers to be himself at x rather than the other individual at y, and prefers to be the other individual at x rather than himself at y. In either case, there is something superior at x vis-a-vis y in terms of his own preference ordering, either retaining the respecting positions or reversing them.

Suppes demonstrates that the ordering relation "more just than" does define a partial strict ordering over the set of pairs of consequences, i.e., the relation is "asymmetric" and "transitive." Suppes then proceeds to use three definitions based on the grading principle of justice to outline two rules of ethical behavior. A *justice-admissible element*[24] for an individual i is a pair of consequences which is not less just than any feasible pair of consequences, according to that individual's preference ordering. A *point of justice* is a set of strategies, one for each player, that leads to a justice-admissible element. A *justice-saturated strategy* for a player is a strategy such that no matter which strategy the other player picks in the two-person game, the result is a point of justice.

Based on these definitions, Suppes suggests two rules of justice-oriented behavior:

> I   If grading principles of justice of the two individuals yield the same partial strict ordering, and if there is a unique point of justice, then the strategy belonging to each point ought to be chosen.
>
> II   If for any player the set of justice-saturated strategies is non-empty, he ought to choose one.

These rules of behavior will make sense only insofar as the *grading principle* of justice defined by Suppes makes sense, though the converse is not necessarily correct, since the rules of behavior are to some extent arbitrary.[25] In what follows, we shall concentrate on the merits of the grading principle itself, which is closer to our concern with collective choice rules.

A merit of Suppes's grading principle of justice is that it seems to satisfy the requirement of "universalizability" as outlined by Hare (1952), (1963), on one interpretation,[26] even in the context of interpersonal interchangeability. Since the rule of comparison is symmetrical between the positions of the individuals, the person can honestly claim that if he maintains that x is more just than y, he does so *irrespective* of being in his own position or that of the

---

[24] Suppes calls it "(J_i) admissible element."

[25] See the example given by Suppes (1966) himself on pp. 304–305 to illustrate a case where a justice-saturated strategy yields what looks like a *less* "equitable and just" solution than the equilibrium point analysis.

[26] There is, however, a different and more appropriate interpretation of Hare for which this is not true. See footnote 28 below.

other person.   Whether the first situation is $[(x, 1), (x, 2)]$ or $[(x, 2), (x, 1)]$ and the second situation is $[(y, 1), (y, 2)]$ or $[(y, 2), (y, 1)]$, makes no difference whatever to the ranking of justice between the two situations.   It seems to pass, therefore, a demanding test.

A second advantage is that the approach of Suppes, unlike those of Harsanyi and of Rawls, does not require interpersonal comparisons of welfare.   We do not have to compare the welfare levels of different persons, and all comparisons are made in terms of the ordering of a given individual with his own tastes and preferences. Furthermore, unlike in the Harsanyi approach, cardinalization of welfare indices of the individuals is not needed.

The avoidance of cardinalization and interpersonal comparisons is, however, achieved at some price.   Unlike the orderings generated by Rawls' criterion, or that of Harsanyi, the rankings yielded by the grading principle of Suppes is *incomplete*.   This need not be a very serious criticism, since the ordering, while incomplete, may nevertheless help to solve a set of important problems involving considerations of justice.

It is possible, however, to have a very serious reservation about the grading principle itself.   As a consequence of doing all the comparisons in terms of the same individual's tastes, personal differences in preferences find little reflection in the principle.   Consider the following example, where the two pairs of consequences are expressed in terms of commodities enjoyed by two individuals without any externalities: To give the sense of the difference in tastes, we take individual 1 to be a devout Muslim and individual 2 to be a devout Hindu, with the commodities in question being pork and beef.   It is assumed that the Muslim likes beef and is disgusted by pork, while the Hindu enjoys pork but cannot bear the thought of eating beef.   Assuming free disposal, the Muslim is indifferent between different amounts of pork, and the Hindu between different amounts of beef.   The two alternative outcomes are given by x and y.

	The Muslim	The Hindu
state x	2 pork, 0 beef	0 pork, 2 beef
state y	0 pork, 1 beef	1 pork, 0 beef

It is clear that y is Pareto-wise better than x, since the Muslim prefers 1 unit of beef to 2 units of pork, while the Hindu prefers 1 unit of pork to 2 units of beef.   What about the grading principle of justice developed by Suppes?   Alas, both individuals find x to be more just than y.   The Muslim prefers $(x, 2)$ rather than $(y, 1)$, i.e., prefers to have 2 units of beef rather than having one unit of it.   Also he is indifferent between $(x, 1)$ and $(y, 2)$, i.e., between having 2 units of pork and having 1 unit of it.   Similarly, the Hindu prefers $(x, 1)$ to $(y, 2)$, and is indifferent between $(x, 2)$ and $(y, 1)$.   So both find x to be preferable to y by the grading principle of justice.   But y is Pareto-wise superior to x.

When the choice is between x and y, x is justice-admissible while y is not.   It is easy to construct a game where x will correspond to the unique point of justice, and to get ethical endorsement in terms of the Suppes model for choosing strategies such that x becomes the outcome.   The result seems extremely perverse.   The source of the problem lies in the procedure whereby each individual can make comparisons in terms of his own tastes on behalf of himself as well as that of the others.[27]   Unlike in the models of Harsanyi and Rawls there is no requirement in the Suppes model that one must take on the subjective features (in particular, tastes) of the other when one places oneself in his position.   This is the source of the trouble.[28]

The problem, however, is easily removed.   Placing oneself in the position of the other should involve not merely having the latter's objective circumstances but also identifying oneself with the other in terms of his subjective features.   We call this the identity axiom in Chapter 9*, and it rules out the difficulty altogether, but at some price.   On this interpretation a comparison of $(x, 1)$ with $(y, 2)$ or of $(x, 2)$ with $(y, 1)$ *is* an interpersonal comparison.   This is not really a major loss, however.   It should be fairly obvious from our earlier discussion that nothing of much interest can be said on justice without bringing in some interpersonal comparability.   The required reformulation of the grading principles of Suppes merely brings this point home.

---

[27] Cf. "Do not do unto others as you would that they should do unto you. Their tastes may not be the same."   "The Golden Rule" in "Maxims for Revolutionists," in George Bernard Shaw, *Man and Superman*, London, 1903.

[28] Since placing oneself in the position of the other in Hare's model is supposed to include *subjective features* of the other, the Suppes criterion does not, in fact, pass the test of "universalizability."

9.5.   Grading Principle, Maximin, and Utilitarianism

The grading principles of Suppes can be extended from his two-person world to n-person societies, which is presented in Chapter 9*. Thus extended (and combined with the identity axiom), the Suppes relation can be seen to be a crucial building block of both the maximin relation and utilitarianism. If x is more just than y in the sense of Suppes (with the identity axiom imposed), then x must have a larger welfare aggregate than y (utilitarian relation) and also the worst-off individual at x must be at least as well off as any individual at y (maximin relation) (see Theorems 9*5 and 9*7).

This is an extremely important property.   As we noted earlier, the conflicting claims of the maximin criterion and of utilitarianism are difficult to resolve.   Each has some attractive features and some unattractive ones.   The grading principle, when suitably constrained, seems to catch the most appealing common elements of the two.

However, since it yields only a strict partial ordering it is an incomplete criterion.   What it does, essentially, is to separate out the relatively noncontroversial part of interpersonal choice.   It takes us substantially beyond the Pareto criterion.   This is especially so in the n-person extension of the Suppes relation; the number of possible interpersonal permutations is given by $n!$, i.e., by $n(n-1)(n-2)\cdots 1$.   There are only two permutations in a two-person world, but as many as 3,628,800 different interpersonal permutations in a ten-man world.   The Pareto relation is concerned with only one particular one-to-one correspondence.   In contrast, there are 3,628,800 *different* ways in which x can be more just than y in a ten-person society, using the extended grading principle.

The extended version of the grading principle is, thus, rich. While it does not yield a complete social ordering, it does squeeze out as much juice as possible out of the use of "dominance" (or vector inequality), which is the common element in the maximin criterion, utilitarianism, and a number of other collective choice procedures involving interpersonal comparability.

Chapter 9*

IMPERSONALITY AND COLLECTIVE
QUASI-ORDERINGS

9*1. Grading Principles of Justice

The notion of justice, as we saw in Chapter 9, is closely connected with "extended sympathy" in the form of placing oneself in the position of another.

DEFINITION 9*1. *Let (x, i) stand for being in the position of individual i in social state x.*

In the discussion so far we have always considered R_i over such alternatives as (x, i), (y, i), etc. Now, R_i will be defined also over such alternatives as (x, i), (y, j), etc., when $i \neq j$. Such an R_i, denoted $\tilde{R}_i$, will be called an *extended* individual ordering.

DEFINITION 9*2. *$\tilde{R}_i$ is the ordering of the i-th individual defined over the Cartesian product of X and H, where X is the set of social states, and H is the set of individuals.*

LEMMA 9*a. *A subrelation of $\tilde{R}_i$ for each i is defined by R_i.*

The proof is obvious from the fact that $x R_i y$ is now defined as $(x, i) \tilde{R}_i (y, i)$. We define $\tilde{P}_i$ and $\tilde{I}_i$ corresponding to $\tilde{R}_i$.

It may be noted that x is Pareto-superior to y, i.e., $x \bar{P} y$, if and only if $\forall i: [(x, i) \tilde{R}_i (y, i)]$ & $\exists i: [(x, i) \tilde{P}_i (y, i)]$.

Suppes (1966) has defined an important criteria of justice by making use of extended sympathy in a two-person case. We present here an n-person extension of the Suppes model. It involves one-to-one correspondences from the set of individuals H to H itself, such that $k = \rho(j)$, where person j is mapped onto person k. Let the set of all such one-to-one correspondences between H and H be called T. Now, $x J_i y$ is defined to be read as "x is more just than y according to person i."

DEFINITION 9*3. *For all pairs x, y in X,*

$$x J_i y \leftrightarrow \exists \rho \in T:$$
$$[\{\forall j: (x, j) \tilde{R}_i (y, \rho(j))\} \ \& \ \{\exists j: (x, j) \tilde{P}_i (y, \rho(j))\}]$$

According to person i, x is more just than y if there is a one-to-one transformation from the set of individuals to itself such that he would prefer to be in the position of someone in x rather than in the position of the corresponding person in y, and also would prefer to, or be indifferent to, being in the position of *each* person in x than to be in the position of the corresponding person in y.

Suppes has shown (his Theorem 2) that for the two-person case that he considers, J_i will be a strict partial ordering over possible social states. The result is generalized below for the n-person case.[1]

THEOREM 9*1. *Each J_i is a strict partial ordering over X, i.e., J_i is asymmetric and transitive, for every logically possible set of extended individual orderings $(\tilde{R}_i)$.*

Proof. For any $x, y, z \in X$, and for any $i \in H$,

$$x J_i y \ \& \ y J_i z$$
$$\rightarrow \exists \rho, \mu \in T: [\{\forall j: (x, j) \tilde{R}_i (y, \rho(j))\}$$
$$\& \ \{\exists j: (x, j) \tilde{P}_i (y, \rho(j))\} \ \& \ \{\forall k: (y, k) \tilde{R}_i (z, \mu(k))\}]$$
$$\rightarrow [\{\forall j: (x, j) \tilde{R}_i (z, \pi(j))\} \ \& \ \{\exists j: (x, j) \tilde{P}_i (z, \pi(j))\}]$$

where $\pi(j) = \mu(\rho(j))$. Since π is also a one-to-one correspondence between H and H, i.e., $\pi \in T$, we can conclude that $x J_i z$, which proves transitivity.

Asymmetry is now proved by contradiction. Suppose $x J_i y$ & $y J_i x$ for some $x, y \in X$. Then there are ρ and μ in T such that

$$\forall j: (x, j) \tilde{R}_i (y, \rho(j)) \tag{1}$$

$$\& \ \forall k: (y, k) \tilde{R}_i (x, \mu(k)) \tag{2}$$

$$\& \ \exists j: (x, j) \tilde{P}_i (y, \rho(j)) \tag{3}$$

Without loss of generality, let a particular person j for whom (3)

---

[1] However, we cannot use Suppes' method of proof since he shows the result by a complete study of all possible cases—a method that works well for his two-person situation, but not well at all for general n-person situations.

holds be called 1. From (2) and (3), we have for $\pi(j) = \mu(\rho(j))$,

$$(x, 1) \, \tilde{P}_i \, (x, \pi(1)) \tag{4}$$

Clearly it is impossible that $\pi(1) = 1$. Without loss of generality, let $\pi(1)$ be called person 2.

From (1) and (2), we obtain

$$(x, 2) \, \tilde{R}_i \, (x, \pi(2)) \tag{5}$$

Obviously, it is impossible that $\pi(2) = 2$, since $\pi(1) = 2$, and π is a one-to-one correspondence. It is also impossible that $\pi(2) = 1$, since (4) and (5) will then be contradictory. Let $\pi(2) = 3$.

Proceeding this way for distinct persons 3, 4, 5, $\ldots$, n, we obtain

$$(x, 3) \, \tilde{R}_i \, (x, 4)$$
$$\vdots$$
$$(x, n - 1) \, \tilde{R}_i \, (x, n) \tag{6}$$

From (4), (5) and (6), we conclude that

$$(x, 1) \, \tilde{P}_i \, (x, n) \tag{7}$$

From (1) and (2), we know that

$$(x, n) \, \tilde{R}_i \, (x, \pi(n)) \tag{8}$$

But since π is a one-to-one correspondence, and $\pi(n)$ cannot be 2, 3, $\ldots$, n, we must have $\pi(n) = 1$. Since (7) and (8) contradict, our initial supposition must be untenable, and hence J_i is asymmetric, which completes the proof.

The Suppes relation of justice J_i is, thus, a strict partial ordering, i.e., "a grading principle" as Suppes defines such a principle (asymmetric and transitive). It is not, however, a collective choice rule as defined in Chapter 2*, since J_i depends not merely on the set of R_i but on $\tilde{R}_i$, with each R_i being merely a subrelation of $\tilde{R}_i$. We redefine a collective choice rule more generally in the next section.

9*2. Suppes and Pareto

DEFINITION 9*4. *A general collective choice rule (hereafter, GCCR) is a functional relation that specifies one and only one social preference relation R over the set of social states X, for any n-tuple of individual orderings $(\tilde{R}_1, \ldots, \tilde{R}_n)$, where each $\tilde{R}_i$ is an ordering over the product of X and H.*

The grading principles of Suppes, as generalized here for the n-person case, are a set of GCCRs. It takes, in fact, the special form of determining $R = J_i$, on the basis of one and only one $\tilde{R}_i$, and thus there are n such alternative principles when there are n individuals.

However, the following result seems disturbing:

THEOREM 9*2. *When the number of individuals is 2 or more, the weak Pareto strict relation $\bar{\bar{P}}$ is incompatible with each J_i, for $i = 1, \ldots, n$, for some logically possible set of individual preferences, $\tilde{R}_1, \ldots, \tilde{R}_n$.*

Proof. Let the individuals be numbered $1, \ldots, n$. Consider $\mu \in T$, such that $\mu(j) = j + 1$, for $j < n$, and $\mu(n) = 1$.

Consider the following preference rankings of each person i for some pair $x, y \in X$, for all j:

$$\left(x, \mu(j)\right) \tilde{P}_i (y, j) \tag{9}$$

$$(y, i) \tilde{P}_i (x, i) \tag{10}$$

Representing the inverse function of μ as μ^{-1}, we obtain the following from (9) and (10) for all i:

$$\left[\left(x, \mu(i)\right) \tilde{P}_i (y, i)\right] \ \& \ \left[(y, i) \tilde{P}_i (x, i)\right] \ \& \ \left[(x, i) \tilde{P}_i \left(y, \mu^{-1}(i)\right)\right] \tag{11}$$

For more than one individual being in the community, i.e., $n > 1$, $\mu(i)$ as defined is not the same as i, nor is i the same as $\mu^{-1}(i)$. Hence there is no contradiction in (9) and (10). For each $\tilde{R}_i$, (9) defines n ordered pairs with no elements in common, and together with (10), we get one strict order of four elements, viz., that given in (11).

We take any set of $(\tilde{R}_i)$ that is compatible with (9) and (10). It is immediate that for each i, $x J_i y$, from (9). Also, it is obvious from (10) that $y \bar{\bar{P}} x$. This proves the theorem.[2]

A corollary is immediate.

COROLLARY 9*2.1. *When the number of individuals is 2 or more, the Pareto strict relation $\bar{P}$ is incompatible with each J_i for $i = 1, \ldots, n$, for some logically possible set of individual preferences, $\tilde{R}_1, \ldots, \tilde{R}_n$.* This follows from: $\forall x, y \in X: x \bar{\bar{P}} y \to x \bar{P} y$. Since the grading

---

[2] A simple example for the two-person case is given by $[\{(x, 2) P_1 (y, 1)\}$ & $\{(y, 1) P_1 (x, 1)\}$ & $\{(x, 1) P_1 (y, 2)\}]$, and $[\{(x, 1) P_2 (y, 2)\}$ & $\{(y, 2) P_2 (x, 2)\}$ & $\{(x, 2) P_2 (y, 1)\}]$, where $x J_i y$ for $i = 1, 2$, but $y \bar{\bar{P}} x$.

principle may contradict the weak Pareto principle, it certainly can contradict the strong Pareto principle.

9*3. Identity Axioms and the Grading Principles

The problem of incompatibility of the Pareto quasi-ordering with the strict partial orderings of justice can be eliminated by imposing certain restrictions on the individuals' extended preferences, $\tilde{R}_i$. The identity axiom discussed in Chapter 9, and which can be justified on ethical grounds as an important part of the exercise of extended sympathy, serves this purpose as well.

AXIOM 9*1. *Identity:* $\forall x, y \in X$:

$$[\forall i : \{(x, i) \, \tilde{R}_i \, (y, i) \leftrightarrow \forall j : (x, i) \, \tilde{R}_j \, (y, i)\}]$$

Each individual j in placing himself in the position of person i takes on the tastes and preferences of i.

THEOREM 9*3. *Under the axiom of identity, for each person i, $\bar{P}$ is compatible with J_i, and further $\forall x, y \in X : [x \, \bar{P} \, y \to x \, J_i \, y]$.*

Proof. For any $x, y \in X$:

$$x \, \bar{P} \, y \to [\{\forall i : (x, i) \, \tilde{R}_i \, (y, i)\} \ \& \ \{\exists i : (x, i) \, \tilde{P}_i \, (y, i)\}]$$
$$\to \forall i : [\{\forall j : (x, j) \, \tilde{R}_i \, (y, j)\} \ \& \ \{\exists j : (x, j) \, \tilde{P}_i \, (y, j)\}]$$
$$\to \forall i : x \, J_i \, y$$

A more demanding assumption is that given by the axiom of complete identity.

AXIOM 9*2. *Complete identity:* $\forall i, j : \tilde{R}_i = \tilde{R}_j$.

It is trivial that under the axiom of complete identity, $J_i = J_j$ for all persons i, j. We can refer to R and J without subscripts under the axiom of complete identity, for the subscript will make no difference.

9*4. The Maximin Relation of Justice

The criteria of justice put forward by Rawls (1958), (1963), (1967), can now be formalized. While Rawls speaks about welfare measures, and finds out the maximin value (see Chapter 9), his criteria are general enough to be expressible in terms of orderings only. We shall refer to $\tilde{R}$, which can be either interpreted as the extended ordering of a certain person i, $\tilde{R}_i$, with the subscript dropped, or alternatively as $\tilde{R}_i$ for all i under the axiom of complete identity. Under the former interpretation, the Rawls relation will reflect judgments on justice by a particular individual, while under the latter, it will reflect everyone's judgments on justice. The maximin relation of justice will be denoted as M.

DEFINITION 9*5.   *For all pairs x, y in X:*

$$x\,M\,y \leftrightarrow [\exists k : \{\forall i : (x, i)\,\tilde{R}\,(y, k)\}]$$

If it is no worse to be anyone in social state x than to be individual k in state y, then x is at least as just as y.

THEOREM 9*4.   *The maximin relation of justice M defines an ordering over the set of social states X, if $\tilde{R}$ is defined over the entire product of X and H.*

Proof.   It is obvious that M is reflexive. It is transitive, since

$\forall x, y, z \in X : x\,M\,y$ & $y\,M\,z$

$\quad \rightarrow ([\exists k : \{\forall i : (x, i)\,\tilde{R}\,(y, k)\}]$ & $[\exists j : \{\forall i : (y, i)\,\tilde{R}\,(z, j)\}]$

$\quad \rightarrow [\exists j : \{\forall i : (x, i)\,\tilde{R}\,(z, j)\}]$

$\quad \rightarrow x\,M\,z$

Finally, the completeness of M is proved by contradiction. Suppose $\sim(x\,M\,y)$ & $\sim(y\,M\,x)$ for some $x, y \in X$. Clearly

$$\sim[\exists k : \{\forall i : (x, i)\,\tilde{R}\,(y, k)\}] \ \& \ \sim[\exists j : \{\forall i : (y, i)\,\tilde{R}\,(x, j)\}]$$

This means that the set $[(x, i) \cup (y, j)]$ with $i = 1, \ldots, n$, and $j = 1, \ldots, n$, has no least ("worst") element with respect to $\tilde{R}$. But this is impossible, since the set is finite and $\tilde{R}$ is an ordering.[3]

For any given $\tilde{R}$, Suppes' relation of justice J implies Rawls' relation of justice M, but not vice versa.

THEOREM 9*5.   *For any given $\tilde{R}$, for all x, y in X: $x\,J\,y \rightarrow x\,M\,y$, but the converse does not hold.*

---

[3] See Lemma 1*j. The existence of a least element is proved in precisely the same way as the existence of a best element.

Proof.

$$x J y \to \exists \rho \in T: \left[\forall j: (x, j) \, \tilde{R} \left(y, \rho(j) \right) \right]$$
$$\to \exists k: \left[\forall j: (x, j) \, \tilde{R} \, (y, k) \right]$$
$$\to x \, M \, y$$

To check the converse, consider the following ordering $\tilde{R}$ in a two-person two-state world: $(y, 1) \, \tilde{P} \, (x, 1)$, $(x, 1) \, \tilde{P} \, (x, 2)$ and $(x, 2) \, \tilde{P} \, (y, 2)$. Clearly, $x \, M \, y$, but $\sim(x \, J \, y)$.

Notice, however, that even under the axiom of complete identity, the Pareto relation $\bar{P}$ (and the Suppes relation J) will not imply the strict preference relation of Rawls.[4]

LEMMA 9*b. *Even under the axiom of complete identity,* $\exists \tilde{R}: [x \, \bar{P} \, y$ & $y \, M \, x]$.

Proof. Consider a pair x, y in X and two individuals 1 and 2 such that $(x, 1) \, \tilde{P} \, (y, 1)$, $(y, 1) \, \tilde{R} \, (x, 2)$, and $(x, 2) \, \tilde{I} \, (y, 2)$. Since $(y, i) \, \tilde{R} \, (x, 2)$ for $i = 1, 2$, we have $y \, M \, x$; but $x \, \bar{P} \, y$. It is trivial to extend the example to any number of individuals.

However, the strict version of Pareto preference $\bar{\bar{P}}$ does imply the strict Rawls relation. And, of course, the weak Pareto preference does imply the weak Rawls relation.

THEOREM 9*6. *Under the axiom of complete identity, for all* x, y *in* X:

(1) $x \, \bar{R} \, y \to x \, M \, y$; and
(2) $x \, \bar{\bar{P}} \, y \to [x \, M \, y$ & $\sim(y \, M \, x)]$.

Proof. For all x, y in X:

$$x \, \bar{R} \, y \to \forall i: (x, i) \, \tilde{R}_i \, (y, i)$$
$$\to \exists k: \left[\forall i: (x, i) \, \tilde{R} \, (y, k) \right]$$
$$\to x \, M \, y$$

Hence (1) holds.

$$(y \, M \, x) \to \exists k: \left[\forall i: (y, i) \, \tilde{R} \, (x, k) \right]$$
$$\to \exists k: (y, k) \, \tilde{R}_k \, (x, k)$$
$$\to \sim(x \, \bar{\bar{P}} \, y)$$

Hence (2) holds, since $x \, \bar{\bar{P}} \, y \to x \, \bar{R} \, y$, and $x \, \bar{R} \, y \to x \, M \, y$, by (1).

---

[4] However, it will imply strict preference under the lexicographic maximin rule, defined in footnote 12 in Chapter 9, p. 138.

9*5. Justice and Aggregation

It is interesting to compare the relations of justice with the aggregation relation discussed in Chapter 7*. For this it is convenient to consider a weaker version of the Suppes relation J.

DEFINITION 9*6. *For all pairs x, y in X:*

$$x \, O_i \, y \leftrightarrow \exists \rho \in T : \left[\forall j : (x, j) \, \tilde{R}_i \left(y, \rho(j) \right) \right]$$

It can be checked that $x \, J_i \, y$ is equivalent to $x \, O_i \, y \;\&\; \sim (y \, O_i \, x)$.

Theorem 9*5 can be strengthened by noting that $x \, O \, y$ is sufficient for $x \, M \, y$, and $x \, J \, y$ is not needed.

COROLLARY 9*5.1. *For any given* $\tilde{R}$*, for all* x, y *in* X*:* $x \, O \, y \rightarrow$ $x \, M \, y$*, but the converse does not hold.*

The same proof holds as in Theorem 9*5.

We note, without proof, the following result:

LEMMA 9*c. *Each* O_i *is a quasi-ordering over* X*, i.e.,* O_i *is reflexive and transitive, for every logically possible set of extended individual orderings* $(\tilde{R}_i)$*.*

Consider any real-valued welfare function $U(x, i)$ defined for all i and all x in X.

DEFINITION 9*7. *For all* x, y *in* X*,* $x \, A \, y$*, i.e.,* x *has at least as great a welfare aggregate as* y*, if and only if*

$$\sum_i \left[U(x, i) - U(y, i) \right] \geqq 0$$

For any U, A is obviously an ordering.

We turn next to the relation between A and O for any particular $\tilde{R}$.

THEOREM 9*7. *If* U *is a real-valued representation of* $\tilde{R}$*, then* O *is a subrelation of* A*.*

Proof. Suppose $x \, O \, y$, and for some ρ, $(x, j) \, \tilde{R} \, (y, \rho(j))$, for all j. Then $\sum_i [U(x, i) - U(y, i)] = \sum_j [U(x, j) - U(y, \rho(j))] \geqq 0$. Hence, $x \, A \, y$. Further, if $x \, J \, y$, then for some j, $(x, j) \, \tilde{P} \, (y, \rho(j))$, and hence $x \, A \, y \;\&\; \sim (y \, A \, x)$.

Now, in terms of the model of Chapter 7* any U corresponds to a particular $W \in L$, so that $W_i(x) = U(x, i)$.

COROLLARY 9*7.1. *For any assumption of measurability and inter-*

personal comparability of individual welfare, if each $W \in \bar{L}$ is a real-valued representation of $\tilde{R}$, then O is a subrelation of R^a.

The proof is immediate from Theorem 9*7.

It is to be noted that the assumption of cardinality is not needed (see Section 7*4). Given strict ordinality, a given $\tilde{R}$ represents a complete interpersonal comparison of ordinal individual welfare levels. Given strict cardinality, however, a particular $\tilde{R}$ can coexist with $\bar{L}$ representing less than full comparability, since those interpersonal variations in origins and units are permitted which do not alter the ordering underlying U.

Chapter 10

MAJORITY CHOICE AND
RELATED SYSTEMS

10.1. The Method of Majority Decision

Of all the collective choice rules, the method of majority decision has perhaps been more studied than any other. As early as 1770, Borda was providing sophisticated studies of voting procedures, and by 1785 Condorcet had sized up many of the analytical problems of majority rule. In the nineteenth century, interest in majority decision widened, and studies of it attracted as diverse scholars as Laplace (1814) and Lewis Carroll (i.e., C. L. Dodgson (1876)).[1]

As a system, majority rule is used in various types of collective choices. It is easy to appreciate its wide appeal. As a CCR, it satisfies the Pareto principles (conditions P and P^*), unrestricted domain (condition U), nondictatorship (condition D), independence of irrelevant alternatives (condition I), neutrality (condition N), anonymity (condition A), positive responsiveness (condition S), and several other appealing conditions. Indeed, the MMD is the only decisive CCR satisfying these conditions (in fact, the only one satisfying conditions U, N, A and S), as was shown in Theorem 5*1.

The deficiencies of the MMD are also important. First, as was pointed out in Chapters 3 and 4, the MMD can lead to intransitivity and, furthermore, to a violation of acyclicity. The famous case of "paradox of voting" discussed in Chapter 3 is a simple example of this. As a SWF, or even as a SDF, it does not work for some configurations of individual preferences.

Second, it violates conditions L and L^*, and gives little scope for personal freedom. If a majority wants me to stand on my head

---

[1] On the history of studies of majority decision see Black (1958) and Riker (1961).

for two hours each morning, the MMD will make this a socially preferred state no matter how I view this exacting prospect. There are presumably areas of choice where even the most ardent supporter of majority rule will hesitate to recommend the MMD as the proper social decision procedure. But if MMD is to be applied for some choices and not for others, problems of inconsistency can arise in much the same way it arose in Chapter 6.[2] The use of one decision procedure for some choices and another for others raises serious problems of consistency. Of course, MMD itself may, on its own, lead to intransitivity and to violations of acyclicity, but its combination with other rules seems to add a new dimension to the problem. Nevertheless, such a hybrid procedure may be preferred by many to an uncompromising use of MMD in every sphere of social choice.

Third, the MMD takes no account of intensities of preference, and it is certainly arguable that what matters is not merely the *number* who prefer x to y and the *number* who prefer y to x, but also *by how much* each prefers one alternative to the other. As was noted in Chapter 8, bringing in cardinality without interpersonal comparability may not help much, but with some comparability (not necessarily much) a lot can be achieved. In Chapter 7, the procedure of aggregation, of which utilitarianism is a special case, was studied with very weak assumptions, and the aggregation procedure may be thought to be a serious rival to the MMD.

Finally, aside from ignoring relative intensities of preference, the MMD also ignores any possible comparison between absolute levels of welfare of different persons. It takes account of such judgments as "I would prefer to be in state x rather than in state y," but not of such judgments as "I would prefer to be Mr. A in state x rather than Mr. B in state y." This is an advantage from some points of view, especially since the latter kind of preferences are rather difficult to collect and work on for practical exercises in collective choice. On the other hand, this characteristic of MMD (and indeed of all CCR, being based on individual orderings R_i rather than on $\tilde{R}_i$) does distract from its attractiveness. The criteria that were discussed in Chapter 9 which incorporate notions of fairness and justice would run counter to the MMD.

As an institutional procedure the MMD has the virtue of making

---

[2] In fact, this is clear from Theorems 6*1–6*3, since the MMD subsumes the Pareto principle.

effective use of individual orderings in a world of imperfect communication.   Intensities of preference and relative measures of
well-being are difficult to handle in an interpersonal context, and
while our value judgments may make use of these concepts, they
are not easy to put together and operate on.   There are also practical difficulties in deciding which choices are really private and which
are the concern of others.   The MMD is a no-nonsense procedure
and ignores all these complications.   Making a virtue out of
independence of irrelevant alternatives, neutrality, and anonymity,
it takes the form of an uncomplicated institution.   While its gross-
ness jars somewhat, its simplicity, symmetry, and primitive logic
would seem to appeal to many.

10.2.   Probability of Cyclical Majorities

How serious is the problem of inconsistency of majority decision?
What is the probability of there being no "majority winner," i.e.,
there being no alternative that has a majority over every other
alternative in the set?   These are difficult questions to answer,
but there have been some attempts to tackle them.[3]   Guilbaud
(1952), Riker (1961), Campbell and Tullock (1965), (1966), Klahr
(1966), Williamson and Sargent (1967), Garman and Kamien (1968),
Niemi and Weisberg (1968), and De Meyer and Plott (1969), among
others, have provided extensive studies of this problem.

In all these calculations some assumptions must be made about
the probability distribution of different individual orderings for each
person.   One assumption is particularly simple and has attracted
many scholars, viz., that all orderings are equally likely for every
individual.[4]   Confining the analysis to strong orderings only,
Guilbaud (1952) calculated that the probability of cyclical majorities was only 8.77%.   Garman and Kamien (1968) and Niemi and
Weisberg (1968) have obtained an exact pattern of probability of
there being no majority winner as the number of voters is varied,
as shown in Table 10.1.   The table is based on there being three

---

[3] See Riker (1961) for a very fine review of problems of inconsistency under
majority rule.
[4] Garman and Kamien (1968) call this an "impartial culture," which seems
a somewhat inappropriate name for a dubious factual assumption.   In this
"impartial culture," given a two-alternative choice between my being beheaded
at dawn and my living on, the probability of my preferring either to the other
will be exactly one-half.   I protest.

Table 10.1. Probability of No Majority Winner for Three Alternatives

Number of persons	Probability	Number of persons	Probability
1	0.0000	17	0.0827
3	0.0556	19	0.0832
5	0.0694	21	0.0836
7	0.0750	23	0.0840
9	0.0780	25	0.0843
11	0.0798	...	...
13	0.0811	∞	0.0877
15	0.0820		

alternatives only, strict preferences of individuals and equiprobability.

It would be noted that the probability of an impasse, while never remarkably high, increases with the number of individuals involved. It increases rapidly to start with, but soon gets very insensitive; an increase in the number of voters from 9 to any figure must increase the probability of failure by less than 1%. Altogether, as Guilbaud had noted, there is less chance than 1 in 11 that no majority winner will emerge.

The probability of failure is, however, very sensitive to the number of alternatives. In Table 10.2 the probabilities of the absence of a majority winner are presented for different numbers of alternatives when the number of individuals is very large. The source is Niemi and Weisberg (1968).

It appears that as the number of alternatives goes up, the probability of cyclical majorities will rise towards 1.

This would appear to be a somewhat depressing fact. But it really is not, for the equiprobability assumption *is* a very special one, and seems to involve a denial of society, in a significant sense.

Table 10.2. Limiting Values of Probabilities of No Majority winner

Number of alternatives	Probability	Number of alternatives	Probability
1	0.0000	20	0.6811
2	0.0000	25	0.7297
3	0.0877	30	0.7648
4	0.1755	35	0.7914
5	0.2513	40	0.8123
10	0.4887	45	0.8292
15	0.6087		

Depending on peoples' values and their personal and group interests there would be a fair amount of link-up between individual preferences. Individual preferences are determined not by turning a roulette wheel over all possible alternatives, but by certain specific social, economic, political, and cultural forces. This may easily produce some patterns in the set of individual preferences. The patterns need not, incidentally, be one of agreement. Sharp disagreements may produce consistent and transitive majority decisions. For example, in a two-class society where "class war" takes the form that all members of one class (e.g., capitalists) have exactly the opposite preference to each member of the other class (e.g., workers), majority decision must be transitive, irrespective of the number of people in each class.[5] Even in the absence of such a sharp contrast, there are patterns of individual preference which will avoid inconsistency of choice.[6]

Taking any probability distribution over possible orderings (not necessarily assuming equiprobability), Garman and Kamien (1968) and Niemi and Weisberg (1968) have obtained general expressions for the probability of there being no majority winner.[7] The results are, however, difficult to interpret. The probability distributions are supposed to apply to all individuals without difference, but depending on the nature of the social alternatives and variations of such things as tastes, class backgrounds, etc., of different individuals, the individuals' probability distributions may really differ substantially. These and other questions of appropriate choice of assumptions are not easy to answer for these probabilistic models.[8]

---

[5] Cultures where the probability of cyclical majorities is greater than under equiprobability ("impartial culture") are called "antagonistic" by Garman and Kamien (1968), p. 314. This is misleading, since antagonism between two classes can make majority rule vigorously consistent.

[6] We discuss these in the next section. On the probability line, an important approach is that of Williamson and Sargent (1967), whereby a slight link-up between the preferences of the different individuals is shown to produce a high probability of transitivity. The definition of slightness remains, however, problematic.

[7] If s_t is the probability that a person will select ordering t, r_t a random variable representing the number of individuals choosing ordering t, in a society of m individuals and n alternatives, the probability p of no majority winner is given by

$$p = \sum_{r \in R} \binom{m}{r_1, r_2, \ldots, r_n!} \prod_{t=1}^{n!} s_t^{r_t}$$

[8] See footnote 6 in Niemi and Weisberg (1968), p. 318. Also Klahr (1966), pp. 385-386.

There is also a fundamental question of motivation and interpretation. It is not altogether clear what a probability distribution of individual orderings stands for. Are these *subjective probabilities* of some outside observer who knows the social states and the individuals, but not their orderings? Or are these *frequencies* of different types of orderings turning up in different periods in the same society or in different societies? If we take the latter interpretaion, in what sense does the set of alternatives remain the same while orderings on them vary, since the set of available choices will change over time and from society to society? If we take the former interpretation, presumably much will depend on the observer's sources of information and indeed on his attitude towards ignorance and uncertainty (e.g., his acceptance or rejection of the principle of "insufficient reason").

A more well-defined and precisely relevant question is to ask: Given the variations over time (between now and period T) of the set of available alternatives X, of the set of individuals H, and of the set of individual orderings (R_i) defined over X by each i in H, for each time period, in what proportion of the cases will the MMD fail to yield a majority winner and in what proportion of the cases will it succeed, between now and period T? It is reasonable to be interested in getting an answer to this question before recommending (or rejecting) the MMD for such a society, but it is not a question that can be answered in terms of the probability formulations over a given set of alternatives for a given set of individuals. However, an extension of these studies to include changes over time (or between societies) of individuals, alternatives, and ordering patterns, is not easy to make, and will require a great deal more empirical study than one can foresee in the subject in the near future.

The probability calculations reported earlier are, however, relevant to the more limited problem of getting an observer's subjective probability of cyclical majorities. This is not to be lightly dismissed, for it certainly may facilitate rational thinking about CCRs, but the relatively limited nature of the exercise should be kept in view.

10.3. Restricted Preferences

An alternative approach to the problem of cyclical majorities was initiated by Black (1948) and Arrow (1951). They demonstrated that if the set of individual preferences satisfy a certain unimodal pattern, which they called "single-peaked preference," then majority decisions must be transitive irrespective of the number of individuals holding any of the possible orderings, provided the total number of persons is odd. The approach makes use of the qualitative pattern of preferences, rather than of a distribution of numbers (unlike the probability approach).

Single-peakedness is a characteristics with a certain amount of political rationality. If individuals classify alternatives in terms of some one dimension (e.g., how "left-wing" is the alternative), and in any pair-wise choice, vote for that alternative which is closer to one's own position, then the individual preference pattern is single-peaked. For example, consider a choice between EL (extreme left). ML (moderate left), JL (just left of center), DC (dead center), JR (just right of center), MR (moderate right), and ER (extreme right). An extreme leftist will order them (in decreasing order) as: EL, ML, JL, DC, JR, MR, ER. An extreme rightist will have the ordering: ER, MR, JR, DC, JL, ML, EL. A dead-centerist will have an ordering which will incorporate two chains, viz., DC, JR, MR, ER, and DC, JL, ML, EL. Similarly, a just-leftist will subscribe to two chains, viz., JL, DC, JR, MR, ER, and JL, ML, EL. And so on. If the number of voters is odd, then irrespective of the total number involved and irrespective of the distribution of that total over the spectrum, majority decisions will be transitive.

The graphic aspect of the expression single-peaked can be understood by arranging the alternatives on a left-right horizontal line and having peoples' welfare levels, or utilities, represented on the vertical axis. All the utility curves will then look single-peaked.

While this bit of pictography may be helpful, some warnings are due. First, even if no utility representation of individual preferences are possible, they can still be single-peaked, because single-peakedness is a property of a set of orderings and not of utility functions. Second, it should be obvious that single-peakedness does not repuire that any arbitrarily chosen way of arranging the alternatives on the horizontal axis will make the utility curves of each uni-modal, but that there *exists* at least one method of sequencing them such that the utility curves will be uni-modal.[9] Third, strictly speaking it is not necessary that all alternatives be arrangeable in a single-peaked manner, but that

---

[9] There will, in fact, be two possible arrangements whenever there is one since uni-modality is direction-independent, and an exact reversing of the arrangement will do as well. For an analysis of single-peakedness in terms of "unfolding theory," see Coombs (1964), Chaps. 9 and 19.

every set of three alternatives ("triples") be so arrangeable. The latter is a weaker condition and is sufficient for the result. Finally, single-peakedness as defined by Arrow (1951) permits one flat portion in the utility curve under certain circumstances. So the nature of the graph is really somewhat more complex than one might be tempted to think.

The real condition is that if x, y, z is a right way of arranging three alternatives, then anyone who finds x at least as good as y, must find y strictly better than z. Similarly, anyone who finds z at least as good as y, must prefer y to x. This is, of course, equivalent to y being not worst according to any, i.e., everyone prefers y to either of the other two alternatives. Depending on other arrangements, viz., (y, z, x) and (z, x, y), single-peakedness will amount to z being not worst and x being not worst, respectively.[10] Thus, single-peakedness is equivalent to the characteristic of a partial agreement, viz., everyone agrees that some particular alternative is not worst in the triple.

This immediately raises the question: What about some alternative not being best, or some alternative not being medium, in anyone's preference ordering? These do equally well, and the generalized condition of "value restriction"[11] requires that all agree that some alternative is not best, or all agree that some alternative is not worst, or all agree that some alternative is not medium in anyone's ranking in the triple. If value restriction (hereafter, VR) holds for every triple, then majority rule will be transitive if the number of voters is odd. It is not necessary that the same subclass of VR holds for each triple. In some triple some alternative may be "not best," in another some alternative may be "not worst," in a third triple some alternative may be "not medium," and so on, and transitivity will still hold. In fact a further weakening of the condition is possible. While persons indifferent over all three alternatives in a triple violate value restriction, they really cause no serious problem for transitivity. So indifferences over entire triples (i.e., "unconcerned" individuals) are permitted and all that is needed is that the number of "concerned" individuals be odd.

---

[10] This exhausts all possibilities, since uni-modality with (z, y, x), (x, z, y) and (y, x, z) are exactly equivalent, respectively, to uni-modality with the three arrangements mentioned.

[11] Sen (1966). See also Vickrey (1960), Inada (1964), Ward (1965) and Majumdar (1969).

This requirement of oddness is, however, disturbing and unattractive. One might think that it would not matter too much if one of the voters could be elevated to an impotent chairmanship should the number of voters be even; but this is no good since the social preference will depend on precisely *who* is chosen for powerless glory. The restriction of oddness *is* serious, and is not easy to dismiss.

Fortunately it can be shown that the oddness restriction is unnecessary if we are interested in generating a social choice function and not a social ordering, i.e., if the MMD is to be a SDF and not a SWF.[12] As long as every triple satisfies VR, majority decisions will be quasi-transitive, irrespective of the number of individuals involved, and hence there will be a best alternative in every subset of alternatives. In fact it can also be shown that if individual orderings are strict (i.e., anti-symmetric), value restriction being satisfied for each triple is the necessary and sufficient condition for the MMD to be a SDF (Theorem 10*8; on the concept of "necessity" see Definition 10*9).

When, however, individual orderings are not necessarily strict, then there are conditions other than value restriction that may work. One such condition is "limited agreement,"[13] which requires that everyone agrees that some alternative (say x) is at least as good as some alternative (say y) in each triple. A third condition is "extremal restriction" (Sen and Pattanaik (1969)), which demands that if someone prefers x to y and y to z, then z is uniquely best in someone's ordering if and only if x is uniquely worst in his ordering.

Limited agreement (or LA) is easy to follow, but some explanatory remarks on extremal restriction (or ER) are in order. Extremal restriction subsumes various interesting cases. First, it covers what Inada (1969) calls "echoic preferences," viz., that if anyone strictly prefers x to y and y to z, then no one strictly prefers z to x. It also covers Inada's "antagonistic preferences," whereby if someone prefers x to y and y to z, then everyone else either has this particular ordering, or holds to its opposite (viz., preferring z to y and y to x), or finds x and z to be equally good. Finally, it covers Inada's "dichotomous preferences," viz., every individual is indifferent

---

[12] Theorem VIII in Sen (1969). This result also occurs in the proof of Theorem I in Pattanaik (1968). Fishburn (1970) has generalized this result for individual preferences that are themselves quasi-transitive.

[13] This is a weakened varsion of Inada's (1969) "taboo preferences"; see Sen and Pattanaik (1969).

between at least one pair of alternatives (not necessarily the same pair for each individual) in each triple.

It can be shown that if any triple satisfies ER, then the social preference generated by MMD must be fully transitive over it. If a triple satisfies LA, then the majority preference relation will be quasi-transitive. In fact, it can also be demonstrated that satisfying either VR, LA or ER, in each triple is the necessary and sufficient condition for majority decision to be a SDF (Theorem 10*6; also Sen and Pattanaik (1969)). And as far as a SWF is concerned, i.e., generating a social ordering rather than a social choice function, the necessary and sufficient condition is that each triple must satisfy ER (Theorem 10*7; also Inada (1969) and Sen and Pattanaik (1969)).

These results clear up the extent to which qualitative patterns (as opposed to numerical distributions) of individual preferences can guarantee transitivity of the majority relation and the existence of a majority winner in each subset.[14] If these conditions are satisfied, then irrespective of the number distribution of individual preferences, rational social choice through majority rule will be possible. If by rational choice we mean the existence of a best alternative in each set (satisfying property α), then anyone of ER, VR and LA, will do. However, if we also want property β to be satisfied, then we must want a social ordering, so that we must demand ER. The question of the necessity of property β, which we found in Chapter 4 to be important for Arrow's general possibility theorem, is crucial also for rational choice through the MMD.

It is worth emphasizing that the patterns of individual preferences that are sufficient to avoid intransitivity or acyclicity do not require uniformity in any strict sense. Antagonism of various types are tolerated and, in fact, of certain types will lead gloriously to the fulfillment of VR or ER. Limited agreement requires some uniformity, but only over one pair in each triple. Value restriction

---

[14] This is a somewhat more demanding requirement than the existence of a majority winner for the entire set only, as in the exercise by Garman and Kamien (1968), and Niemi and Weisberg (1968). Pattanaik (1968) has shown that if all triples consisting of only *Pareto-optimal alternatives* are value restricted, then there is a majority winner. Extending this result, it is shown in Sen and Pattanaik (1969) that if all triples consisting of Pareto-optimal alternatives satisfy *either* VR *or* ER, then a majority winner must exist.

requires agreement about some alternative's relative position, but in a very weak sense. People may disagree as to whether x is best or is worst, but as long as they agree that it is not medium, it will do. Similarly, they may agree that some alternative is not best (or not worst), but no more. Extremal restriction permits a wide variety of relations, viz., "echoic" (partly similar), "antagonistic" (sharply opposite), or "dichotomonus" (just requiring one indifference for all in each triple, but not necessarily indifference between the *same* two alternatives).

Nevertheless, these conditions must be recognized to be fairly restrictive. and these restrictions may or may not be satisfied by specific societies. This is a question for empirical investigation. It would appear that in many economic problems of distribution and allocation none of the conditions will work in the absence of externalities.[15] For example, the division of a homogeneous cake between three persons with each person concerned only about his own share of the cake will beat all the conditions and produce cyclical majorities. One of the objectives in obtaining the necessary and sufficient conditions for rational choice under majority decision is to motivate purposive research on actual patterns of preferences.

10.4. Conditions on Collective Choice Rules and Restricted Preferences

It was noted in Chapter 5 that the MMD is the only decisive CCR with an unrestricted domain satisfying conditions *I*, *N*, *A* and *S*. It is interesting to ask whether the conditions on individual preferences, e.g., VR, ER or LA, that are sufficient for rational choice under the MMD, are also sufficient for collective choice rules that satisfy some but not all of these five conditions. This way the results can be generalized for wider classes of CCRs.

It is shown in Chapter 10* that any decisive CCR that is independent of irrelevant alternatives and neutral (N), and nonnegatively responsive (R), must yield a quasi-transitive social preference rela-

---

[15] This is, however, not a great tragedy since the MMD is, in any case, an unsatisfactory basis for distributional decisions as it ignores preference intensities and avoids interpersonal comparisons (cf. Chapters 7 and 7*). The main appeal of the MMD is for political choices over a few fixed packages (e.g., party programs) with distributional questions thoroughly mixed up with other issues.

tion if individual preferences are value restricted for each triple. Thus, VR works for a wide class of collective choice rules, e.g., two-thirds majority rule,[16] many-staged majority decisions,[17] strict majority rule,[18] semistrict majority rule.[19] Similarly, LA works for any decisive CCR that is independent of irrelevant alternatives and neutral (N), nonnegatively responsive (R), and Pareto-inclusive (P^*). This too will apply to many CCRs, though not to all for which VR will work.

On the other hand, ER is not easily extendable to other collective choice rules. A CCR may be neutral (N), anonymous (A), nonnegatively responsive (R), and Pareto-inclusive (P^*), but still violate quasi-transitivity for individual preferences satisfying ER. If we strengthen nonnegative responsiveness (R) to make it positive responsiveness (S), then we shall simply be back to the MMD.

We can, in some sense, get intermediate positions and in fact semistrict majority rule permits us to get indefinitely close to the MMD, but as long as the CCR is not exactly the MMD, extremal restriction does not even guarantee quasi-transitivity (Theorem 10*5). But once we take the MMD, ER is sufficient for full transitivity. Extremal restriction seems to be cut out precisely for majority decisions. In this it differs sharply from value restriction and limited agreement.

---

[16] This CCR is widely used. To generate a complete ordering we may define that x is at least as good as y if and only if y is not preferred to x by a two-thirds majority.

[17] This includes representative democracy if the elected representative will represent the majority views of his constituents. See Murakami (1966), (1968), and Pattanaik (1968b).

[18] This is defined to mean that x is preferred to y if and only if it is not the case that at least 50% of all persons (and not merely of the nonindifferent ones) prefer y to x.

[19] This is a mixture of majority rule and strict majority rule. See Definition 10*7.

Chapter 10*

RESTRICTED PREFERENCES AND RATIONAL CHOICE

10*1. Restricted Domain

Black (1948) and Arrow (1951) have noted that if individual preferences have a certain pattern of "similarity," then the MMD will yield transitive results. This amounts to a relaxation of condition U as applied to CCRs. The consequences of relaxing the condition of unrestricted domain by considering restrictions on the patterns of individual orderings are investigated in this chapter. The problem is interpreted more broadly than by Black (1948) and Arrow (1951) in three respects.[1] First, we are interested not merely in the transitivity of social preference, but also in generating a social choice function, i.e., we are interested in the MMD as a SDF and not merely in it as a SWF. Second, MMD has certain properties, e.g., neutrality, as was noted in Chapter 5*. Some of the sufficiency conditions for majority decision are, in fact, sufficiency conditions for a wider class of collective choice rules satisfying a few but not all of the properties of the MMD. We study the sufficiency conditions in this more general setting. Third, for a certain class of restrictions, we identify the necessary and sufficient conditions for rational choice under the MMD.

Before some restrictions are specified, it will be covenient to separate out those persons who are indifferent between all the alternatives, for they introduce peculiar logical problems.

DEFINITION 10*1. *A concerned individual for a set of alternatives is one who is not indifferent between every pair of elements in the set.*

We now define three specific restrictions.

---

[1] This chapter relies heavily on Sen (1966), (1969), and Sen and Pattanaik (1969).

DEFINITION 10*2.   *Value restriction (VR):*[2] *In a triple* (x, y, z) *there is some alternative, say* x, *such that all the concerned individuals agree that it is not worst, or agree that it is not best, or agree that it is not medium, i.e., for all concerned* i:

$$[\forall i: x\,P_i\,y \lor x\,P_i\,z] \lor [\forall i: y\,P_i\,x \lor z\,P_i\,x]$$
$$\lor\,[\forall i: (x\,P_i\,y \ \& \ x\,P_i\,z) \lor (y\,P_i\,x \ \& \ z\,P_i\,x)]$$

DEFINITION 10*3.   *Extremal restriction (ER):*[3] *If for an ordered triple* (x, y, z), *there is someone who prefers* x *to* y *and* y *to* z, *then anyone regards* z *to be uniquely best if and only if he regards* x *to be uniquely worst, i.e.,*

$$(\exists i: x\,P_i\,y \ \& \ y\,P_i\,z) \to (\forall j: z\,P_j\,x \to z\,P_j\,y \ \& \ y\,P_j\,x)$$

A triple satisfies ER if and only if the above condition holds for every ordered triple obtainable from that triple.

DEFINITION 10*4.   *Limited agreemet (LA):*[4] *In a triple there is an ordered pair* (x, y) *such that everyone regards* x *to be at least as good as* y, *i.e.,* $\forall i: x\,R_i\,y$.

We shall refer to the number of individuals for whom $x\,P_i\,y$ as $N(x\,P\,y)$, the number for whom $x\,R_i\,y$ as $N(x\,R\,y)$, the number for whom $x\,P_i\,y$ & $y\,R_i\,z$ as $N(x\,P\,y\,R\,z)$, and so on.

Certain preliminary results are recorded next.

LEMMA 10*a.   *ER, VR and LA are comletely independent of each other, i.e., any pair of these three could be satisfied without the third, and any one of these could be satisfied without the remaining pair.*

Proof.   The proof follows from the following six examples:
(1) $x\,P_1\,y\,P_1\,z$
       $z\,P_2\,y\,P_2\,x$
       $y\,P_3\,x\,I_3\,z$
       $x\,I_4\,z\,P_4\,y$
ER is satisfied, but VR and LA are violated by this set of in-

---

[2] In Sen (1966) value restriction was defined as a condition on the preferences of *all* individuals, concerned or unconcerned, but in the "possibility theorem on value-restricted preferences" it was shown that it was sufficient to apply the restriction only to the concerned individuals.   Here value restriction is defined in such a manner that only concerned individuals are involved.

[3] See Sen and Pattanaik (1969).   See also Inada (1969).

[4] This is a weaker version of "taboo preference" of Inada (1969).   See Sen and Pattanaik (1969).

dividual preference patterns.

(2) $x P_1 y P_1 z$
 $z P_2 x P_2 y$

ER is violated, but VR and LA are both satisfied.

(3) $x P_1 y P_1 z$
 $z P_2 y P_2 x$
 $y P_3 z P_3 x$

VR is satisfied, but ER and LA are violated.

(4) $x P_1 y P_1 z$
 $y P_2 z I_2 x$
 $z I_3 x P_3 y$

VR is violated, but ER and LA are both satisfied.

(5) $x P_1 y P_1 z$
 $y P_2 z P_2 x$
 $x P_3 y I_3 z$
 $x I_4 y P_4 z$
 $y I_5 z P_5 x$

LA is satisfied, but ER and VR are violated.

(6) $x P_1 y P_1 z$
 $z P_2 y P_2 x$

LA is violated, but ER and VR are both satisfied.
The next result concerns the joint denial of VR, ER and LA.

LEMMA 10*b. *If a set of orderings over a triple violates VR, ER and LA, then there is a subset of three orderings in that set which itself violates VR, ER and LA.*

Proof. Over a triple, x, y, z, there are thirteen logically possible orderings, and there are 8192 ($= 2^{13}$) different subsets of the set of these thirteen orderings, of which one is empty. We label these orderings in a special manner for convenience, and drop subscript i in the preference relation, e.g., P is written for P_i, on grounds of aesthetics and convenience.

(1.1) $x P y P z$	(1.2) $x P y I z$	(1.3) $x I y P z$
(2.1) $y P z P x$	(2.2) $y P z I x$	(2.3) $y I z P x$
(3.1) $z P x P y$	(3.2) $z P x I y$	(3.3) $z I x P y$
(4) $x P z P y$	(5) $z P y P x$	(6) $y P x P z$
(7) $x I y I z$		

If ER is to be violated, at least one of these orderings must be a chain, i.e., satisfy anti-symmetry. Without loss of generality, ordering 1.1 is chosen, i.e., $x\,P\,y\,P\,z$. It may first be noted that there is no other ordering which, when combined with 1.1, will form a pair that violates VR and LA. Hence, the smallest set of orderings that violate VR, ER and LA, must have at least three elements.

It is easy to check that the only three-ordering sets inclusive of 1.1 that violate VR are given by [1.1, 2.1 or 2.2 or 2.3, 3.1 or 3.2 or 3.3]. There are nine such sets. Each of these violates ER, and only one satisfies LA, viz., [1.1, 2.2, 3.3], where $x\,R_i\,z$ for all i. There are, thus, eight three-ordering sets that violate VR, ER and LA, and this class of eight sets we call Ω.

Next, consider sets inclusive of 1.1, but having more than three orderings that violate VR, ER and LA. If these sets include any member of Ω, then the result follows immediately. It is easily checked that in order to violate VR without including any member of Ω, a set of orderings inclusive of 1.1 must include at least one of the following four-ordering sets:[5]

(I) 1.1, 1.2, 1.3, 2.3   (III) 1.1, 1.2, 2.2, 2.3

(II) 1.1, 1.2, 1.3, 3.2   (IV) 1.1, 1.3, 3.2, 3.3

None of these four-ordering sets, it may be noted, violates LA. For example, $y\,R\,z$ holds in every ordering in I. To include an ordering with $z\,P\,y$, either (a) we must include 3.1, 3.2, or 3.3, in which case the set will then include some member of Ω, or (b) we must include ordering 4 or 5, in which case again the set can be seen to include some member of Ω except for formal interchange of y and z, and of x and z, respectively. Similarly, II lacks $y\,P\,x$ III lacks $z\,P\,y$, and IV lacks $y\,P\,x$, and in each case the inclusion of any ordering filling this gap brings in some member of Ω. This establishes the lemma.

10*2. Value Restriction and Limited Agreement

First, we present a mundane but useful lemma involving value restriction.

---

[5] This might appear to be not so if we include ordering 4 or 5 or 6, e.g., [1.1, 4, 5 or 3.2 or 2.3, 6 or 2.2 or 1.3]. But the last three elements of each of these possibilities do form a member of Ω except for the substitution of x and y, or y and z, or z and x.

LEMMA 10*c.   *If a set of individual preferences is value restricted over a triple (x, y, z), at least one of equations (1), (2) and (3), and at least one of equations (4), (5) and (6) hold:*

(1) $N(x I y I z) = N(x R y R z)$ (4) $N(x I y I z) = N(y R x R z)$

(2) $N(x I y I z) = N(y R z R x)$ (5) $N(x I y I z) = N(x R z R y)$

(3) $N(x I y I z) = N(z R x R y)$ (6) $N(x I y I z) = N(z R y R x)$

Proof. Suppose x is not best. Then those who hold $(x R_i y \ \& \ y R_i z)$, or $(x R_i z \ \& \ z R_i y)$ must be unconcerned. Hence, (1) and (5) hold. Similarly, (2) and (4) hold if y is not best, and (3) and (6) hold if z is not best. Similarly, it is checked that if one of the alternatives is not worst, or not medium, at least two of conditions (1)–(6) must hold, one from (1)–(3), and one from (4)–(6).

THEOREM 10*1.   *If a decisive collective choice rule is independent of irrelevant alternatives and neutral (N), and nonnegatively responsive (R), and if individual preferences are value-restricted over a triple, then the rule must yield social preference relations that are all quasi-transitive over that triple.*

Proof. If quasi-transitivity is violated over a triple (x, y, z), then for some one-to-one correspondence between (x, y, z) and (u, v, w) we must have $u P v$, $v P w$ and $w R u$. It is now shown that if one of the equations (1)–(3) and one of (4)–(6) of Lemma 10*3 hold, then this configuration is impossible.

First consider (1). We can check that

$$(1) \to \forall i: \{ \sim(x I_i y I_i z) \to \sim(x R_i y \ \& \ y R_i z)\}$$
$$\to \forall i: \{\sim(x I_i y I_i z)$$
$$\to [(x R_i y \to z P_i y) \ \& \ (y R_i z \to y P_i x)]\}$$
$$\to \forall i: \{[(x P_i y \to z P_i y) \ \& \ (x I_i y \to z R_i y)]$$
$$\& \ [(y P_i z \to y P_i x) \ \& \ (y I_i z \to y R_i x)]\}$$
$$\to [(x R y \to z R y) \ \& \ (y R z \to y R x)]$$

by neutrality and nonnegative responsiveness,[6]

$$\to [(x R y \ \& \ y R z \ \& \ z R x) \to (x I y \ \& \ y I z)]$$

---

[6] This is easily checked. If $(x P_i y \leftrightarrow z P_i y) \ \& \ (x I_i y \leftrightarrow z I_i y)$, then by neutrality, $(x P y \to z P y) \ \& \ (x I y \to z I y)$. Therefore, if $(x P_i y \to z P_i y) \ \& \ (x I_i y \to z R_i y)$, then by nonnegative responsiveness, $(x P y \to z P y) \ \& \ (x I y \to z R y)$, so that $x R y \to z R y$. Similarly, $y R z \to y R x$.

Similarly,

$$(2) \rightarrow [(x\,R\,y\ \&\ y\,R\,z\ \&\ z\,R\,x) \rightarrow (y\,I\,z\ \&\ z\,I\,x)]$$
$$(3) \rightarrow [(x\,R\,y\ \&\ y\,R\,z\ \&\ z\,R\,x) \rightarrow (z\,I\,x\ \&\ x\,I\,y)]$$

Thus, if at least one of the three implications (1), (2) or (3) holds, then it is impossible to have $u\,P\,v$, $v\,P\,w$ and $w\,R\,u$, assigning (u, v, w) as (x, y, z), or as (y, z, x), or as (z, x, y). Similarly, if one of (4), (5) or (6) holds, then $u\,P\,v$, $v\,P\,w$ and $w\,R\,u$ is impossible for the assignments of (u, v, w) as (y, x, z), or as (x, z, y), or as (z, y, x). But there is no other possible assignment. Hence, if value restriction is satisfied by individual preferences over every triple, then the social preference relation must be quasi-transitive for every triple.

THEOREM 10*2.   *If a decisive collective choice rule is independent of irrelevant alternatives and neutral* (N), *nonnegatively responsive* (R), *and satisfies the strong Pareto criterion* (P^*), *then it must yield a quasi-transitive preference relation over a triple if individual preferences satisfy limited agreement over that triple.*

Proof.   Let x, y, z be any triple. Without loss of generality, let $\forall i: x\,R_i\,y$. Hence, $\forall i: (y\,P_i\,z \rightarrow x\,P_i\,z)\ \&\ (y\,I_i\,z \rightarrow x\,R_i\,z)$, so that be neutrality and nonnegative responsiveness,[7] we have $y\,R\,z \rightarrow x\,R\,z$. Similarly, $z\,R\,x \rightarrow z\,R\,y$. Thus, $(x\,R\,y\ \&\ y\,R\,z\ \&\ z\,R\,x) \rightarrow (x\,R\,y\ \&\ y\,I\,z\ \&\ x\,I\,z)$. Consider now the hypothesis $y\,R\,x$. Since $\forall i: x\,R_i\,y$, clearly the strong Pareto criterion implies that $\forall i: x\,I_i\,y$. Hence,

$$y\,R\,x \rightarrow \forall i: \{[(x\,P_i\,z \rightarrow y\,P_i\,z)\ \&\ (x\,I_i\,z \rightarrow y\,I_i\,z)]\}$$
$$\&\ \forall i: \{[(z\,P_i\,y \rightarrow z\,P_i\,x)\ \&\ (z\,I_i\,y \rightarrow z\,I_i\,x)]\}$$
$$\rightarrow [(x\,R\,z \rightarrow y\,R\,z)\ \&\ (z\,R\,y \rightarrow z\,R\,x)]$$

Thus,

$$(y\,R\,x\ \&\ x\,R\,z\ \&\ z\,R\,y) \rightarrow (y\,R\,x\ \&\ x\,I\,z\ \&\ z\,I\,y)$$

Relation R cannot violate quasi-transitivity without at least one of the two "circles" $(x\,R\,y\ \&\ y\,R\,z\ \&\ z\,R\,x)$ or $(y\,R\,x\ \&\ x\,R\,z\ \&\ z\,R\,y)$ holding, and if either of them holds, then at least two indifferences must rule in this set of three relations. This means that violation of quasi-transitivity is impossible, which establishes the theorem.

---

[7] The reasoning is given in footnote 6.

We do not, of course, need a special proof of the sufficiency of VR and LA for the method majority decision.

THEOREM 10*3. *If individual preferences satisfy either VR or LA over each triple, then the method of majority decision is a SDF over a finite set of alternatives for every possible configuration of individual preferences.*

Proof. By Theorem 5*1, the MMD is a pair-wise-decisive collective choice rule which satisfies neutrality and positive responsiveness and, by Lemma 5*d, this means that it also satisfies the strong Pareto principle and nonnegative responsiveness. Hence, by Theorems 10*1 and 10*2, social preferences generated by the MMD must be quasi-transitive when individual preferences satisfy VR or LA over each triple. But then, by Lemma 1.k, each of the social preference relations generated by the MMD will yield a choice function. Hence the MMD is a social decision function over all possible sets of individual preferences.

10*3. Extremal Restriction

Extremal restriction is now shown to be sufficient for the transitivity of the majority preference relation R.

THEOREM 10*4. *All logically possible sets of individual preferences satisfying extremal restriction for any triple are in the domain of the majority-decision SWF over that triple.*

Proof. If every individual is indifferent between at least two alternatives in a triple, then ER will be fulfilled for that triple trivially. Transitivity is easily proved in this case. Of the thirteen possible orderings over a triple (x, y, z) recorded in the proof of Lemma 10*b, only seven include at least one indifference, viz., (1.2), (1.3), (2.2), (2.3), (3.2), (3.3), and (7). Referring to the number of individuals holding any of the respective preference orderings as $N(1.2)$, $N(1.3)$, etc., it is clear that

$$(x \, R \, y \,\, \& \,\, y \, R \, z)$$
$$\rightarrow [\{N(1.2) + N(3.3) - N(2.2) - N(2.3)\} \geq 0$$
$$\& \,\, \{N(1.3) + N(2.2) - N(3.2) - N(3.3)\} \geq 0]$$
$$\rightarrow \{N(1.2) + N(1.3) - N(2.3) - N(3.2)\} \geq 0$$
$$\rightarrow x \, R \, z$$

Similarly, $u \, R \, v$ & $v \, R \, w \rightarrow u \, R \, w$, for any one-to-one correspondence between (x, y, z) and (u, v, w).

We now consider nontrivial fulfillment of ER; let someone hold (1.1). Suppose that contrary to the theorem, ER holds over this triple, but majority decisions are still intransitive. We know then that exactly one of the following must be true: $[x \, R \, y, \, y \, R \, z, \, z \, R \, x]$, "the forward circle," and $[y \, R \, x, \, x \, R \, z, \, z \, R \, y]$, "the backward circle." Suppose the former holds. Since there is an individual such that $x \, P_i \, y \, P_i \, z$, we have:

$$z \, R \, x \rightarrow [N(z \, P \, x) \geq N(x \, P \, z)]$$
$$\rightarrow [N(z \, P \, x) \geq 1]$$
$$\rightarrow [\exists i : z \, P_i \, y \ \& \ y \, P_i \, x], \quad \text{by ER}$$

The last is a strict ordering over this triple, and applying ER once again, we are left only with a set of four orderings that satisfy ER, which are (1) $x \, P_i \, y \, P_i \, z$; (2) $z \, P_i \, y \, P_i \, x$; (3) $y \, P_i \, z \, I_i \, x$; and (4) $x \, I_i \, z \, P_i \, y$. Referring to the number of persons holding each of these orderings as N_1, N_2, N_3 and N_4, respectively, we obtain

$$(x \, R \, y \ \& \ y \, R \, z \ \& \ z \, R \, x) \rightarrow [\{N_1 + N_4 \geq N_2 + N_3\}$$
$$\& \ \{N_1 + N_3 \geq N_2 + N_4\} \ \& \ \{N_2 \geq N_1\}]$$
$$\rightarrow [\{N_1 = N_2\} \ \& \ \{N_3 = N_4\}]$$
$$\rightarrow (y \, R \, x \ \& \ x \, R \, z \ \& \ z \, R \, y)$$

Thus, the forward circle implies the backward circle, and intransitivity is impossible.

The only remaining possibility is that the backward circle holds alone.

$$(z \, R \, y \ \& \ y \, R \, x) \rightarrow [N(z \, P \, y) - N(x \, P \, y)] + [N(y \, P \, x) - N(y \, P \, z)] \geq 0$$
$$\rightarrow [N(z \, P \, y \, R \, x) - N(x \, P \, y \, R \, z)$$
$$+ \, N(z \, R \, y \, P \, x) - N(x \, R \, y \, P \, z)] \geq 0$$
$$\rightarrow N(z \, P \, y \, R \, x) + N(z \, R \, y \, P \, x) > 0$$

since $N(x \, P \, y \, R \, z) > 0$, as someone holds $x \, P_i \, y \, P_i \, z$ by assumption. Further, due to ER we must have

$$N(z \, P \, y \, I \, x) = N(z \, I \, y \, P \, x) = 0$$

Obviously, therefore, $N(z \, P \, y \, P \, x) > 0$.

Since we now know that someone holds $z\,P_i\,y\,P_i\,x$, in addition to someone holding $x\,P_i\,y\,P_i\,z$, the only permissible individual preference orderings are those numbered (1), (2), (3) and (4) above. The rest of the proof consists of showing that under these circumstances, the backward circle implies the forward circle, and it is omitted here since it is exactly similar to the proof of the converse given above. Thus, intransitivity is impossible if ER is fulfilled.

While ER is sufficient for transitivity of majority decision, it is not so for rules that lie indefinitely close to the MMD. Consider a decisive collective choice rule that satisfies conditions U, N, A and R. It falls short of being the MMD by virtue of the difference between R (nonnegative responsiveness) and S (positive responsiveness), as we know from Theorem 5*1. We may even go some of the way towards the MMD by imposing condition P^* as well. Can we get still closer to the MMD without going all the way?

An example of a decision rule that is neutral, anonymous, and nonnegatively responsive, is the following:

DEFINITION 10*5. *The strict majority rule:*

$$\forall x, y \in X: [N(x\,P\,y)/N] > \tfrac{1}{2} \leftrightarrow x\,P\,y$$

where N is the total number of individuals. Further, $x\,R\,y \leftrightarrow \sim(y\,P\,x)$.
The following lemma is immediate:

LEMMA 10*d. *If $x\,P\,y$ according to the strict majority rule, then $x\,P\,y$ according to the method of majority decision.*

In fact, it may be noted that $x\,P\,y$ under majority decision requires that $N(x\,P\,y)$ be larger than $\tfrac{1}{2}N^*$, where N^* is the number of nonindifferent individuals in the relation between x and y. Lemma 10*d thus follows simply from the fact that $N^* \leq N$.

We know that the strong Pareto criterion will be implied by positive responsiveness in the presence of neutrality by Lemma 5*d, but the converse does not hold. Since positive responsiveness will also usher in majority decision, given the other conditions, one way of moving towards majority decision without getting there is to incorporate the strong Pareto criterion as well. Consider a Pareto-inclusive version of the strict majority rule.

DEFINITION 10*6. *The Pareto-inclusive strict majority rule:* $\forall x, y \in X:\ x\,P\,y$ *if and only if* $[\{N(x\,P\,y)/N\} > \tfrac{1}{2}] \lor [\forall i:\ x\,R_i\,y\ \&\ \exists i:\ x\,P_i\,y]$. *Further, $x\,R\,y \leftrightarrow \sim(y\,P\,x)$.*
A continuum of group decision rules can now be defined, which

will lie intermediate between the strict majority rule (in either the Pareto-inclusive form or not) and the method of majority decision. We can require $N(x\,P\,y)$ to be greater than some convex combination of N and N^*.

DEFINITION 10*7.   *Semistrict majority rule:*

$$\forall x, y \in X:\ N(x\,P\,y)/[pN + (1 - p)N^*] > \tfrac{1}{2} \leftrightarrow x\,P\,y$$

for some given p chosen from the open interval $]0, 1[$. *Further,* $x\,R\,y \leftrightarrow \sim(y\,P\,x)$.

Clearly, if $p = 0$, then this is the majority rule, and if $p = 1$, then this is the strict majority rule.   However, since we confine p to the *open* interval $]0, 1[$, these possibilities are ruled out, though we can come indefinitely near either the majority rule, or the strict majority rule.

Since within the class of semistrict majority rule we can come indefinitely close to the method of majority decision, the question arises as to whether extremal restriction may be sufficient for some cases of semistrict majority rule.   It is now shown that ER is not sufficient for semistrict majority rule no matter how close we are to the method of majority decision.

THEOREM 10*5.   *Extremal restriction is not a sufficient condition for the quasi-transitivity of the semistrict majority rule over any triple no matter which p we select.*

Proof.   Since we are interested in the strong Pareto criterion also, we prove this theorem with a line of reasoning that will not be disturbed if we were to impose additionally Pareto-inclusiveness. Consider a triple x, y, z, and the following four individual preference orderings, which is a set that satisfies ER:

$$(1)\quad x\,P_i\,y\,P_i\,z \qquad (3)\quad y\,P_i\,z\,I_i\,x$$
$$(2)\quad z\,P_i\,y\,P_i\,x \qquad (4)\quad x\,I_i\,z\,P_i\,y$$

Let N_j be the number of individuals holding ordering j, for $j = 1$, 2, 3, 4.   Take $N_1 = 2$, $N_2 = 1$, and $N_3 = N_4 = q$, where q is a positive integer such that $0 < 1/q < p$.   It is easy to check that such a q always exists no matter how small $p > 0$ is.   By construction, $x\,P\,y$, $y\,P\,z$, and $x\,I\,z$, which violates quasi-transitivity.   This completes the proof.

We can, thus, get as close as we like to the majority rule, by taking p indefinitely close to 0, but ER remains insufficient. It is also clear that the Pareto criterion (weak or strict) will make no difference, since both are satisfied (trivially) by the group decisions specified above.

However, as soon as p instead of being close to 0 becomes 0, i.e., as soon as we have the method of majority decision, ER becomes a sufficient condition for not merely quasi-transitivity, but even for full transitivity, as shown in Theorem 10*4.

10*4. Necessary and Sufficient Conditions for Rational Choice

The necessary and sufficient conditions for deriving a social choice function or a social ordering through the method of majority decision for a finite set of alternatives are now derived. The definitions of sufficiency and necessity are first stated. Since these definitions will be applied to both SWF and SDF we shall refer to the domain of f, which will be interpreted appropriately in the respective cases.

DEFINITION 10*8. *A condition on the set of individual preferences is sufficient if every set of individual preferences satisfying this condition must be in the domain of f.*

DEFINITION 10*9. *A condition on the set of individual preferences is necessary if every violation of the condition yields a list of individual orderings such that some assignment of these orderings over some number of individuals[8] will make the individual preference pattern lie outside the domain of f.*

The definition of sufficiency was used by Arrow (1951), and that of necessity was first proposed by Inada (1969). These are not the only possible definitions of necessary and sufficient conditions, but they do make sense if restrictions have to be about the list of permissible orderings for individuals and not about the distribution of the number of individuals over possible orderings. If more than 50% of the concerned electors share the same chain, then no matter what orderings the others hold, majority decision will yield a social ordering. However, the restrictions that we consider are those that apply only to types of permissible preference orderings and not on numbers holding them.

---

[8] Each individual must have one and only one ordering, but any given ordering can, of course, be assigned to as many individuals as we like, or to none at all.

THEOREM 10*6.   *The necessary and sufficient condition for a set of individual orderings over a finite set of alternatives to be in the domain of the majority-decision SDF is that every triple of alternatives must satisfy at least one of the conditions VR, ER and LA.*

Proof.   Sufficiency of VR, LA and ER follows immediately from Theorem 10*1, 10*2 and 10*4.   We need concern ourselves only with necessity.

We know from Lemma 10*b that if a set of individual orderings violates VR, ER and LA, then that set must include a three-ordering subset, which also violates those three restrictions.   Further, from the proof we know that there are essentially eight three-ordering subsets[9] that violate VR, ER and LA, viz., [1.1, 2.1 *or* 2.2 *or* 2.3, 3.1 *or* 3.2 *or* 3.3], excluding [1.1, 2.2, 3.3], where

(1.1) $x P y P z$

(2.1) $y P z P x$ (2.2) $y P z I x$ (2.3) $y I z P x$

(3.1) $z P x P y$ (3.2) $z P x I y$ (3.3) $z I x P y$

We have to show that in each of these eight cases some assignment of these orderings over some number of individuals will produce a majority preference relation that does not yield a choice function.

First consider the cases represented by [1.1, 2.1 *or* 2.3, 3.1 *or* 3.2]. Let N_1 be the number of persons holding 1.1, N_2 the number holding 2.1 or 2.3, and N_3 the number holding 3.1 or 3.2.   If we assume $N_1 > N_2$, $N_1 > N_3$ and $(N_2 + N_3) > N_1$, then we must have $x P y$, $y P z$ and $z P x$.   A simple example is $N_1 = 3$, $N_2 = N_3 = 2$.

This leaves four cases.   Consider next the following two sets, viz., [1.1, 2.1 *or* 2.3, 3.3].   With the same convention on numbering, if we take $N_2 > N_1 > N_3$, and $N_1 + N_3 > N_2$, we have again $x P y$, $y P z$ and $z P x$.   A simple example is $N_1 = 3$, $N_2 = 4$ and $N_3 = 2$.   Finally, we take the cases given by [1.1, 2.2, 3.1 *or* 3.2]. Taking $N_3 > N_1 > N_2$ and $N_1 + N_2 > N_3$, we get $x P y$, $y P z$ and $z P x$, as for example with $N_1 = 3$, $N_2 = 2$ and $N_3 = 4$.   This completes the proof of necessity, which establishes the theorem.

Next the necessary and sufficient conditions for full transitivity of majority decisions are obtained.

---

[9] There are, in fact, forty-eight such subsets if we treat x, y and z as constants. But the remaining ones are all exactly like the one described below, but for the substitution of x for y; or y for z; or z for x; or y for x and z for y and x for z; or z for x and x for y and y for z.   Exactly the same analysis applies in each case.

THEOREM 10*7. *The necessary and sufficient condition for a set of individual orderings to be in the domain of the majority-decision SWF is that every triple of alternatives must satisfy extremal restriction.*

Proof. Consider the necessity of ER. Suppose ER is violated. This means that there is (say) some individual i such that $x P_i y P_i z$, while there is another whose preference satisfies *either* of the following patterns: (1) $z P_j x$, $z P_j y$ and $x R_j y$, or (2) $z P_j x$, $y P_j x$ and $y R_j z$. Let there be one individual i and one individual j. If j holds (1), then majority decision will yield $x P y$, $y I z$ and $x I z$, which implies a choice function but is not an ordering. Similarly, if j holds (2), then $x I y$, $y P z$ and $x I z$, which is also not an ordering. Hence the necessity of ER is proved. The sufficiency of ER has already been proved in Theorem 10*4 and the proof is now complete.

10*5. The Special Case of Anti-Symmetric Preferences

We may now consider a special case, viz., when individual preferences are chains, i.e., the orderings are anti-symmetric.

LEMMA 10*e. *If individual orderings are anti-symmetric, then $ER \rightarrow VR$ and $LA \rightarrow VR$.*

Proof. Suppose ER is satisfied over some triple. Since indifference is impossible, the case of trivial fulfillment of ER does not arise. Let us assume $x P_i y P_i z$ for some i. We know from ER that $\forall i: z P_i x \rightarrow z P_i y$ & $y P_i x$. If there is no individual such that $z P_i x$, then z is not best in anyone's ordering, since $\sim (z P_i x) \rightarrow x P_i z$, in the case of anti-symmetric ordering. In this case, VR holds. If, on the other hand, there is someone who holds $z P_i x$, and therefore $z P_i y P_i x$, then anyone holding $x P_i z$ must hold $x P_i y P_i z$ by ER. Since $\forall i: x P_i z \underline{\vee} z P_i x$, it follows that in this case $\forall i: \{x P_i y P_i z\} \underline{\vee} \{z P_i y P_i x\}$. Once again, VR is satisfied since y is not best (nor indeed worst) in anyone's ordering. Hence, $ER \rightarrow VR$.

Suppose LA is satisfied over some triple. Without loss of generality, let $x R_i y$ hold for all i, which in this case means $\forall i: x P_i y$. Hence, x is not worst (nor indeed is y best) in anyone's ordering. Thus VR holds, which completes the proof.

It may be noted that the converse does not hold. VR does not imply either ER or LA. This is readily checked by looking at the following configuration: $x P_1 y P_1 z$, $z P_2 y P_2 x$, and $y P_3 z P_3 x$. Both ER and LA are violated, but y is not worst in anyone's ordering, and hence VR holds.

The relevant theorems about the MMD as SDF and SWF, respectively, can now be derived for this special case.

THEOREM 10*8. *The necessary and sufficient conditions for a set of individual chains over a finite set of alternatives to be in the domain of the majority-decision SDF is that every triple must satisfy value restriction.*[10]

Proof. Since ER, VR and LA are sufficient for all individual orderings, strict or not, VR is clearly sufficient in the case of strict orderings. By Theorem 10*6, VR or ER or LA must hold for every triple as a necessary condition for the existence of a social choice function, and by Lemma 10*e if ER or LA holds, then so must VR, in the case of chains. Hence, VR is both sufficient *and* necessary.

THEOREM 10*9. *A necessary condition for a set of individual chains to be in the domain of a majority-decision SWF is that every triple of alternatives must satisfy value restriction, but it is not a sufficient condition.*

The proof of necessity is obvious from Theorem 10*7 and Lemma 10*e. The following example shows the insufficiency of VR: Let there be two individuals such that $x P_1 y P_1 z$ and $z P_2 x P_2 y$, which yields $x P y$, $y I z$ and $x I z$. Value restriction is satisfied, but there is an intransitivity.[11] Incidentally, the necessary and sufficient condition is still given by Theorem 10*7.

---

[10] This theorem holds even with the original definition of value restriction in Sen (1966), and not merely for the modified Definition 10*2 given above.

[11] It becomes also sufficient if the number of individuals is odd; see Sen (1966).

Chapter 11

THEORY AND PRACTICE

11.1. Systems of Collective Choice

It is clear that there are a number of radically different ways of basing social preference on the preferences of the members of the society. They differ from each other not merely in their exact procedures, but also in their general approach.

One particular approach has been formalized in the literature more than the others, and this is the case of a "social welfare function" in the sense of Arrow (1951), where a social ordering R is specified for every set of individual orderings (R_i). A somewhat more choice-oriented category is what we called a "social decision function," where a choice function is generated by a social preference relation R that is determined by the set of individual orderings (R_i). In general, a SWF is a special category of SDF, but there are exceptions.[1] In any case, if choice is our object, a SDF seems the appropriate starting point.

The demands of consistency of a SDF may be less than that of a SWF, and this affects various results, including the famous "impossibility" theorem of Arrow (Chapters 3 and 4). However, there are similar problems in combining different principles of choice even for a SDF (Chapters 4, 5, and 6). While social preferences need not be transitive and may satisfy merely quasi-transitivity, or acyclicity, SDFs still have difficulty in incorporating a set of reasonable looking conditions on collective choice. As it happens, some of these conditions are not really very reasonable, and the underlying conflicts can be clarified by taking different types of SDFs that bring out the precise properties of these conditions (Chapters 5 and 6).

---

[1] See Chapter 4. In this and subsequent references, the mention of an unstarred chapter should be taken to include a reference also to the corresponding starred chapter. The converse is, however, not intended.

Another approach is to demand less than a SDF, i.e., not to require that the social preference relation must generate a choice function. A quasi-ordering, which violates completeness but does give guidance to collective choice in many situations, is often helpful, since it may incorporate weaker (and more universally accepted) principles of collective choice, free from some of the maddening dilemmas. The alternatives are not all or none, and there are lots of reasonable intermediate possibilities (Chapters 7 and 9).

Individual preferences may also take different forms. Various collective choice systems are indeed based on more complete information on individual attitudes to social alternatives than will be conveyed by orderings only. Instead of orderings, utility functions may be used in an ordinal, or cardinal, form, or in some intermediate form which we categorized as ordinal-type (Chapter 7); and these utility, or welfare, measures can be used without interpersonal comparability (Chapter 8), or with it (Chapters 7 and 9). Further, comparability can be of various types, and under some assumptions a continuum of partial comparability of welfare units can be defined varying from noncomparability to complete comparability of units (Chapter 7).

Also, the concentration may not be on comparability of *units* of welfare, but of welfare *levels*. Instead of taking individual orderings R_i defined over social states ("I would prefer state x to state y"), collective choice may make use of individual orderings defined over the position of being any individual in any social state ("I would prefer to be Mr. A in state x rather than Mr. B in state y"). This permits the use of various criteria of fairness and justice (Chapter 9).

Diagram 11.1 gives a pictorial representation of different formulations of collective choice based on different types of information on individual preferences.[2] An arrow with a double head points to a special case, and a dotted line represents near equivalence in the sense that all collective choice systems that have been considered which belong to one category, also belong to the other.[3] Examples of each approach in terms of some well-known collective choice systems are noted in parentheses.

---

[2] The notation is as defined before, viz., R and R_i as in Chapter 2*, L and $\overline{L}$ as in Chapter 7*, and $\tilde{R}$ and $\tilde{R}_i$ as in Chapter 9*.

[3] This is, however, not necessarily so far all *conceivable* collective choice systems.

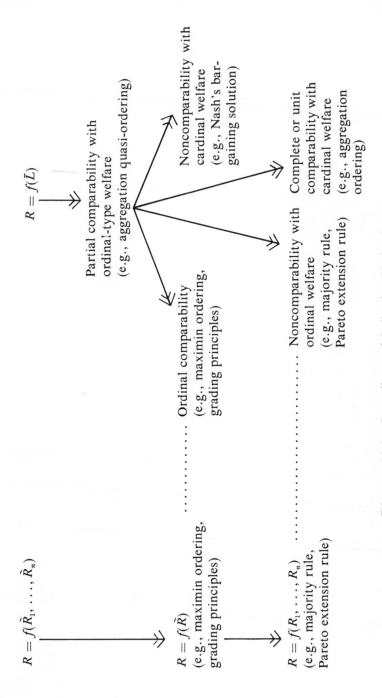

$R = f(\tilde{R}_1, \ldots, \tilde{R}_n)$

$R = f(\tilde{R})$
(e.g., maximin ordering,
grading principles)

$R = f(R_1, \ldots, R_n)$
(e.g., majority rule,
Pareto extension rule)

$R = f(\tilde{L})$

Partial comparability with
ordinal-type welfare
(e.g., aggregation quasi-ordering)

Ordinal comparability
(e.g., maximin ordering,
grading principles)

Noncomparability with
ordinal welfare
(e.g., majority rule,
Pareto extension rule)

Noncomparability with
cardinal welfare
(e.g., Nash's bar-
gaining solution)

Complete or unit
comparability with
cardinal welfare
(e.g., aggregation
ordering)

Diagram 11.1. Ingredients of Collective Choice Systems

The diagram should be clear from our preceding analysis. Two explanatory remarks may, however, be useful. First, it may not be obvious that making social preference R a function of the set of individual orderings $(R_1, \ldots, R_n)$ is a special case of basing it on an extended ordering $\tilde{R}$, but it is so. It is clear that in $(R_1, \ldots, R_n)$ we have n separate orderings of m elements, each defined over $(x_1, i), \ldots, (x_m, i)$ for each individual i, whereas an R is an ordering over all these mn elements (Chapter 9*). Hence, an $\tilde{R}$ contains *inter alia* such n orderings $(R_1, \ldots, R_n)$. Thus, basing social preference on $(R_1, \ldots, R_n)$ is a special case of basing it on $\tilde{R}$, since the former type of information is contained in the latter.[4]

Second, basing social preference on the set of individual orderings is not precisely the same thing as basing it on the set of individual ordinal utility functions with noncomparability, since not all orderings are representable even by an ordinal utility. However, they are more or less equivalent for our purpose, since we did not consider any collective choice system that makes essential use of noncomparable ordinal representations of individual preference. The same applies to the near-equivalence of basing social preference on $\tilde{R}$ and basing it on ordinally comparable individual utility functions.[5]

11.2. Institutions and Framework

While there are such wide varieties of approaches to collective choice, part of the variation simply reflects the different fields or contexts in which problems of collective choice arise. The problem may be one of choosing an institutional mechanism of decision taking, e.g., elections based on the majority rule or the rank-order method. Or it may be a problem faced by an individual, or a group, or a party, in making its own recommendations for social choice based on individual preferences. While calculations of the type involved in $\tilde{R}_i$ may be difficult to use in purely institutional mechanisms, for which it is easier to concentrate on the set of R_i,

---

[4] Further, if the identity axiom is assumed, then *every* individual $\tilde{R}_i$ will incorporate the entire set $R_1, \ldots, R_n$ (Chapter 9*).

[5] This is not strictly right, since ordinal interpersonal comparability may go with personal cardinal measurement, and we can then make some use of cardinality (e.g., in using Nash's (1950) bargaining solution, or solutions of Raiffa (1953) or Braithwaite (1955)).

it may be quite appropriate to bring in $\tilde{R}_i$ in making recommendations.

Similarly, it may be difficult to find a means of reflecting cardinal welfare measures of individuals in a purely institutionalized choice system, but it may be quite possible for a planner to base his policy recommendations on his evaluation of *aggregate* gains and losses for the nation as a whole. This is especially so with systems that permit a considerable latitude in aggregation, e.g., with "partial comparability" (Chapter 7). A planner may find it convenient in making up his mind to specify a subset $\bar{L}$ in L, whereas it may be impossible to devise a satisfactory mechanical procedure for specifying $\bar{L}$ for a purely institutionalized choice.

The existence of great varieties of collective choice procedures is, therefore, somewhat illusory. They may be relevant to different types of collective choice exercises. Since the field is so vast, it may indeed be useful to list a few different types of exercises that all come under the broad hat of the theory of collective choice, but which differ essentially from each other.

(1) *Institutional mechanisms* of social choice are based on some theory of collective choice. For example, the use majority rule will imply some implicit attachment to principles of anonymity, neutrality, and positive responsiveness (Chapter 5).[6] Similarly, a complete adherence to a free market system in the absence of externalities may be justified on grounds of Pareto optimality and to require no more than that may involve the implicit use of the Pareto extension rule, with its implied principles (Chapter 5). Similarly, social institutions may include provisions for individual freedom for certain choices in the lines of condition L (Chapter 6).

(2) *Planning decisions*, typically taken by a committee responsible to some political body (e.g., a parliament), require some theories of relating goals of planning to individual preferences. Criteria like the aggregation rule (Chapter 7), or the maximin rule (Chapter 9), may be used implicitly or explicitly. Concern for "aggregate welfare," or for "welfare of the worst-off group," is quite common in public policy, even though the exercise may not usually be carried out very systematically.

(3) In making *social criticism*, or in *arguing on social policy*, one has to evaluate systems of collective choice. *Conditions* on collec-

---

[6] There is also the question of transitivity and that of generating a choice function (Chapter 10).

tive choice systems are especially relevant here (e.g., those discussed in Chapters 3–9). This is a wide basket of problems varying from advising the existing government to arguing for its revolutionary overthrow. Many of the major advances on collective choice theories seem to have come from such eminently practical pursuits, especially the latter.[7] Social criticism and protest typically take the form of postulating principles of collective choice which the existing mechanisms do not satisfy.

(4) Problems of *committee decisions* are special cases of collective choice. Committees may be large or small, formal or informal, and institutions have to vary. With smaller groups, various institutional procedures are possible that may not be open to large groups, e.g., having informal systems of taking account of the intensities of preference (typical of many committees), or using an informal system of vote trading (typical of legislative bodies). The question of transitivity is especially transparent for committee decisions (Chapter 10).

(5) Problems of *public cooperation* are dependent on collective choice procedures and their evaluation by the people. For many problems it is important not merely that justice should be done but also that it must be seen to be done. Planning for economic development may require imposing sacrifice on the population, and the division of the burden (e.g., of taxation) may involve considerations of fairness, justice, and measurements of relative gains and losses (Chapter 7 and 9). What is relevant here is not merely the problem of *achieving* fairness, justice, etc., but also of *making clear* that the choices made have these characteristics when seen from the point of view of the population at large. The difference between success and failure in planning is often closely related to public enthusiasm and cooperation, and while the so-called "realists" not infrequently seem to pooh-pooh "vague normative considerations" like fairness or justice, these considerations seem eminently relevant to success or failure even in terms of most crude indices.

11.3. Expression of Individual Preferences

There are several difficulties with devising systems of expression

---

[7] Cf. Gramsci (1957), pp. 140–42.

of individual preferences for the purpose of collective choice. First, there are game considerations which could distort preferences in the process of expression. "Honest voting" is often not in a person's best interest.[7]

This is a perfectly general difficulty, but its relevance will vary greatly with the system of collective choice. As Murakami has argued, with those collective choice systems that are nonnegatively responsive to individual preferences the scope of what voters can achieve by distorting their preferences is very limited.[8] This applies in particular to the MMD. By distorting his preferences a person cannot increase the weight on his most preferred alternative, for the greatest weight he can put on it is to vote sincerely.

An example in terms of the MMD may help to bring out this problem. Consider three individuals, viz., 1, 2 and 3, with person 1 preferring x to y and y to z, person 2 preferring y to x and x to z, and person 3 preferring z to x and x to y. Majority ordering will yield x socially preferred to y and z, and y socially preferred to z. Person 2 can disrupt the ordering by pretending to prefer y to z and z to x, which will create cyclical majorities of x over y, y over z, and z over x. But he cannot bring y into the choice set this way, since the most he can do to help y into the choice set is to vote honestly. He can knock x out of the choice set by dishonest voting, but he cannot put y into it.

From this, however, it should not be presumed that strategic distortion can never help an individual or a group to improve the social outcome under a mechanism that is nonnegatively responsive. Even under the MMD insincere voting can help the selection of a preferred alternative. The following illustration brings this out.[9] Let there be three alternatives and four persons. Person 1 prefers x to both y and z between which he is indifferent; person 2 is indifferent between x and y and prefers each of these to z; person 3 prefers z to x and x to y; and person 4 ranks y above z

---

[7] See Arrow (1951), pp. 80–81, Majumdar (1956), and Luce and Raiffa (1957), Section 14.8.

[8] Murakami (1968), Chapter 4, Section 10.

[9] Suggested by Bengt Hansson. This case requires that two persons join hands. A case in which the insincerity of one is sufficient is the following. 1 and 2 prefer x to y and y to z; 3 prefers z to x and x to y, and 4 prefers y to z and z to x. With sincere voting the MMD yields x as the unique best element. If instead 4 pretends to prefer z to y and y to x, then z will be a majority winner also, and for him this is better.

and z above x. The MMD will yield under sincere voting: x preferred to y, y preferred to z, and x and z indifferent. Thus x is the sole element in the social choice set. Both 3 and 4 prefer z to x, even though for person 4 the most preferred alternative is not z. If 3 and 4 now pretend that they both prefer z to y and y to x, then the MMD will yield: z preferred to y, y preferred to x, and x and z indifferent. Now z is the sole member of the social choice set so that both 3 and 4 are better off through their sharp practice.[10] Thus nonnegative responsiveness or even positive responsiveness is no guarantee against insincere voting being an efficient strategy.

Incidentally, under some circumstances game considerations and vote trading may help to bring in some measures of intensities of individual preferences, and a vote-trading equilibrium does reflect a compromise of conflicting interests.[11] While there are problems in accepting these solutions as ethically optimal and fair (as discussed in Chapters 2 and 8), these models have much to commend as plausible representations of social choice, and they also help to clarify the ethical bases of these choices.

There have also been some attempts to get measures of cardinal intensities of preference of the individuals by examining their voting behavior. It is certainly correct, as Coleman (1966a) has pointed out, that a voter may view his act of voting in terms of its probable effects, and given his preferences over the set of social alternatives his action will depend on his estimation of the probability distribution of the voting behavior of the others, and also on the probability distribution of the consequences of the chance mechanisms that may be employed by the choice system, e.g., in breaking deadlocks. Thus, individual acts of voting can be viewed as a choice between lotteries, and will involve revelation of individual intensities of preference. However, the lotteries will, in fact, be severely limited in variety, so that any hope of constructing a utility function on this basis is not easy to entertain. We also have to know the subjective probability distributions of each

---

[10] When, however, the social preference relation has to be an *ordering* this possibility is less open; see Murakami (1968). Murakami, therefore, recommends voting being done in a "round-robin" manner, i.e., putting every alternative against every other alternative in pairwise voting, which would reveal intransitivities if there were any.

[11] See Buchanan and Tullock (1962), Coleman (1966), (1966a), and Wilson (1968), (1968a).

individual concerning the others' voting behavior to be able to calculate the utility measures. Thus it may not be possible to construct cardinal measures for practical social choices on the basis of merely observing actual voting behavior. The approach is, however, enlightening.[12]

There is, of course, a more primitive question as to whether individuals actually do behave in the manner postulated, i.e., maximizing the expected utility from voting by considering the probabilistic impact on actual social choices. This question needs further empirical investigation, but a preliminary doubt may be worth expressing at this stage. When a large number of voters are involved (e.g., in national elections), the probability that any individual's vote will affect the outcome is very small indeed, and even a tiny cost of voting (e.g., transport cost) may easily overcompensate that. Nevertheless, the turn-out in voting in such elections may be quite high.[13] This might indicate that the individuals are guided not so much by maximization of expected utility, but by something much simpler, viz., just a desire to record one's true preference.[14]

It may, of course, be that people just enjoy voting. This could explain why people vote in large elections, but once this type of consideration is brought in, even the ordinal correspondence between votes and preferences is damaged. A person may be indifferent and still vote for one or the other alternative if he gets delight in voting. If, on the other hand, there is some cost from voting, he may abstain even through he may prefer one alternative to another, but not sufficiently strongly. In fact, the problem is present even when voting is a source neither of cost nor of delight.

---

[12] For maximizing aggregate utility, we need in addition to measures of individual cardinal utility, some system of interpersonal comparability. Coleman notes this as an arbitrary element. For descriptive models, one can treat this as a set of parameters, as in Coleman (1966), (1966a). For normative models, however, systematic judgments on this have to be performed. (See Chapters 7, 8 and 9.)

[13] It is also possible that people are interested in the outcome not merely in terms of who (or which) wins, but by what margin, which always changes with one's vote. This will tend to complicate models of utility revelation very considerably. Further, since the impact of one more vote on the winning (or losing) margin is small, the incentive of the voter to exercise his vote would still seem to require some explaining, if we must confine ourselves to the expected utility framework.

[14] Cf. Robinson (1964), p. 10.

196

A person who is indifferent may then just as easily vote for either candidate as abstain. Thus whether the cost of voting is negative, positive, or zero, there will not be a one-to-one correspondence between (a) voting for x, (b) voting for y, and (c) abstaining, vis-a-vis (a) preferring x, (b) preferring y, and (c) being indifferent.[15] While analytically valid, this is not a terribly serious problem. If cost of voting is zero, then for *large* groups of voters, the overall result may be very close to what would happen under the one-to-one correspondence. The real problem arises if there are costs or delight from voting, and if these magnitudes are relatively large. Even in this form this is just one of many problems that infest this problem-ridden branch of choice theory.

11.4. Efficiency and Pareto Optimality

The problems of communication (and use) of cardinal measures are more serious than those of orderings. This has been partly responsible for the usual concentration on only orderings in dealing with collective choice.[16] The most widely used approach, at least in economics, is that of Pareto optimality and of "economic efficiency" (Chapter 2).

---

[15] In Sen (1964) this lack of one-to-one correspondence is shown to hold generally for all cases of continuous utility maximization. Honest expression of one's preference conflicts with maximizing a continuous utility function, which seems a little sad.

[16] Of course, in doing aggregation for such purposes as planning one can introduce certain variations in possible utility functions of an individual, and still get a quasi-ordering, in the same line as the approach developed in Chapter 7. An alternative, which is more demanding, is to supplement the planner's ignorance by a probability distribution, e.g., as proposed by Lerner (1944) in the context of the pure problem of distribution. Lerner assumes that the planner works on the basis of the same probability distribution for each individual over the possible utility functions (concave), and given the problem of division of a given total of homogeneous income, must therefore recommend an equal division on grounds of maximizing expected utility. The equiprobability assumption needed is, however, quite strong (see Friedman (1947), and Samuelson (1964)), but one can generalize Lerner's approach through using any combination of probability distributions. One can also use decision criteria that do not use probability, e.g., the maximin strategy, and the Lerner conclusion about equality holds in this case as well under very general assumptions, as shown in Sen (1966b). However, problems of interpretation of ignorance and uncertainty remain, as do the problems of choice of one decision criteria among many possible ones.

On the basis of the analyses in Chapters 5 and 6, the underlying assumptions of concentrating on Pareto optimality are clear. If one takes the view that Pareto optimality is the only goal, and as long as that is achieved, we need not worry further (an approach that is implicitly taken in much of modern welfare economics, but rarely explicitly), then one is demanding precisely a CCR generating quasi-transitive social preference and satisfying condition U (unrestricted domain), I (independence of irrelevant alternatives), P^* (strong Pareto principle), and A (anonymity). These conditions together imply that we must declare all Pareto-optimal points as indifferent, as shown in Theorem 5*3. This result gives an axiomatization of an approach that is implicit in a substantial part of modern welfare economics.

In some respects Theorem 5*3 is quite disturbing. All the imposed conditions are superficially appealing, but the conclusion that all Pareto-optimal points are indifferent, irrespective of distributional considerations, is very unattractive. In fact, it is this aspect of modern welfare economics that is most often separated out for special attack.

What this result possibly reveals (as do other results in the book) is an important difficulty in postulating general conditions on collective choice rules, viz., these conditions are essentially opaque. It is easier to secure acceptance of these conditions than the acceptance of all of their implications. Arrow's (1951) general possibility theorem may also be interpreted in that light.[17]

We found difficulties with even a very limited use of Pareto optimality, viz., treating it as a necessary but not a sufficient condition of overall optimality. In this case, Pareto optimality is usually thought to have compelling appeal.[18] But it turns out that

---

[17] Similar difficulties would seem to arise in axiomatic attempts at establishing specific decision rules, e.g., Koopmans' (1960) elegant demonstration of the necessity of "impatience" for rational accumulation programs given certain axioms of decision making. See also Koopmans, Diamond and Williamson (1964). The axioms used are apparently appealing, but the approach is subject to the difficulty discussed above.

[18] Arguments for rejecting Pareto optimality over the choice of *actions* have been constructed by Zeckhauser (1968) and Raiffa (1968), making use of interpersonal differences of probabilistic expectations about the *consequences* of action. These are, however, not arguments for rejecting the Pareto relation over the set of consequences, or the set of social states completely specified. We are concerned with this latter question.

even the weak version of the Pareto relation conflicts (Theorem 6*3) with a very weak condition of individual liberty, which gives individuals the freedom to do certain personal things (e.g., choosing what one should read). Even if only two individuals are given such freedom and over one pair each, the Pareto relation may still have to be violated to ensure acyclicity, which is weaker than transitivity. The conflict between individual freedom and the weak Pareto relation cannot, of course, arise in a choice over a pair, but it can arise whenever more than two alternatives are involved. Hence, Pareto optimality even as a necessary but not sufficient condition is open to some question. That Pareto optimality is not easily achievable in the presence of externalities is widely known (see Koopmans (1957)), but what emerges from the analysis of Chapter 6 is a serious doubt about its *merit* as a goal in the presence of some types of externalities.

11.5. Concluding Observations

Of the conditions on collective choice, the Pareto principle is thought to be the mildest of the mild. The difficulties that we encounter in making universal use of even the Pareto rule outlines the severeness of the problem of postulating absolute principles of collective choice that are supposed to hold in every situation. The simple principles that are normally put forward tend to be essentially "nonbasic" (Chapter 5). By a suitable choice of facts (e.g., by choosing specific configurations of individual preferences, or by selecting specific motivations behind individual orderings) it seems possible to play havoc with practically all the general principles that are usually recommended for universal application.

This position might appear to be at variance with the need for "generalization" and "universalization" that is emphasized in ethical theories from Kant onwards,[19] and which we discussed in Chapter 9. However, this contradiction is only superficial. It is not being argued here that no general principles exist that would secure total adherence of a person, but that the simple principles usually recommended are not of that type. Conditions of the type of "anonymity" and "neutrality" are based on very limited views of "relevant similarity," leaving out, among other things, informa-

---

[19] "Act always on such a maxim as thou canst at the same time will to be a universal law" (Kant (1785)). In Abbot's translation, Kant (1907), p. 66.

tion on the relation between individuals and the nature of the alternatives (Chapters 5 and 6) and information on preference intensities (Chapter 7). "Independence of irrelevant alternatives," while less restrictive, also concentrates on similarity in a narrow sense, viz., of individual rankings over the relevant pair. Preference intensities do not count (Chapter 7), nor does any indirect information that we get from observing rankings of other (but related) alternatives, which might indicate something about a person's motivation (Chapter 6). This last, rather than any consideration of preference intensities, seems crucial in our reservation about the Pareto principle (Section 6.5). What is in dispute is not the approach that in "similar situations similar judgments must be made," but the criteria to decide which situations *are* similar. To make a completely general statement of "relevant similarity" we may have to go into an enormously complicated criterion. Simple principles may be devised which will catch the essentials in many cases but not in all, and while these principles (e.g., conditions I, N, A, P and others) may superficially have the form of universal principles, they are in fact nonbasic in most value systems.

Even nonbasic principles, if sufficiently widely applicable, are helpful in understanding and evaluating collective choice procedures. Only a masochist can enjoy having to deal with the full array of details in every choice situation. Simple principles provide convenient shortcuts, and as long as we recognize these principles as useful guidelines rather than as masters to be obeyed to the bitter end, there is no problem. Arrow's general possibility theorem (Theorem 3*1), and other impossibility theorems (Theorems 4*3, 4*5, 5*1.1, 5*2, 6*1–6*3, 8*1.1, 8*2, 9*2, 9*2.1, 10*5), presented in this book, are to be viewed not as arguments for nihilism, but as positive contributions aimed at clarifying the role of principles in collective choice systems. The same is true of theorems that assert positive results about choice mechanisms (Theorems 4*1, 4*2, 4*4, 5*1, 5*3, 7*1–7*9, 8*1, 9*1, 9*3–9*7, 9*5.1, 9*7.1, 10*1–10*4, 10*6–10*9).

Once the nonbasic nature of the usual principles of collective choice are recognized, some of the rigid distinctions must go. For example, in traditional welfare economics it is conventional to distinguish between Paretian judgments, which are treated as compelling, and non-Paretian judgments, which are treated as "arbitrary." This clear-cut dichotomy seems to be inopportune both because the Pareto principle is also partly arbitrary (Chapter 6) as well as because some of the other principles are also compelling in many situations (Chapters 5–7 and 9). An almost exclusive concentration on Paretian considerations has, on the one hand, confined traditional welfare economics into a very narrow box, and has, on the other hand, given it a sense of ethical invulnerability which does not seem to survive a close scrutiny.

A closely related point concerns the relative acceptability of different collective choice systems. Since the simple principles that the different systems satisfy seem to be essentially nonbasic, it is quite clear that an evaluation of the relative desirability of different systems will depend on the nature of the society. One way of interpreting the various "impossibility" results is to say that there is no "ideal" system of collective choice that works well in every society and for every configuration of individual preferences (as proposed by the use of the condition of "unrestricted domain" employed in virtually all the impossibility theorems). Some choice procedures work very well for some types of choice and some sets of individual preferences but not for others (see Chapters 5–7, 9, and 10), and naturally our evaluation of these procedures must depend on the the type of society for which they may be considered. There is nothing outstandingly defeatist in this modest recognition.

Finally, it is worth emphasizing that while "pure" systems of collective choice tend to be more appealing for theoretical studies of social decisions, they are often not the most useful systems to study. With this in view, this book has been much concerned with "impurities" of one kind or another, e.g., *partial* interpersonal comparability (Chapters 7 and 9), *partial* cardinality (Chapter 7), *restricted* domains (Chapters 6 and 10), *intransitive* social indifference (Chapters 4 and 10), *incomplete* social preference (Chapters 7 and 9), and so on. The pure procedures, which are more well-known, seem to be the limiting cases of these systems with impurities.

Both from the point of view of institutions as well as that of frameworks of thought, the impure systems would appear to be relevant. The relative allocation of space in this book reflects a belief, which we have tried to defend, that while purity is an uncomplicated virtue for olive oil, sea air, and heroines of folk tales, it is not so for systems of collective choice.

BIBLIOGRAPHY

Allen, R. G. D., *Mathematical Economics*, Macmillan, London, 1959.

Archibald, G. C., "Welfare Economics, Ethics, and Essentialism," *Economica*, N.S., **26**, 1959.

Aristotle, *The Nicomachean Ethics*, edited by J. A. K. Thomson, Allen and Unwin, London, 1953.

Armstrong, W. E., "A Note on the Theory of Consumer's Behavior," *Oxford Economic Papers*, N.S., **2**, 1950.

———, "Utility and the Theory of Welfare," *Oxford Economic Papers*, N.S., **3**, 1951.

Arrow, K. J., "A Difficulty in the Concept of Social Welfare," *Journal of Political Economy*, **58**, 1950.

———, *Social Choice and Individual Values*, Wiley, New York, 1951; 2nd ed. 1963.

———, "An Extension of the Basic Theorems of Classical Welfare Economics," in Neyman, 1951 (1951a).

———, "Little's Critique of Welfare Economics," *American Economic Review*, **41**, 1951 (1951b).

———, "Le Principe de Rationalité dans les Décisions Collectives," *Économie Appliquée*, **5**, 1952.

———, "Rational Choice Functions and Orderings," *Economica*, N.S., **26**, 1959.

———, "Economic Welfare and the Allocation of Resources for Invention," in K. J. Arrow et al., *The Rate and Direction of Inventive Activity*, Princeton University Press, Princeton, 1962.

———, "Uncertainty and the Welfare Economies of Medical Care," *American Economic Review*, **53**, 1963.

———, *Aspects of the Theory of Risk-Bearing*, Yrjö Jahnssonin Säätiö, Helsinki, 1965.

———. "Values and Collective Decision Making," in Laslett and Runciman, 1967.

———, "Public and Private Values," in Hook, (1967) (1967a).

———, "The Place of Moral Obligation in Preference Systems," in Hook (1967) (1967b).

Arrow, K. J., S. Karlin and P. Suppes, eds., *Mathematical Methods in Social Sciences, 1959*, Stanford University Press, Stanford, 1960.

Aumann, R. J., "Utility Theory without the Completeness Axiom," *Econometrica*, **30**, 1962.

——, "Utility Theory without the Completeness Axiom: A Correction," **32**, 1964.

Ayer, A. J., *Philosophical Essays*, Macmillan, London, 1959.

Banerji, D., "Choice and Order: Or First Things First," *Economica*, N.S., **31**, 1964.

Barone, E., "The Ministry of Production in the Collectivist State," in F. A. von Hayek, ed., *Collective Economic Planning*, Routledge, London, 1935.

Barry, D., *Political Argument*, Humanitarian Press, New York, 1965.

Bator, F. M., "The Anatomy of Market Failure," *Quarterly Journal of Economics*, **72**, 1958.

Baumol, W. J., "Community Indifference," *Review of Economic Studies*, **14**, 1946.

——, *Welfare Economics and the Theory of the State*, Harvard University Press, Cambridge, Mass., 1952; 2nd ed., 1966.

——, "The Cardinal Utility Which is Ordinal," *Economic Journal*, **68**, 1958.

Bentham, J., *An Introduction to the Principles of Morals and Legislation*, Payne, 1789; Clarendon Press, Oxford, 1907.

Bergson, A., "A Reformulation of Certain Aspects of Welfare Economics," *Quarterly Journal of Economics*, **52**, 1938.

——, "Socialist Economics," in H. S. Ellis, ed., *A Survey of Contemporary Economics*, Vol. I, Blakiston, Philadelphia, 1948.

——, "On the Concept of Social Welfare," *Quarterly Journal of Economics*, **68**, 1954.

——, *Essays in Normative Economics*, Harvard University Press, Cambridge, Mass., 1966.

Bernoulli, D., "Specimen Theoriae Novae de Mensura Sortis," *Commentarii Academiae Scientiarum Imperialis Peropolitanae*, 1730, 1731, 1738; trans. by L. Sommer, "Exposition of a New Theory of the Measurement of Risk," *Econometrica*, **22**, 1954.

Birkhoff, G., *Lattice Theory*, American Mathematical Society, 1940.

Bishop, R. L., "A Zeuthen-Hicks Theory of Bargaining," *Econometrica*, **32**, 1964.

Black, D., "On the Rationale of Group Decision Making," *Journal of Political Economy*, **56**, 1948.

——, "The Decisions of a Committee Using a Simple Majority," *Econometrica*, **16**, 1948 (1948a).

——, *The Theory of Committees and Elections*, Cambridge University Press, Cambridge, 1958.

Black, M., "The Gap Between Is and Should," *Philosophical Review*, **73**, 1964.

Blackwell, D., and M. A. Girschik, *Theory of Games and Statistical Decisions*, Wiley, New York, 1954.

Blanche, R., *Axiomatics*, trans. by G. B. Keene, Free Press of Glencoe, New York, 1962.

Blau, J. H., "The Existence of a Social Welfare Function," *Econometrica*, **25**, 1957.

Borda, J. C., "Mémoire sur les Élections as Scrutin," *Mémoires de l'Académie Royale des Sciences*, 1781; English translation by A. de Grazia, *Isis*, **44**, 1953.

Boulding, K. E., "Welfare Economics," in B. F. Haley, ed., *A Survey of Contemporary Economics*, Vol. II, Blakiston, Philadelphia, 1952.

Bourbaki, N., *Éléments de Mathématique*, Hermann, Paris, 1939; English translation, *General Topology*, Parts I and II, Addison-Wesley, Reading, Mass., 1966; *Theory of Sets*, Addison-Wesley, Reading, Mass., 1968.

Bowen, H. R., "The Interpretation of Voting in the Allocation of Economic Resources," *Quarterly Journal of Economics*, **58**, 1943.

Braithwaite, R. B., *Theory of Games as a Tool for the Moral Philosopher*, Cambridge University Press, Cambridge, 1955.

Brandt, R. B., *Ethical Theory*, Prentice-Hall, Englewood Cliffs, N.J., 1959.

——, ed., *Social Justice*, Prentice-Hall, Englewood Cliffs, N, J., 1961.

——, review of Hare's *Freedom and Reason*, *Journal of Philosophy*, **61**, 1964.

Broad, C. D., "On the Function of False Hypotheses in Ethics," *International Journal of Ethics*, **26**, 1916.

Buchanan, J. M., "Individual Choice in Voting and the Market," *Journal of Political Economy*, **62**, 1954.

——, "Simple Majority Voting, Game Theory, and Resource Use," *Canadian Journal of Economics and Political Science*, **27**, 1961.

Buchanan, J. M., and G. Tullock, *The Calculus of Consent*, University of Michigan Press, Ann Arbor, 1962.

Campbell, C. D., and G. Tullock, "A Measure of the Importance of Cyclical Majorities," *Economic Journal*, **75**, 1965.

——, "The Paradox of Voting—A Possible Method of Calculation," *American Political Science Review*, **60**, 1966.

Carnap, R., *Introduction to Symbolic Logic and Its Application*, Dover, New York, 1958.

Cassen, R., "Alternative Approaches to the Theory of Social Choice," mimeographed, 1967.

Chakravarty, S., "Alternative Preference Functions in Problems of Investment Planning on the National Level," in E. Malinvaud and M. Bacharach, eds., *Activity Analysis in the Theory of Growth and Planning*, Macmillan, London, and St. Martin's Press, New York, 1967.

Chernoff, H., "Rational Selection of Decision Functions," *Econometrica*, **22**, 1954.

Chipman, J. S., "The Foundations of Utility," *Econometrica*, **28**, 1960.

———, "The Lexicographic Representation of Preference Orderings," in Minnesota Symposium (1969).

Church, A., *Introduction to Mathematical Logic*, Princeton University Press, Princeton, 1956.

Coleman, J. S., "Foundations for a Theory of Collective Choice," *American Journal of Sociology*, **71**, 1966.

———, "The Possibility of a Social Welfare Function," *American Economic Review*, **56**, 1966 (1966a).

Condorcet, Marquis de, *Essai sur l'Application de l'Analyse à la Probabilité des Décisions Rendues à la Pluralité des Voix*, Paris, 1785.

Contini, B., "A Note on Arrow's Postulates for a Social Welfare Function," *Journal of Political Economy*, **74**, 1966.

Coombs, C. H., "Psychological Scaling without a Unit of Measurement," *Psychological Review*, **57**, 1950.

———, *A Theory of Data*, Wiley, New York, 1964.

Criswell, J. H., H. Solomon and P. Suppes, *Mathematical Methods in Small Group Processes*, Stanford University Press, Stanford, 1962.

Curry, H. B., and R. Feys, *Combinatory Logic*, North-Holland, Amsterdam, 1958.

Dahl, R. A., *A Preface to Democratic Theory*, University of Chicago Press, Chicago, 1956.

Dahl, R. A., and C. E. Lindbloom, *Politics, Economics and Welfare*, Harper, New York, 1954.

Davidson, D., and P. Suppes, "A Finitistic Axiomatization of Subjective Probability and Utility," *Econometrica*, **24**, 1956.

Davis, R. G., "Comment on Arrow and the 'New Welfare Economics'," *Economic Journal*, **68**, 1958.

Debreu, G., "Representation of a Preference Ordering by a Numerical Function," in Thrall, Coombs and Davis (1954).

———, *The Theory of Value*, Wiley, New York, 1959.

———, "Topological Methods in Cardinal Utility Theory," in Arrow, Karlin and Suppes (1960).

de Grazia, A., "Mathematical Derivation of an Election System," *Isis*, **44**, 1953.

De Meyer, F., and C. R. Plott, "The Probability of a Cyclical Majority," *Econometrica*, in press.

Diamond, P., "Cardinal Welfare, Individualistic Ethics, and Interpersonal Comparisons of Utility: A Comment," *Journal of Political Economy*, **75**, 1967.

Dobb, M. H., *On Economic Theory and Socialism*, Routledge, London, and International Publishers, New York, 1955.

———, "A Note on Index Numbers and Compensation Criteria," *Oxford Economic Papers*, N.S., **8**, 1956.

———, "A Further Comment on the Discussion of Welfare Criteria," *Economic Journal*, **73**, 1963.

———, *Welfare Economics and the Economics of Socialism*, Cambridge University Press, Cambridge, 1969.

Dodgson, C. L., (Lewis Carroll), *A Method of Taking Votes on More than Two Issues*, Clarendon Press, Oxford, 1876, reprinted in Black (1958).

Downs, A., *An Economic Theory of Democracy*, Harper, New York, 1956.

———, "In Defence of Majority Voting," *Journal of Political Economy*, **69**, 1961.

Dummett, M., and R. Farquharson, "Stability in Voting," *Econometrica*, **29**, 1961.

Dunford, N., and J. T. Schwartz, *Linear Operators*, Interscience, New York, 1958.

Edgeworth, F. T., *Mathematical Psychics*, Kegan Paul, London, 1881.

Eilenberg, S., "Ordered Topological Spaces," *American Journal of Mathematics*, **63**, 1941.

Ellman, M. J., "Individual Preferences and the Market," *Economics of Planning*, **6**, 1966.

Ellsberg, D., "Classic and Current Notions of 'Measurable Utility'," *Economic Journal*, **64**, 1954.

———, "Risk, Ambiguity and the Savage Axioms," *Quarterly Journal of Economics*, **75**, 1961.

———, "Risk, Ambiguity and the Savage Axioms: Reply," *Quarterly Journal of Economics*, **77**, 1963.

Fagen, R. R., "Some Contributions of Mathematical Reasoning to the Study of Politics," *American Political Science Review*, **55**, 1961.

Farquharson, R., "An Approach to the Pure Theory of Voting Procedure," *Ph. D. Thesis*, Oxford University, 1957–1958.

Farrell, M. J., "Mr. Lancaster on Welfare and Choice," *Economic Journal*, **69**, 1959.

Fenchel, W., *Convex Cones, Sets and Functions*, Department of Mathematics, Princeton University (mimeographed), 1953.

Fleming, M., "A Cardinal Concept of Welfare," *Quarterly Journal of Economics*, **66**, 1952.

———, "Cardinal Welfare and Individualistic Ethics: A Comment," *Journal of Political Economy*, **65**, 1957.

Fishburn, P. C., "Interdependence and Additivity in Multivariate Unidimensional Expected Utility," *International Economic Review*, **8**, 1967.

Fishburn, P. C., "Intransitive Individual Indifference and Transitive Majorities," *Econometrica*, **38**, 1970.

Fisher, F. M., "Income Distribution, Value Judgments and Welfare," *Quarterly Journal of Economics*, **70**, 1956.

Fisher, F. M., and J. Rothenberg, "How Income Ought to be Distributed: Paradox Lost," *Journal of Political Economy*, **69**, 1961.

———, "How Income Ought to be Distributed; Paradox Enow," *Journal of Political Economy*, **70**, 1962.

Friedman, M., "Lerner on the Economics of Control," *Journal of Political Economy*, **55**, 1947.

———, "The Expected-Utility Hypotheses and the Measurability of Utility," *Journal of Political Economy*, **60**, 1952.

———, *Essays in Positive Economics*, University of Chicago Press, Chicago, 1953.

Friedman, M., and L. J. Savage, "The Utility Analysis of Choices Involving Risk," *Journal of Political Economy*, **56**, 1948.

Frisch, R., *New Methods of Measuring Marginal Utility*, Mohr, Tübingen, 1932.

———, *Maxima and Minima: Theory and Economic Applications*, Rand McNally, New York, 1966.

Garman, M., and M. Kamien, "The Paradox of Voting: Probability Calculations," *Behavioral Science*, **13**, 1968.

Gauthier, D. P., "Morality and Advantage," *Philosophical Review*, **74**, 1967.

———, "Hare's Debtors," *Mind*, **77**, 1968.

Georgescu-Roegen, N., *Analytical Economics*, Harvard University Press, Cambridge, Mass., 1966.

Goodman, L. A., and H. Markowitz, "Social Welfare Functions Based on Individual Rankings," *American Journal of Sociology*, **58**, 1952.

Gorman, W. M., "Community Preference Fields," *Econometrica*, **21**, 1953.

———, "The Intransitivity of Certain Criteria Used in Welfare Economics," *Oxford Economic Papers*, N.S., **7**, 1955.

———, "Are Social Indifference Curves Convex?" *Quarterly Journal of Economics*, **73**, 1959.

———, "The Structure of Utility Functions," *Review of Economic Studies*, **35**, 1968.

Graaff, J. de V., "On Optimum Tariff Structures," *Review of Economic Studies*, **17**, 1949.

———, *Theoretical Welfare Economics*, Cambridge University Press, Cambridge, 1957.

———, "On Making Recommendations in a Democracy," *Economic Journal*, **72**, 1962.

Gramsci, A., *The Modern Prince and Other Writings*, trans. by L. Marks, Lawrence & Wishart, London, 1967.

Granger, G.-G., *La Mathématique Social du Marquis de Condorcet*, Presses Universitaires de France, Paris, 1956.

Guilbaud, G.-Th., "Les Théories de l'Intérêt Général et la Problème Logique de l'Aggrégation," *Économie Appliquée*, **5**, 1952.

Halmos, P. R., *Algebraic Logic*, Chelsea, New York, 1962.

Hansson, B., "Choice Structures and Preference Relations," *Synthese*, **18**, 1968.

———, "On Group Preferences," *Econometrica*, **37**, 1969.

———, "Voting and Group Decision Functions," *Synthese*, in press.

Hare, R. M., *The Language of Morals*, Clarendon Press, Oxford, 1952; 2nd ed., 1961.

———, *Freedom and Reason*, Clarendon Press, Oxford, 1963.

Harsanyi, J. C., "Cardinal Utility in Welfare Economics and in the Theory of Risk Taking," *Journal of Political Economy*, **61**, 1953.

———, "Cardinal Welfare, Individualistic Ethics, and Interpersonal Comparisons of Utility," *Journal of Political Economy*, **63**, 1955.

———, "Approaches to the Bargaining Problem Before and After the Theory of Games: A Critical Discussion of Zeuthen's, Hicks', and Nash's Theories," *Econometrica*, **24**, 1956.

———, "Ethics in Terms of Hypothetical Imperatives," *Mind*, **67**, 1958.

———, "A General Theory of Rational Behavior in Game Situations," *Econometrica*, **34**, 1966.

Herstein, I. N., and J. Milnor, "An Axiomatic Approach to Measurable Utility," *Econometrica*, **21**, 1953.

Herzberger, H., "Ordinal Choice Structures," mimeographed, 1968; *Econometrica*, forthcoming.

Hicks, J. R., *Value and Capital*, Clarendon Press, Oxford, 1939.

———, "The Foundations of Welfare Economics," *Economic Journal*, **48**, 1939a.

———, "The Valuation of Social Income," *Economica*, N.S., **7**, 1940.

———, "The Rehabilitation of Consumers' Surplus," *Review of Economic Studies*, **8**, 1941.

———, "Consumers' Surplus and Index Numbers," *Review of Economic Studies*, **9**, 1942.

———, "The Valuation of Social Income: A Comment on Professor Kuznets' Reflections," *Economica*, N.S., **15**, 1948.

Hilbert, D., and W. Ackermann, *Principles of Mathematical Logic*, Chelsea, New York, 1960.

Hildreth, C., "Alternative Conditions for Social Ordering," *Econometrica*, **21**, 1953.

Hobsbawm, E. J., "Where Are British Historians Going?", *The Marxist Quarterly*, **2**, 1955.

Hook, S., ed., *Human Values and Economic Policy*, New York University Press, New York, 1967.

Houthakker, H. S., "Revealed Preference and the Utility Function," *Economica*, **17**, 1950.

——, "On the Logic of Preference and Choice," in A.-T. Tyminieniecka, ed., *Contributions to Logic and Methodology in Honor of J. M. Bocheński*, North-Holland, Amsterdam, 1965.

Hurwicz, L., "Optimality Criteria for Decision Making under Ignorance," *Cowles Commission Discussion Paper, Statistics*, **370**, 1951.

——, "Optimality and Informational Efficiency in Resource Allocation Processes," in Arrow, Karlin and Suppes (1960).

Inada, K., "Alternative Incompatible Conditions for a Social Welfare Function," *Econometrica*, **23**, 1955.

——, "On the Economic Welfare Function," *Econometrica*, **32**, 1964.

——, "A Note on the Simple Majority Decision Rule," *Econometrica*, **32**, 1964a.

——, "On the Simple Majority Decision Rule," *Econometrica*, **37**, 1969.

International Economic Association, *Economics of the Public Sector*, papers presented at the Round-Table Conference at Biarritz, 1966; J. Margolis and H. Guitton, eds., *Public Economics*, Macmillan, London, 1969.

Jensen, N. E., "An Introduction to the Bernoullian Utility Theory," *Swedish Journal of Economics*, **69**, 1967.

Johansen, L., *Public Economics*, North-Holland, Amsterdam, 1965.

Kahn, R. F., "Some Notes on Ideal Output," *Economic Journal*, **45**, 1935.

Kaldor, N., "Welfare Propositions in Economics," *Economic Journal*, **49**, 1939.

——, "A Comment [on Baumol]," *Review of Economic Studies*, **14**, 1946.

Kant, I., *Grundlegung zur Metaphysik der Sitten*, 1785; English translation by T. K. Abbott, *Fundamental Principles of the Metaphysics of Ethics*, 3rd ed., Longmans, London, 1907.

——, *Critik der practischen Vernunft*, 1788; English translation by L. W. Beck, *Critique of Practical Reason*, Liberal Arts Press, New York, 1956.

Kemp, M. C., "Arrow's General Possibility Theorem," *Review of Economic Studies*, **21**, 1954.

Kemp, M. C., and A. Asimakopulos, "A Note on 'Social Welfare Functions' and Cardinal Utility," *Canadian Journal of Economics and Political Science*, **18**, 1952.

Kenen, P. B., and F. M. Fisher, "Income Distribution, Value Judgments and Welfare: A Correction," *Quarterly Journal of Economics*, **71**, 1957.

Kennedy, C. M., "The Common Sense of Indifference Curves," *Oxford Economic Papers*, N.S., **2**, 1950.

———, "The Economic Welfare Function and Dr. Little's Criterion," *Review of Economic Studies*, **20**, 1953.

———, "Comments [on Little and Sen]," *Economic Journal*, **73**, 1963.

Klahr, D. A., "Computer Simulation of the Paradox of Voting," *American Political Science Review*, **60**, 1966.

Knight, F. H., *The Ethics of Competition*, Allen and Unwin, London, 1935.

Kolm, S. Ch., "The Optimum Production of Social Justice," in International Economic Association, see above, 1966.

Koopmans, T. C., "Efficient Allocation of Resources," *Econometrica*, **19**, 1951.

———, *Three Essays on the State of Economic Science*, McGraw-Hill, New York, 1957.

———, "Stationary Ordinal Utility and Impatience," *Econometrica*, **28**, 1960.

———, "Structure of Preferences over Time," *Cowles Foundation Discussion Paper 206*, 1966.

Koopmans, T. C., P. A. Diamond and R. E. Williamson, "Stationary Utility and Time Perspective," *Econometrica*, **32**, 1964.

Kuhn, H. W., and A. W. Tucker, *Contributions to the Theory of Games*, Princeton University Press, Princeton, Vol. I, 1950, and Vol. II, 1953.

Kuznets, S., "On the Valuation of Social Income: Reflections on Professor Hicks' Article," *Economica*, N.S., **15**, 1948.

Lancaster, K., "Welfare Propositions in Terms of Consistency and Extended Choice," *Economic Journal*, **68**, 1958.

———, "Welfare and Expanded Choice: Proof of the General Case," *Economic Journal*, **69**, 1959.

Lancaster, K., and R. G. Lipsey, "The General Theory of the Second Best," *Review of Economic Studies*, **24**, 1957.

Lange, O., "The Foundations of Welfare Economics," *Econometrica*, **10**, 1942.

———, "The Scope and Method of Economics," *Review of Economic Studies*, **13**, 1945.

Lange, O., and F. M. Taylor, *On the Economic Theory of Socialism*, University of Minnesota Press, Minneapolis, 1952.

Laplace, P.-S., *Théorie Analytique des Probabilités*, 2nd ed., 1814.

Laslett, P., and W. G. Runciman, *Philosophy, Politics, and Society, First Series*, Blackwell, Oxford, and Macmillan, New York, 1958; *Second Series*, Blackwell, Oxford, and Barnes and Noble, New York, 1962; *Third Series*, Blackwell, Oxford, and Barnes and Noble, New York, 1967.

Leibenstein, H., "Notes on Welfare Economics and the Theory of Democracy," *Economic Journal*, **72**, 1962.

——, "Long-Run Welfare Criteria," in Margolis, 1965.

Leiberman, B., "Combining Individual Preferences into Social Choice," *Research Memorandum SP-111.3*, Department of Sociology, University of Pittsburgh, Pittsburgh, 1967.

Lenin, V. I., *The State and Revolution*, Foreign Languages Publishing House, Moscow, 1966.

Leontief, W., "A Note on the Interrelations of Subsets of Independent Variables of a Continuous Function with Continuous First Derivatives," *Bulletin of American Mathematical Society*, **53**, 1947.

——, "Introduction to a Theory of the Internal Structure of Functional Relationships," *Econometrica*, **15**, 1947a.

Lerner, A. P., *Economics of Control*, Macmillan, New York, 1944.

Little, I. M. D., "A Reformulation of the Theory of Consumer's Behavior," *Oxford Economic Papers*, N.S., **1**, 1949.

——, "The Foundations of Welfare Economics," *Oxford Economic Papers*, N. S., **1**, 1949 (1949a).

——, "*A Critique of Welfare Economics*, Clarendon Press, Oxford, 1950; 2nd ed., 1957.

——, "Social Choice and Individual Values," *Journal of Political Economy*, **60**, 1952.

——, "Welfare Criteria: An Exchange of Notes," *Economic Journal*, **72**, 1962.

——, "Comments [on Dobb and Sen]," *Economic Journal*, **73**, 1963.

Lorimer, P., "A Note on Orderings" *Econometrica*, **35**, 1966.

Lucas, J. R., "Moralists and Gamesmen," *Philosophy*, **34**, 1959.

Luce, R. D., "Semi-orders and a Theory of Utility Discrimination," *Econometrica*, **24**, 1956.

——, "Two Extensions of Conjoint Measurement," *Journal of Mathematical Psychology*, **3**, 1966.

Luce, R. D., and H. Raiffa, *Games and Decisions*, Wiley, New York, 1957.

Luce, R. D., and J. W. Tukey, "Simultaneous Conjoint Measurement: A New Type of Fundamental Measurement," *Journal of Mathematical Psychology*, **1**, 1964.

Madell, G., "Hare's Prescriptivism," *Analysis*, **26**, 1965.

Majumdar, T., "Choice and Revealed Preference," *Econometrica*, **24**, 1956.

——, "Armstrong and the Utility Measurement Controversy," *Oxford Economic Papers*, N.S., **9**, 1957.

——, *The Measurement of Utility*, Macmillan, London, 1958; 2nd ed., 1962.

Majumdar, T., "Sen's General Theorem on Transitivity of Majority Decisions: An Alternative Approach," in T. Majumdar, ed., *Choice and Growth*, Oxford University Press, Calcutta, 1969.

———, "A Note on Arrow's Postulates for a Social Welfare Function: A Comment," *Journal of Political Economy*, 77, 1969 (1969a).

Malinvaud, E., "Note on von Neumann-Morgenstern Strong Independence Axiom," *Econometrica*, 20, 1952.

———, "Capital Accumulation and Efficient Allocation of Resources," *Econometrica*, 21, 1953; "A Corrigendum," *Econometrica*, 30, 1962.

Manne, A. S., "The Strong Independence Assumption—Gasoline Blends and Probability Mixtures," *Econometrica*, 20, 1952.

Marglin, S. A., "The Social Rate of Discount and the Optimal Rate of Investment," *Quarterly Journal of Economics*, 77, 1968.

Margolis, J., ed., *The Public Economy of Urban Communities*, Johns Hopkins Press, Baltimore, 1965.

Marschak, J., "Rational Behavior, Uncertain Prospects, and Measurable Utility," *Econometrica*, 18, 1950; "Errata," *Econometrica*, 18, 1950.

Marshall, A., *Principles of Economics*, Macmillan, London, 1890; 9th (variorum) ed., Macmillan, London, 1961.

Marx, K., *Economic and Philosophic Manuscript of 1844*, Foreign Languages Publishing House, Moscow, 1959.

———, *Critique of the Gotha Programme*, 1875; Foreign Languages Publishing House, Moscow, 1967.

Marx, K., and F. Engels, *Manifesto of the Communist Party*, 1848; Foreign Languages Publishing House, Moscow, 1948.

May, K. O., "A Set of Independent, Necessary and Sufficient Conditions for Simple Majority Decision," *Econometrica*, 20, 1952.

———, "A Note on Complete Independence of the Conditions for Simple Majority Decision," *Econometrica*, 21, 1953.

———, "Intransitivity, Utility and Aggregation in Preference Patterns," *Econometrica*, 41, 1966.

McGarvey, D. C., "A Theorem in the Construction of Voting Paradoxes," *Econometrica*, 21, 1953.

Meade, J. E., "Welfare Criteria: An Exchange of Notes," *Economic Journal*, 72, 1962.

Mill, J. S., *On Liberty*, 1859; Gateway, New York, 1959.

———, *Utilitarianism*, 1863; Dent, London, 1929.

Mills, C. W., *The Power Elite*, Oxford University Press, New York, 1953.

Minnesota Symposium, *Consumption Theory without Transitive Indifference*, unpublished, 1969.

Mishan, E. J., "An Investigation into Some Alleged Contradictions in Welfare Economics," *Economic Journal*, 67, 1957.

Mishan, E. J., "Arrow and the 'New Welfare Economics': A Restatement," *Economic Journal*, **68**, 1958.

——, "A Survey of Welfare Economics, 1939–59," *Economic Journal*, **70**, 1960.

——, "Welfare Criteria: An Exchange of Notes," *Economic Journal*, **72**, 1962.

——, "The Welfare Criteria that Aren't," *Economic Journal*, **74**, 1964.

Montague, R., "Universalizability," *Analysis*, **25**, 1965.

Morris, W. E., "Professor Sen and Hare's Rule," *Philosophy*, **41**, 1966.

Murakami, Y., "A Note on the General Possibility Theorem of Social Welfare Functions," *Econometrica*, **29**, 1961.

——, "Formal Structure of Majority Decisions," *Econometrica*, **34**, 1966.

——, *Logic and Social Choice*, Macmillan, London, and Dover, New York, 1968.

Myint, H., *Theories of Welfare Economics*, Harvard University Press, Cambridge, Mass., 1948.

Myrdal, G., *The Political Elements in the Development of Economics*, Harvard University Press, Cambridge, Mass., 1954.

——, *Value in Social Theory*, edited by P. Streeton, Routledge, London, 1958.

Nanson, E. J., "Methods of Elections," *Transactions and Proceedings of the Royal Society of Victoria*, **18**, 1882.

Nash, J. F., "The Bargaining Problem," *Econometrica*, **18**, 1950.

——, "Two-Person Cooperative Games," *Econometrica*, **21**, 1953.

Neumann, J. von, and O. Morgenstern, *Theory of Games and Economic Behavior*, Princeton University Press, Princeton, 1947.

Newman, P., "Mr. Lancaster on Welfare and Choice," *Economic Journal*, **69**, 1959.

Neyman, J., ed., *Proceedings of the Second Berkeley Symposium on Mathematical Statistics and Probability*, University of California Press, Berkeley, 1951; *Third Symposium*, University of California Press, Berkeley, 1956.

Nicholson, M. B., "Conditions for the 'Voting Paradox' in Committee Decisions," *Metroeconomica*, **42**, 1965.

Niemi, R., "Majority Decision-Making with Partial Unidimensionality," *American Political Science Review*, **63**, 1969.

Niemi, R., and H. Weisberg, "A Mathematical Solution for the Probability of the Paradox of Voting," *Behavioral Sciences*, **13**, 1968.

Nowell-Smith, P. H., *Ethics*, Penguin Books, Harmondsworth, 1954.

Olafson, F. A., ed., *Justice and Social Policy*, Prentice-Hall, Englewood Cliffs, N.J., 1961.

Olson, M. N., *The Logic of Collective Action*, Harvard University Press, Cambridge, Mass., 1964.

Pareto, V., *Cours d'Économie Politique*, Rouge, Lausanne, 1897.

——, *Manuale di Economia Politica*, Societa Editrice Libraria, Milano, 1906; French translation (revised), *Manuel d'Économie Politique*, Giard, Paris, 1909.

Park, R. E., "Comment [on Coleman]," *American Economic Review*, **57**, 1967.

Parsons, T., and E. Shils, *Toward a General Theory of Value*, Harvard University Press, Cambridge, Mass., 1951.

Pattanaik, P. K., "Aspects of Welfare Economics," *Ph. D. Thesis*, Delhi University, 1967.

——, "A Note on Leibenstein's 'Notes on Welfare Economics and the Theory of Democracy'," *Economic Journal*, **77**, 1967 (1967a).

——, "A Note on Democratic Decisions and the Existence of Choice Sets," *Review of Economic Studies*, **35**, 1968.

——, "Risk, Impersonality and the Social Welfare Functions," *Journal of Political Economy*, **76**, 1968 (1968a).

——, "Transitivity and Choice under Multi-Stage Majority Decisions," *Discussion Paper 52*, Harvard Institute of Economic Research, 1968b.

——, "Sufficient Conditions for the Existence of a Choice Set under Majority Voting"; *Working Paper 14*, Delhi School of Economics, 1966. *Econometrica*, forthcoming.

——, "A Generalization of Some Theorems on the Transitivity of Social Decisions with Restricted Individual Preferences," mimeographed, 1969.

Pigou, A. C., *The Economics of Welfare*, Macmillan, London, 1920.

Plott, C. R., "A Notion of Equilibrium and Its Possibility under Majority Rule," *American Economic Review*, **57**, 1967.

Pratt, J. W., H. Raiffa and R. O. Schlaifer, *Introduction to Statistical Decision Theory*, McGraw-Hill, New York, 1965.

Quine, M. V., *Mathematical Logic*, Harvard University Press, Cambridge, Mass., 1940; rev. ed., 1951; Harper, New York, 1962.

Rader, T., "The Existence of a Utility Function to Represent Preferences," *Review of Economic Studies*, **31**, 1963.

Radner, R., and J. Marschak, "Note on Some Proposed Decision Criteria," in Thrall, Coombs and Davis, 1954.

Raiffa, H., "Arbitration Schemes for Generalized 2-person Games," in Kuhn and Tucker, 1953.

——, *Decision Analysis*, Addison-Wesley, Reading, Mass., and London, 1968.

Ramsey, F. P., *The Foundations of Mathematics*, Harcourt, Brace, New York, and Trubner, Borden, London, 1931.

Rapoport, A., *Fights, Games, and Debates*, University of Michigan Press, Ann Arbor, 1960.

Rawls, J., "Outline of a Decision Procedure for Ethics," *Philosophical Review*, **60**, 1951.

———, "Two Concepts of Rules," *Philosophical Review*, **64**, 1955.

———, "Justice as Fairness," *Philosophical Review*, **67**, 1958; reprinted in Olafson, 1961, and Laslett and Runciman, 1962.

———, "Constitutional Liberty and the Concept of Justice," in C. J. Friedrich and J. Chapman, eds., *Justice: Nomos 8*, Atherton Press, New York, 1963.

———, "The Sense of Justice," *Philosophical Review*, **72**, 1963 (1963a).

———, "Distributive Justice," in Laslett and Runciman, 1967.

———, "Chapters on Justice," materials for Philosophy 171 at Harvard University, unpublished, 1968.

Reder, M. W., *Studies in the Theory of Welfare Economics*, Columbia University Press, New York, 1947.

———, "Theories of Welfare Economics," *Journal of Political Economy*, **58**, 1950.

Rescher, N., ed., *The Logic of Decision and Action*, University of Pittsburgh Press, Pittsburgh, 1967.

Richter, M. R., "Revealed Preference Theory," *Econometrica*, **34**, 1966.

Riker, W., "Voting and the Summation of Preferences: An Interpretative Bibliographical Review of Selected Developments during the Last Decade," *American Political Science Review*, **55**, 1961.

———, "Arrow's Theorem and Some Examples of the Paradox of Voting," in Ulmer, 1965.

Robbins, L., *An Essay on the Nature and Significance of Economic Science*, Macmillan, London, 1932.

Robertson, D. H., *Utility and All That*, Macmillan, London, 1952.

———, "Utility and All What?", *Economic Journal*, **64**, 1954.

Robinson, J., *Economic Philosophy*, Aldine, Chicago, 1962.

Ross, W. D., *The Right and the Good*, Clarendon Press, Oxford, 1930.

Rosser, J. B., and A. R. Turquette, *Many-Valued Logics*, North-Holland, Amsterdam, 1952.

Rothenberg, J., "Conditions for a Social Welfare Function," *Journal of Political Economy*, **61**, 1953.

———, "Marginal Preference and the Theory of Welfare," *Oxford Economic Papers*, N.S., **5**, 1953a.

———, "Non-convexity, Aggregation and Pareto Optimality," *Journal of Political Economy*, **68**, 1960.

———, *The Measurement of Social Welfare*, Prentice-Hall, Englewood Cliffs, N.J., 1961.

Rousseau, J.J., *Du Contrat Social*, 1763; English translation by M. Cranston, *The Social Contract*, Penguin Books, Harmondsworth, 1968.

Ruggles, N., "The Welfare Basis of Marginal Cost Pricing Principle," *Review of Economic Studies*, **17**, 1949.

Runciman, W. G., *Social Justice*, Cambridge University Press, Cambridge, 1965.

Runciman, W. G., and A. K. Sen, "Games, Justice, and the General Will," *Mind*, **74**, 1965.

Russell, B., *Principles of Mathematics*, 2nd ed., Cambridge University Press, Cambridge, 1938.

———, *Philosophical Essays*, Longmans, London, 1910; Allen and Unwin, London, 1966; Simon and Schuster, New York, 1967.

Samuelson, P. A., *Foundations of Economic Analysis*, Harvard University Press, Cambridge, Mass., 1947.

———, "Consumption Theory in Terms of Revealed Preference," *Economica*, N.S., **15**, 1948.

———, "Evaluation of Real National Income," *Oxford Economic Papers*, N.S., **2**, 1950.

Samuelson, P. A., "The Problem of Integrability in Utility Theory," *Economica*, N.S., **17**, 1950 (1950a).

———, "Probability, Utility and the Independence Axiom," *Econometrica*, **20**, 1952.

———, "Social Indifference Curves," *Quarterly Journal of Economics*, **70**, 1956.

———, "A. P. Lerner at Sixty," *Review of Economic Studies*, **31**, 1964.

———, *Collected Scientific Papers*, edited by J. Stiglitz, Vols. I and II, M.I.T. Press, Cambridge, Mass., 1966.

———, "Arrow's Mathematical Politics," in Hook, 1967.

Savage, L. J., "Note on the Strong Indepence Assumption," *Econometrica*, **20**, 1950.

———, *The Foundations of Statistics*, Wiley, New York, 1954.

Scitovsky, T., "A Note on Welfare Propositions in Economics," *Review of Economic Studies*, **9**, 1941.

———, "A Reconsideration of the Theory of Tariffs," *Review of Economic Studies*, **9**, 1942.

———, "The State of Welfare Economics," *American Economic Review*, **41**, 1951.

———, *Papers on Welfare and Growth*, Stanford University Press, Stanford, 1964.

Scott, D., and P. Suppes, "Foundational Aspects of Theories of Measurement," *Journal of Symbolic Logic*, **23**, 1958.

Searle, J. R., "How to Derive 'Ought' from 'Is'," *Philosophical Review*, **73**, 1964.

Searle, J. R., *Speech Acts*, Cambridge University Press, London, 1969.

Sen, A. K., "Distribution, Transitivity, and Little's Welfare Criteria," *Economic Journal*, **73**, 1963.

——, "Preferences, Votes and the Transitivity of Majority Decisions," *Review of Economic Studies*, **31**, 1964.

——, "Mishan, Little, and Welfare: A Reply," *Economic Journal*, **75**, 1965.

——, "A Possibility Theorem on Majority Decisions," *Econometrica*, **34**, 1966.

——, "Hume's Law and Hare's Rule," *Philosophy*, **41**, 1966 (1966a).

——, "Planners' Preferences: Optimality, Distribution, and Social Welfare," in International Economic Association, see above, 1966 (1966b).

——, "The Nature and Classes of Prescriptive Judgments," *Philosophical Quarterly*, **17**, 1967.

——, "Isolation, Assurance, and the Social Rate of Discount," *Quarterly Journal of Economics*, **81**, 1967 (1967a).

——, "Quasi-Transitivity, Rational Choice and Collective Decisions," *Review of Economic Studies*, **36**, 1969.

——, "The Impossibility of a Paretian Liberal," *Journal of Political Economy*, **78**, 1970.

——, "Interpersonal Aggregation and Partial Comparability," *Econometrica*, **38**, 1970 (1970a).

Sen, A. K., and P. K. Pattanaik, "Necessary and Sufficient Conditions for Rational Choice under Majority Decision," *Journal of Economic Theory*, **1**, 1969.

Shubik, M., ed., *Essays in Mathematical Economics*, Princeton University Press, Princeton, 1967.

Sidgwick, H., *The Method of Ethics*, Macmillan, London, 1907; Dover, New York, 1966.

Siegel, S., and L. E. Fouraker, *Bargaining and Group Decision Making*, McGraw-Hill, New York, 1960.

Singer, M. S., *Generalizations in Ethics*, Knopf, New York, 1961.

Sonnenschein, H., "The Relationship between Transitive Preference and the Structure of Choice Space," *Econometrica*, **33**, 1965.

——, "Reply to 'A Note on Orderings,'" *Econometrica*, **35**, 1967.

Stevens, S. S., "Mathematics, Measurement and Psychophysics," in S. S. Stevens, ed., *Handbook of Experimental Psychology*, Wiley, New York, 1951.

——, "Psychophysics of Sensory Function," *The American Scientist*, **48**, 1961.

Stevenson, C. L., *Ethics and Language*, Yale University Press, New Haven, 1944.

217

Stevenson, C. L., *Facts and Values: Studies in Ethical Analysis*, Yale University Press, New Haven, 1963.

Stigler, G. J., "A Note on the New Welfare Economics," *American Economic Review*, **30**, 1943.

Streeton, P., "Economics and Value Judgment," *Quarterly Journal of Economics*, **64**, 1950.

———, "Introduction," in Myrdal, 1958.

Strotz, R. H., "How Income Ought to be Distributed; A Paradox in Distributive Ethics," *Journal of Political Economy*, **66**, 1958.

———, "How Income Ought to be Distributed: Paradox Regained," *Journal of Political Economy*, **69**, 1961.

Suppes, P., "The Role of Subjective Probability and Utility in Decision Making," in Neyman, 1956.

———, *Introduction to Logic*, Van Nostrand, Princeton, N.J., 1958.

———, "Some Formal Models of Grading Principles," *Synthese*, **6**, 1966.

Suppes, P., and D. Davidson, "A Finitistic Axiomatization of Subjective Probability and Utility," *Econometrica*, **24**, 1956.

Suppes, P., and M. Winet, "An Axiomatization of Utility Based on the Notion of Utility Differences," *Management Science*, **1**, 1955.

Szpilrajn, E., "Sur l'Extension de l'Ordre Partiel," *Fundamenta Mathematicae*, **16**, 1930.

Tarski, A., *Introduction to Logic*, Oxford University Press, New York, 1941; 2nd ed., 1946; 3rd ed., 1965.

Theil, H., "On the Symmetry Approach to the Committee Decision Problem," *Management Science*, **9**, 1963.

Thrall, R. M., D. H. Coombs and R. L. Davis, eds, *Decision Processes*, Wiley, New York, 1954.

Thrustone, L. L., "A Law of Comparative Judgment," *Psychological Review*, **34**, 1927.

Tintner, G., "A Note on Welfare Economics," *Econometrica*, **14**, 1946.

Tullock, G., "Problems of Majority Voting," *Journal of Political Economy*, **67**, 1959.

———, "Reply to a Traditionalist," *Journal of Political Economy*, **69**, 1961.

———, "The Irrationality of Intransitivity," *Oxford Economic Papers*, N.S., **16**, 1964.

———, "The General Irrelevance of the General Impossibility Theorem," *Quarterly Journal of Economics*, **81**, 1967.

———, *Towards a Mathematics of Politics*, University of Michigan Press, Ann Arbor, 1968.

Ulmer, S., *et al.*, *Mathematical Applications in Political Science*, Southern University Press, 1965.

Uzawa, H., "Preference and Rational Choice in the Theory of Consumption," in Arrow, Karlin and Suppes, 1960.

Veblen, T., *The Theory of the Leisure Class*, Macmillan, London, 1899.

Vickrey, W., "Measuring Marginal Utility by Reactions to Risk," *Econometrica*, **13**, 1945.

———, "Utility, Strategy, and Social Decision Rules," *Quarterly Journal of Economics*, **74**, 1960.

Ward, B., "Majority Voting and Alternative Forms of Public Enterprise," in Margolis, 1965.

Weldon, J. C., "On the Problem of Social Welfare Functions," *Canadian Journal of Economics and Political Science*, **18**, 1952.

Whitehead, A. N., and B. Russell, *Principia Mathematica*, Cambridge University Press, Cambridge, 1913.

Wicksell, K., *Lectures on Political Economy*, Routledge, London, 1935.

Williamson, O. E., and J. G. Sargent, "Social Choice: A Probabilistic Approach," *Economic Journal*, **77**, 1967.

Wilson, J. Q., and E. C. Banfield, "Public Regardingness as a Value Premise and Voting Behavior," *American Political Science Review*, **52**, 1958.

Wilson, R., "An Axiomatic Model of Logrolling," *Working Paper No. 3*, Graduate School of Business, Stanford University, 1968.

———, "A Class of Solutions for Voting Games," *Working Paper No. 156*, Graduate School of Business, Stanford University, 1968 (1968a).

———, "A Game Theoretic Analysis of Social Choice," *Discussion Paper No. 2*, Institute of Public Policy Analysis, Stanford University, 1968 (1968b).

Wright, G. H. von, *The Logic of Preference*, Edinburgh University Press, Edinburgh, 1963.

Zeckhauser, R., "Group Decision and Allocation," *Discussion Paper No. 51*, Harvard Institute of Economic Research, 1968.

———, "Majority Rule with Lotteries on Alternatives," *Quarterly Journal of Economics*, **83**, 1969.

Zeuthen, F., *Problems of Monopoly and Economic Warfare*, Routledge, London, 1930.

INDEXES

NAME INDEX

SUBJECT INDEX